HISTORY OF THE GLOSTER JAVELIN

THE FIRST ALL WEATHER BRITISH FIGHTER

IAN SMITH WATSON

Fonthill Media Language Policy

Fonthill Media publishes in the international English language market. One language edition is published worldwide. As there are minor differences in spelling and presentation, especially with regard to American English and British English, a policy is necessary to define which form of English to use. The Fonthill Policy is to use the form of English native to the author. Ian Smith Watson was born and educated in the United Kingdom; therefore, British English has been adopted in this publication.

Fonthill Media Limited
Fonthill Media LLC
www.fonthill.media
office@fonthillmedia.com

First published in the United Kingdom and the United States of America 2018

British Library Cataloguing in Publication Data:
A catalogue record for this book is available from the British Library

Copyright © Ian Smith Watson 2018

ISBN 978-1-78155-374-9

The right of Ian Smith Watson to be identified as the author of this work has been asserted by him in accordance with the Copyright, Designs and Patents Act 1988.

All rights reserved. No part of this publication may be reproduced, stored in a retrieval system or transmitted in any form or by any means, electronic, mechanical, photocopying, recording or otherwise, without prior permission in writing from Fonthill Media Limited

Typeset in 8pt on 13pt Sabon
Printed and bound in England

Preface

So, I trust you, the reader, find that you have an informative and worthwhile read put together in the pages ahead, so well supported by the many images, diagrams, and indeed the cartoon images, which, although the artist remains unknown, are included here as they convey a contemporary lighter side of the Gloster Javelin through the eyes of an artist. Writing this book has been rather like tucking into an all you can eat buffet; to put it more plainly, the amount of data has proved overwhelming and while I have endeavoured to be comprehensive and inclusive, there will be some instances and events concerning the subject matter that did not make it into these pages or received only a passing reference—including some Javelin operators who, while covered in the text, are not counted among the images—but any such omissions are very much in a minority. As intended, this is a comprehensive and, I hope, sufficiently definitive account of the RAFs first true all-weather fighter. Read on and enjoy.

Acknowledgements

I have to admit, when I first set out to write this book back in the spring of 2015 just as *Northern 'Q'* became available, the one thing that started to dawn on me was the contact with the 'first party': never the easiest thing to do but then again, somehow managed in the end. What I mean of course is the problem of tracking down those who actually had first-hand knowledge and experience of the subject matter—in this case, the Gloster Javelin. Now if I was to write about the Harrier or the Lightning still, access to such people would possibly prove much easier, but the Javelin was never the household name that the Harrier especially is. When the SDSR 2010 was published, the press and many others, the ordinary layman among them, reacted with dismay that the 'Harrier' was for the chop, such was the charisma and media folklore about the 'jumpjet'. When the Javelin passed from service after a much shorter, but arguably more adventurous and certainly controversial service career, I doubt if many in the RAF outside the very units and commands associated with the beast were at all anything other than oblivious. Yet alas, some were tracked down so many years on. Also, as this book headed off to the printers, it did so in an era that has seen a handful of others get the same idea about writing books about the Gloster Javelin. Therefore, the assistance of the following has proved all the more precious:

I will start with Ed Durham. Ed had become far more associated with the Lightning during his career and featured in *Northern 'Q'*, having flown non-stop in that aircraft, not known for its long legs, across the Atlantic to Canada in 1968 supported entirely by in-flight refuelling and bite-sized chicken sandwiches. However, Ed flew the Javelin on 85 Sqn and was able to provide some images. Keith Deal was involved with the Javelin from the maintenance side of things, being a navigation instruments technician and former Apprentice. Keith was able to provide some interesting stories and photos from his tour on 3 Squadron at Geilenkirchen and had the great misfortune to be bear witness to two separate tragic events. Brian Henwood, who served on 151 and 87 Squadrons and as an instructor on 228 OCU at Leuchars, came in handy for attaching some names to faces in the OCU staff photo.

Next are three individuals from the Javelin force whom I have probably driven to the point of plotting to kill me as a result of my being a constant source of discomfort in the nether region over the last several months, while constantly reassuring each that the book was almost ready. They are: Peter Goodwin, who flew with 25 Squadron and remained with them when they moved from Leuchars to Germany and became 11 Sqn. Peter has been instrumental in providing his memories and some technical details of the Javelin, as well as some personal photographs including his pilot's notes. Barry Mayner, ex-29 Sqn, was so helpful with *Northern 'Q'* and has stepped up to the plate once again with an array of images and a further array of anecdotes. Roy Evans, ex-25 and 11 Squadrons, has likewise proved an invaluable source of detail and a direct link with service on the Javelin force, including some interesting memories.

Further afield, thanks to Andy Renwick at the RAF Museum, Hendon, for his assistance in identifying the content of images from that location, and Lee Harper at the Air Historical Branch, who, as always, is a ready source of images. Ian White, who contacted me quite recently having read *Fading Eagle*, made some images from his own collection available. Once again, Peter March, aviation writer and historian, provided images so early on for the original book submission at Fonthill Media.

I must also make a special mention of Paul Johnson and Hugh Alexander at the National Archives, who have been most helpful over the provision of images from that particular source, not to mention the vast amount of data held by the National Archives themselves. I have also relied upon one of the images supplied several years back by John Wharam, who usually has at least one of his images appear in the pages of my books; this is no exception. I must make mention of one David Downey who was a navigator on 85 Squadron and provided the rare images of the arrival at West Malling and the start up on the Stradishall pan for the weather aborted Queen's Birthday Flypast. Finally, with regards to rare images, one source came to my attention on the point of handing everything over to the commissioning editor, Jay Slater—that is the two photos taken at Leuchars of the 228 OCU display team, of which Brian Henwood was a member. These images were taken by a Mr R. A. Stitchell, and are kindly made available by his son, Scott. All of these gentlemen, and the establishments mentioned, are the source of the body of this book.

Contents

Preface — 3
Acknowledgements — 5
Introduction — 9

1. Cats Eyes, Carrots, and Intruders — 11
2. Post-War to Cold War — 22
3. Cold War Night Fighter — 36
4. Service Debut — 46
5. Duncan Sandys and the Javelin — 63
6. The Javelin Operational — 79
7. Overseas Theatre — 137
8. Staying On — 180
9. The Last Days — 194
10. Javelin Postscript — 200

Appendix I: Flat Iron Comparisons — 201
Appendix II: Javelin Squadrons and Post History — 203
Appendix III: Fighter Command Order of Battle as of 1 September 1957 — 214
Appendix IV: Chart Depicting Fighter Command Planned Deployment as of 30 September 1958 — 216

Introduction

Flat Iron, Flying Blow Lamp, Harmonious Dragmaster, and Drag Queen are all references to the Gloster Javelin, at once a significant aircraft in RAF history and for all its imposing appearance, one of the easiest to be forgotten. As for the nicknames, these are likely even less familiar terms, with the possible exceptions of Flat Iron and Drag Queen, but I would be surprised for sure if any but the hardcore aviation expert or enthusiast would instantly make the connection with the aircraft itself. This is one aircraft that served with the Royal Air Force that did not attract the kind of public notoriety which others have, such as the Spitfire, Hurricane, Lightning, Hunter, Meteor, Vampire, Tornado, Phantom, Typhoon, and even before becoming the victim of the acrimonious 2010 Strategic Defence and Securty Review, everyone has certainly heard of the Harrier, which drew astonishment and critique from even those critically disposed toward the efficacy of air power anyway. They are all familiar names and there is a pretty darn good chance that quite a broad number of even the most remotely familiar people can recognise them.

The same could not honestly be said of the Javelin. There are others through aviation history that enjoyed little in the way of celebrity, and for many aircraft types, it can easily be understood why. I will try to shed some light on at least why the Javelin did not achieve this fame along the way, but it is possibly the case that the Javelin received a rather worse press than was perhaps deserved. By rights, it should have gone down in aviation history with rather more of a flattering valediction than it received, given the era in which it entered service and all the more so, given its significance as the first of a kind—that is the first wholly, from the drawing board up, all-weather fighter and the first in the RAF to be missile armed, eventually. Again, all will be revealed. One might have expected it to last a little longer on the RAF's inventory than it did and one thing is for sure—it would cock-a-hoop the aviation enthusiasts' world if someone somewhere with more money (a lot more money in fact) than sense would somehow find a way to bring one back to life, just as has been the case with a number of other rare and exotic jet-powered Cold War warriors. Then again, it is almost certainly the case that the opportunity to do this alas has long since been lost—more's the pity.

Born to meet the ever-increasing demands of the Cold War, to stay a step or two ahead of Soviet arms technology, and to be prepared to counter the Kremlin's growing reach (which would inevitably see British airspace vulnerable once again to the threat of the long-range bomber, this time possibly with air dropped or launched nuclear weapons), the need for a long range, all-weather fighter that could intercept supersonic targets at high altitude became a pressing priority. The Gloster Javelin was one embryo design that the Gloster aircraft company expected would address this. The problem was that early shortcomings proved difficult to overcome. When they were, at least in sight, the company's endeavours were overtaken by events; this included the burgeoning cost of defence against the increased costs to maintain peacetime Britain in a manner to which a great many aspired and have come to see as only reasonable (your author one of them). It is therefore easy to understand how better social and health care, and to have access to public services only dreamed a short few years earlier, meant that compromise would always need to be negotiated, regardless of the merits of the argument. Unlike the war years, new arms developments could not all be pursued with seemingly unlimited resource. There was no war for national survival, as serious a concern as the Cold War became; despite occasionally seeing the big hand of the Doomsday Clock shifted a minute or two closer to midnight on occasion, we still were not at war. So, however, worrying at times as a result, to have the population live in constant fear of a very near imminent Soviet invasion of the West and Armageddon could not be justified, meaning ever more elaborate defence projects had to fight for a sympathetic hearing from many a chancellor over the second half of the twentieth century. To be honest, nothing has changed.

The intended ultimate version of the Javelin (there were nine altogether)—a thin-winged version that would be truly supersonic—never got as far as the prototype stage.

The Javelin saw operational service with no fewer than eighteen operational squadrons with four operational commands of the RAF between 1956 and 1968. An impressive sounding list if a short number of years despite the fact that the more promising thin-winged version, examined in the pages ahead along with a bomber variant, never got to fly. Truth be known, for the era, eighteen squadrons was not a particularly big number; furthermore, the peak of Javelin operations reached around 1960 had seen squadrons form and disband ahead of full deployment as they fell victim in turn to the rash, misplaced, futuristic, and less costly, visions of politicians convinced of the rationale of an all missile defence force. The decision to pursue this radical doctrine (The 'Sandys Review') lost momentum through the early 1960s, but not before it had decimated Fighter Command and the Royal Air Force in Germany and cut short the development and full potential of the Javelin. The intervening years quickly forgot the Flat Iron. It was never quite what it promised; it was never truly supersonic; and the final two definitive versions, the Mark 8 and Mark 9, had belatedly been fitted with reheated engines, but this had no effect below 20,000 feet, where the use of reheat was not to be used (above this, ceiling performance was significantly improved with reheat but not encouraged). The reheat could not be engaged below 20,000 feet without draining fuel from the engine supply, therefore diminishing any expected boost to performance. The RAF could at the very least fill a short gap between the Hunter, Meteor, and Venom on the early side and the Lightning and Phantom in more recent times. That said, the Javelin, for all its variants and for all the squadrons equipped with the type, served for only twelve years, which for aircraft entering service from the late 1950s forward was brief. The chapters ahead will give some insight into the aircraft's awkward development then equally messy introduction to RAF service, but also its unsettling operational history.

1
Cats Eyes, Carrots, and Intruders

With the German Army carrying all before it and all the remnants of resistance holed up in Britain, it is no wonder that the British Government was contemplating seeking an accommodation with Berlin. The early summer of 1940 had seen the last of the British Expeditionary Force and as much as could be salvaged from the French Army safely extracted from the continent, which was now completely under the Nazi yolk from the most northern tip of Norway down through Denmark, the Low Countries, and France. Austria was subsumed into Germany by annexation; Italy became an ally; and Spain, if not a part of the German Axis, was at least a benign state to Germany, courtesy of General Franco. The big question was just how would the *Führer* go about his next move and when. It was almost certain that, with his eastern border being alongside the USSR, with whom the non-aggression pact was holding out for the time being, the United Kingdom was to brace for a likely invasion or seek accommodation.

There has been much revisionist debate about just whether Hitler was convinced of the need to destroy British resistance once and for all, seek an accommodation (seemingly his most favoured route), or, believing that the British were irreversibly isolated, seize the opportunity to plot his more strategically important attack on Soviet Russia. Stalin seemed surprisingly faithful to the non-aggression pact, not that he had blind faith in the *Führer*'s word but that such a vast and comprehensive invasion by Germany would at all materialise certainly caught him even more off guard than the response from London to Berlin following the 1939 invasion of Poland surprised Hitler.

Britain's new Prime Minister, Winston Churchill, was, regardless of the circumstances, determined not only to refuse any accommodation with Berlin but determined upon a most unlikely course to bring about the defeat of Nazi Germany. Britain needed to brace itself, for a battle for national survival and that of hundreds of years of civilised development was waiting in the wings and the outcome looked far from certain, indeed, bleak.

The expected response was that Hitler would indeed attempt a seaborne invasion and that this was quite imminent. That this may be preceded or accompanied by air attacks was not unexpected. When the opening phase of air attacks came, they were by day and concentrated on destroying the very means of threatening any future landings of troops; this principally meant attacks against the RAF, its assets, and its infrastructure. It has always been argued that a reprisal air raid by Bomber Command over Berlin at night was the spur that prompted Hitler to go down the inadvisable path of switching to the bombing of British cities and increasingly by night. Indeed, the bombing of Berlin was very much a reprisal in response to bombs falling on London at night, supposedly unintentionally. The likelihood of night bombing was likely enough to see night fighter squadrons in operation from very early on; of course, by the 1930s, aircraft design now predominantly served military interests but those interests were still intended to serve essentially two fundamental requirements: the fighter and the bomber. The idea or concept of a night fighter *per se* in an age when trying to get radar, or rather radio direction and range as a concept in its own right, to work might seem to be ambitious. Radar, such as it was, involved land-based static structures, the associated paraphernalia of an ops room, oscilloscopes, and plotting table, meaning that the night fighter of the Battle of Britain would not be something designed with such a thing as a radar system condensed into a typical fighter fuselage. Yet such was the speed of frantic development that what would ordinarily be more than a decade away was less than a year's gestation away before aircraft designed often for another purpose or role on both sides of the war would have radar antenna, rather like latter-day TV aerials, bristling from the nose.

This was a new and specialised concept. The aircraft used were typically obsolescent bombers, initially with no radar. The Bristol Blenheim Mark 1 aircraft for the Battle of Britain was the night fighter mainstay. Far too vulnerable to venture out during the day, they enjoyed very little success in hunting down German bomber formations at night, unlike the devastation inflicted on Bomber Command's Lancasters and Halifaxes two to five years later. The night fighter of 1940 was not an effective instrument of war; in fact, it was quite difficult to justify the rationale for sending them aloft each night, but the need to get to grips with being able to successfully intercept, identify, engage, and destroy enemy aircraft by night was an ever-growing imperative. So as German night sorties over British cities increased toward the *Blitzkrieg*, some kind of response, no matter how unrealistic, had to be attempted.

Radar, the key to night interception, was already playing its part as the nation's saviour, allowing sufficient time for fighters to be scrambled against day targets. To equip aircraft with the means of detecting other aircraft out to a significant distance and also provide information on range and bearing was to take a fairly big step forward. No one could quite visualise the smooth lines of the Spitfire, or the Hurricane for that matter, bulging with antenna, or, as was the case initially, sprouting out of what was usually the nose. However, the traditional day fighter and the less orthodox night fighter continued to diverge through the war, certainly unto the onlooker, mostly due to the night fighter types being utilised twin-engine bombers both RAF and Luftwaffe. The USAAF did not pursue night fighters in any widespread sense, but did build one single twin-prop night fighter: the Northrop P-61 Black Widow. This was deployed in every theatre but was used in a far more covert sense, therefore if the Javelin was the RAF's first purpose-built all-weather fighter, the Black Widow was perhaps the first overall; indeed, a P-61 is credited with claiming the final Allied air-to-air victory, in the Far East, shortly before V-J Day. Otherwise, the USAAF concentrated instead on longer-range fighters, better suited to escort the large bomber formation by day. US military air operations managed to step aside largely from the need to fly operations at night through the war.

In 1940, of course, the means to intercept in all weather, engage, and destroy had to be done, if at all, without radar for airborne interception. Night fighters, such as they were, had an almost impossible task during the crucial period of the Battle of Britain and *Blitzkrieg*. The task was quite fruitless, the Blenheim squadrons, the principal night fighter of the few claimed few enemy aircraft but whatever the lacklustre tally from night fighter operations, the move toward this concept intensified and expanded through the war. The Luftwaffe, in particular, were, as a result of the war's conduct, forced to concentrate the lion's share of resources on defending Germany against the overwhelming allied bomber raids, with RAF Bomber Command concentrating its effort on night operations in order to minimise detection and to avoid the heavier expense for heavier defensive armament something, which did not trouble the US Army Air Force, who did the exact opposite. The USAAF were drawn to the logic of daytime bombing accompanied with fighter escorts and bombers bristling with 0.5 calibre guns, the ultimate perhaps being the Boeing B-17G Flying Fortress and B-24 Liberator, in the European theatre leastways. These heavies were armed with nine to thirteen 0.5-inch calibre guns depending on the mark of say B-17, either 'E', 'F', or 'G' (one of the guns on the 'E' was a .3 calibre). Compared to the British bomber with the heaviest defensive armament, the Handley Page Halifax, carrying ten 0.303-inch calibre guns but grouped in three positions, it is easy to see why Bomber Command preferred bombing by night. Night fighter operations both during and immediately after the Battle of Britain relied not on radar to see the target but through judicious use of navigation lights, a system in use on both sides. By November 1940, in the aftermath of the battle, new regulations and procedures were issued by Fighter Command. Enemy aircraft continued using their navigation lights for recognition when crossing the French coast while at the same time trying to pick up coastal beacons. Conversely, RAF night fighters operating near the coast were under orders not to shoot anything down unless they could see navigation lights glowing. Of course, group controllers were to contact Bomber Command (in particular, No. 2 Group) to ascertain whether any friendly bombers would be operating in the area of any night fighter patrol lines, in this case regarding the French coast. It was also of paramount importance not to allow Defiants and Beaufighters, replacement types for the Blenheims, to operate in the same area. All this to keep the situation as clear as possible, Allied bombers were to operate without using navigation lights, but resin lights could be switched on within 20 miles of the British coast.

It was with no amount of flippancy that the British authorities claimed that eating carrots could help you see in the dark. The idea of promoting such notions, along with taking railings down with the expressed intention of melting them down to make more aeroplanes, was complete nonsense to reassure everyone that all was being done to beat the Hun when in truth, all was being done to support public moral. The carrots story encouraged the hard-pressed population to make the effort to grow their own vegetables in the back garden, but the claim about improving night vision was further promoted by suggesting that this was how the RAF's night flyers were able to see in the dark, such was the given explanation as to how RAF notorieties like 'Cats' Eyes' Cunningham managed such a high score—carrots were the secret.

The true secret was the plan to carry radar on board both night fighters and eventually bombers as well. The first of the radar night fighters, Bristol Beaufighters, were equipped with the AI Mk IV identifiable by its arrow-tip aerial protruding from the nose, the set was in the rear gunner's position and operated, of course, by a navigator, not the gunner, who had a closed cockpit unlike the latter, who had to contend with the partially open rear cockpit. The idea of flying like this at 15,000 feet would not appeal to most. Apart from the Spitfire and Hurricane no RAF aircraft, during the first year of the war, possessed sufficient performance to reach a significantly greater altitude; the Beaufighter's ceiling performance was not great. However, one such aircraft that could be considered as indeed the very first purpose-built night fighter were it not for its general utility as a bomber, photo recce, anti-ship, and covert operations mount was the de Havilland Mosquito. However, for now, the Blenheim was effectively the mainstay.

As for the Germans, they probably took the concept of the all-weather night fighter furthest, operating both the Bf 110 and Ju 88 as the most prominent designs to be converted, the latter being a quite successful bomber during the Battle of Britain earning the accolade 'Wonder Bomber'. The Bf 110 twin-engine escort fighter during the early stages of the war enjoyed a less than glowing success rate in its day job and, like the Stuka, was seen as easy meat for the RAF fighters. In these early stages, any aircraft design selected by the RAF to fulfil the role of night fighter likewise typically fell short of the original remit, whether intended as a bomber or fighter. As far as its original assignment went, these aircraft never truly met expectations. In addition to the Blenheim Mark 1, the Boulton Paul Defiant was converted to the NF role. The Boulton Paul Defiant had proved a disaster as a day fighter during the Battle of Britain, with one of only two formed squadrons being decimated in a single engagement over the coast near Dover. The Blenheim Mk 1 had already been superseded as a bomber by more capable types at the outbreak of war, such as the Blenheim Mk IV, Vickers Wellington, and a couple of older airframes including the Handley Page Hampden and Armstrong Whitworth Whitley. Agility and speed were the attributes of the day fighter, the night fighter required first and foremost the ability to see, detect, and hunt down what were almost always lone enemy aircraft, usually stragglers from a night raid or a solo special sortie. The likelihood of finding a gang of Bf 109s was utterly remote, meaning agility and performance could be sacrificed to make room for whatever night flying aids could be crammed into the airframe, while an additional pair of eyes or more would not go amiss either. Just the same, the air staff expected some tangible success from night interceptions. On one particular occasion on the evening of 14–15 November 1940, the reports from the NF units were paltry to the extent that the CAS (Chief of the Air Staff) requested an explanation for the low figures. Fighter Command reported back that there had been a total of 121 such sorties flown. Ten Beaufighters, by this stage the latest design and now radar-equipped, had obtained five AI returns (blips); a further thirty-nine Beaufighters between them had picked up just six AI returns. These resulted in a total of five sightings of enemy aircraft of which one was closed in on; the ensuing encounter resulted in the enemy aircraft being damaged. Other fighters, ill-equipped for such operations, also took part, including twenty-two Defiants. These saw five illuminated targets but made no successful pursuits and as many as forty-five Hurricanes were ordered aloft but faired even worse, illuminating a single aircraft, which evaded them. Four Gladiators and a solitary Spitfire were also involved but reported nothing seen.

Fighter Command's SASO (senior air staff officer) sought to point out that this at least showed the superior performance of the Mark IV AIR (airborne intercept radar) currently equipping the Blenheim, further praise was afforded the RDF stations, in particular the Kenley Sector for providing 'more' accurate raid information. However, the explanation for how this high level of accurate data resulted in a single engagement out of eleven AI radar returns was accounted for by blaming 'the well-known poor view from these aircraft.' Of ten Beaufighters in the first sortie, it was admitted that these came from a force of forty-three aircraft and that the reason for the low turnout was the result of difficulty in maintaining the new undeveloped Beaufighters currently being delivered to service squadrons. The marginally better result for the Defiants was attributed to the simple advantage of two pairs of eyes, one pair of which can be devoted permanently to searching for enemy aircraft; the cockpit design was also seen as an advantage. The best results for all concerned, however, lay with the fitting of exhaust manifolds to prevent the glare of flickering light from exhaust flame.

With AIR still being a new-fangled instrument, equipping all those aircraft to which it was rationally applicable still fell short of being regarded as what you would describe as standard. Therefore, the method of aiding interceptions at night still relied, significantly, on a combination of co-operation between different contributors: the ground RDF (radar) stations and the Observer Corps being the principal two. Yet with the reporting of plots derived being slow, a degree of lag developed. One idea was to involve Army gun control units for obtaining information to throw into the mix. An exercise was performed in October 1940. Experiments were carried out in the Humber area, in co-operation with the Hull gun operations room, using fighter aircraft from the Kirton Sector. A controller was sent from Kirton to the operations room at Hull, together with an R/T tender. On the approach of enemy aircraft, or an aircraft playing the part of an enemy, the sector operations room retained the responsibility to order up patrols to a suitable position within, or close to the area covered by the gun sets. When the fighter arrived in the area and the target enemy aircraft approached close to the area, control was handed over to the Hull controller, in this instance, so that he might guide the fighter to an intercept by means of information passed by the gun fire control room plotting table. The information from the Army Gun control table was considered to be around two minutes more up to date than that obtained through RDF or Observer Corps channels. However, as the gun fire control tables could only be used for plotting enemy aircraft positions, fighter movement information still had to be relayed from the sector controller. When information of both plots approached one another, vectors would then be given to the fighter from either the sector controller directly or indeed direct from the local controller using his own R/T tender. The limitations of this exercise were soon evident as enemy aircraft seldom ventured near the area in question. Therefore, no intercepts of enemy aircraft took place. As a result, numerous experiments were carried out using RAF aircraft to represent the enemy, the result being that it was found possible to direct fighters to within 400 yards of the target; equally importantly, the gun team were able to provide accurate height information.

A 'phrase' in use many years later was employed from this time: 'Pigeons' was used in R/T messages (although used by fighter crews under radar control in later years simply when requesting range and bearing information in relation to a given point), in the event of an actual hostile raid during training exercises to refer to friendly aircraft representing enemy aircraft instead of the usual 'Bandits'. The gun teams and observer corps searchlights would be directed toward the target by means of sound locators then alerting the next cone of searchlights along the way. Searchlights were operated in groups of three. This was deemed sufficient for simplifying information to the fighter by providing height and position of the target and bomber clearly and to give some idea of its track, requiring a high degree of skill and therefore practice on the part of the searchlight operators, which was seldom achieved. The aim was to find an intersection of the three beams, usually meeting between 5,000 feet and 10,000 feet. The higher the intersection, the shorter the range, naturally, but this mode of interception of targets at night was becoming a headache as the searchlights were getting as much in the way as being of any help. It had frequently occurred that when a night fighter was stalking an enemy bomber, the attack had been frustrated by searchlights, which always seemed to expose the fighter and not the bomber. If searchlights were not used at all, it was deemed possible, but difficult, to still get airborne interceptions on dark nights but the enemy bomber would not, of course, be seen until it was very close indeed, with the much greater chance of the fighter overshooting the target, especially as these intercepts, otherwise unaided, required exceptional skill, while the bomber, 'fingers crossed', maintained a steady and largely predictable course. So, at the height of the Battle of Britain, September 1940, AI was still to make any real impact at all and the best means had yet to be fully determined.

As a device that might provide the answers to night time intercepts, the ability for an AI operator to determine the range and height of a target from behind was truly revolutionary. What was for sure, single-engine fighters were far from suitable for night intercepts. All were suffering the same common problem—that of exhaust flames on either side of the engine. This could create severe obscuration of the pilot's forward view and not one single-engine fighter existed that could carry radar in 1940. As it was expected to fare better (which it did, relatively speaking), an order from HQ 11 Group to four of its stations—Debden, Tangmere, Biggin Hill, and Gravesend—on 23 November 1940 permitted the Group Controller to order Defiant aircraft to patrol near the French coast and in the path of returning bombers or those outgoing, but only in exceptional weather conditions. This was a particularly closely controlled affair with the Defiants in question operating from Gravesend and only if fitted with VHF (very high frequency) radio. Still, the best way forward depended on the availability of RDF, not just on the ground but in the air. The night fighter would not just need radar to intercept targets at night, but a suitable airframe.

Like most endeavours to create a machine for a particular purpose, to meet requirements in the interim, and often long term, the first thing to do is find an existing working design which lends itself to meeting the new requirement. This was seen extensively with a wide range of military aircraft during the Second World War. The need for night fighters in the early stages of the Second World War became increasingly apparent during the Battle of Britain and the Blitz. Later in the war, night fighters, such as they were, often carried out searches for other enemy night fighters, a form of fighter escort, or 'night intruder' for the RAF night time bomber formations. For all the inventiveness of the era, at no stage did any of the principal protagonists design and develop a purpose-built machine, with the notable exception of the Northrop P-61. Instead, many aircraft were developed to suit a raft of roles with varying degrees of speciality. As the successful day fighter was a night fighter flop conversely, those fighters picked to be night fighters tended to be something of a dead loss in day light, the classic early example being the Boulton Paul Defiant. This contemporary of the Spitfire and Hurricane was, if anything, a ruined additional single-seat fighter to go with the aforementioned types. Instead of putting guns in the wings and leaving it at that, the designers were clearly looking to meet a requirement for rearward-facing armament and so a perfectly adequate single-seat fighter with what would have been reasonable performance was, if anything, saddled (literally) with a weighty handicap in the form of a gun turret, which was perched immediately aft of the pilot. Of course, it had to have a crewman to operate it.

The Defiant had not been designed to taking on lumbering bombers trying to find targets over the UK; at night, it was to fly alongside the other nimbler Spitfires and Hurricanes to confront both light and medium bombers alongside the Luftwaffe's Bf 109s. Not long into the Battle of Britain, it became clear that the two Defiant squadrons operated by Fighter Command, 141 and 264, the former of which was destined to fly Javelins, had virtually no fine hour. The disastrous ordeal of 141 Squadron engaging 109s over Kent with many of the aircraft lost at sea; one buried itself into one of the residential areas of Dover, in particular seemed to settle the move from day fighter to night fighter for the Defiants. The Battle of Britain is of course well branded in the subconsciousness of even the most remotely interested mindset as a stand-off between the Luftwaffe's Bf 109s, Stukas, and Heinkels on the one hand with the RAF's Spitfires and Hurricanes on other side of the centre line. As true as it is that the latter two were to claim the bulk of enemy aircraft down, especially the Hurricane, Fighter Command operated 11 Squadrons in the night fighter role; the two Defiant units were later assigned to this task which was already being addressed by nine squadrons of Bristol Blenheim 1Fs. Thus, the low priority night fighter became all the more in demand as the Germans switched tactics from daylight raids on airfields to night bombing of the cities and industrial targets. As the war progressed and the air offensive was waged in the opposite direction, the Germans, rather than develop a specialised all-weather fighter which one would have thought prudent given the experiences of the Blitzkrieg, chose instead to follow the makeshift approach of the

RAF and develop existing bomber and heavy fighter designs to confront the streams of heavy night time raids. As such, the Ju 88 and Bf 110 became the two most prominent *Nachtjägers* (night fighters) on the Luftwaffe's inventory.

Regardless of the increasing demand throughout the war, night fighters remained what they would be in the RAF until 1956: derivatives.

The best available aircraft to be assigned as a night fighter during the war was undoubtedly the de Havilland Mosquito, 'The Wooden Wonder'. The Mark II being the first to be utilised as such, the Mosquito existed through thirty-eight versions, most of the later models being assigned as night fighters, but alas, still all derivatives of what was essentially a reconnaissance bomber design. As with the German JU-88, the Mossie was as good as it got when hunting down enemy bombers at night. The Mosquito's success as a night fighter was in no small part due to its tremendous gun group fitted in the nose: four 20-mm Hispano cannons and four .303 Browning guns. The light guns were removed from the later NF variants in order to make room for the radar antenna, which, after the Mark II, no longer sat exposed on the tip of the nose but needed to be housed in a large nose cone with what is best described as a broad snout, but the four cannons could still be embedded underneath facing through the ports, the edge of which were in line with the curve of the nose. Together with the radar, this was the definitive Mosquito NF format through to the end of the war and then continuing through to the first jet fighter converts. Whatever the success of night fighters, by midway through the war, AOC-in-C Fighter Command put forward proposals in December 1942 to the Prime Minister advising a re-adjustment of the night fighter force—that is to say he wanted to reduce the relatively tiny Mosquito element, at the time twenty-two squadrons to twenty. However, he also wanted to increase the establishment of the squadrons by adding six Mosquitoes to each.

This was expected to increase both the striking and defensive capability of the night fighter forces. The role of intruder was an elaborate form of fighter escort for which the Mosquitoes were well suited, during both day and night. As such, the Mosquito proved its worth beyond compare. Very low fast approach was the Mossie's forte no matter what role. As an intruder, the low approach below radar best suited attacks on those German airfields from which their own night fighters operated to harass the Allied bomber formations. The squadron reduction therefore was simply to split the available assets between the remaining twenty squadrons, but also in due course to re-establish the missing two. Indeed, ten more squadrons, which flew either earlier Mosquitoes or night fighter converts, were all to re-equip with Mosquito NFs in the fullness of time, subject to the Prime Minister's approval.

These were to be:

No. 25: Current types: Beaufighter I and Mosquito NF.II
No. 29: Current type: Beaufighter IF
No. 85: Current type: Mosquito NF.II
No. 151: Current types: Defiant II and Mosquito NF.II
No. 157: Current type: Mosquito NF.II
No. 256: Current type: Beaufighter VI

No. 264: Current type: Mosquito NF.II
No. 307: Current types: Beaufighter VI and Mosquito NF.II
No. 410: Current types: Beaufighter II and Mosquito NF.II
No. 456: Current types: Beaufighter II/VI and Mosquito NF.II

As can be seen, the process of re-equipment had already begun, but further production would need to be approved to completely re-equip all night fighter units with expected later developed Mosquito NF variants.

Three more squadrons, 3 (Hurricane IIC), 245, and 247 (Hurricane IIB and IIC) were also a part of the AOC-in-C's list of NF squadrons but single-seat equipped. The Hurricane, along with the Hawker Typhoon, were the two better known single-seat fighters that had been used in the NF role, but briefly, not surprisingly, and found wanting. The Hawker Hurricane was too slow to operate against the latest German bombers and the Hawker Typhoon was possessed of such a large nose that forward view, when landing and taking off, was heavily restricted and was unsuitable for flying on dark nights, except by experienced pilots. As a result, the three NF-assigned Hurricane squadrons were recommended to be returned to the day fighter role.

Despite the lack of faith in single-seat night fighters, the AOC-in-C recommended that testing of the Mark VI airborne intercept radar already begun with the Typhoon should continue at the FIU (Fighter Interception Unit). However, these three squadrons continued in the day and tactical fighter role with various single-seaters—Spitfires, Typhoons, then Tempests—until the end of the war. Post war, No. 3 Squadron operated the Gloster Javelin for a brief period before the radical realignment of the RAF front line determined a move to tactical strike and then close support through much of the Cold War and after. The unique Mosquito can perhaps claim fourth place after the Spitfire, Lancaster, and Hurricane as the most prominent British-built aircraft during the Second World War, despite its versatility and application; if you follow the rule 'jack of all trades, master of none', there was not a better night fighter. A derivative it may have been, but speed, ceiling performance, and indeed simplicity when it came to supplying materials to build Mossies, being made to a large degree of wood, had the Mosquito been designed solely as a night interceptor and utilised for little or nothing else would so easily have justified any suggestion of its being a thoroughbred design with a single purpose. Despite all, the number of night fighter units in existence by late 1944 remained pitifully few, but their value did not pass without notice. As of 10 November, the DGO (Director General Organisation) was trying to deal with what he was prepared to describe as an emergency regarding training and operational requirements for Mosquito night fighter units. Desperate to get as many Mk 30 Mosquitoes out to replace those equipped with earlier model Mk XIIs and XIIIs, there was a delay in production centred on the fitting of the new radar, AI X. The problem was an instruction directing that only AI X-equipped Mosquitoes should reach the front line from here forward, this meaning of course only aircraft capable of carrying the AI X should be available, including to the OTUs. Herein lay the problem: five Fighter Command units were equipped with the Mosquito XIII. With supply of Mk XXXs leaden, the DGO was pondering temporary measures to accommodate the delay impacted on supply of spares for the older equipped units. This was to the degree of concern that the DGO was prepared to proceed with a plan to delay the formation of more Mosquito bomber squadrons assigning them to the night fighter role instead. This did not last too long before someone pointed out the lack of defensive armament on the bomber version. Therefore, the disbandment of an existing squadron and delaying the replacement of Mark XIII squadrons was thought to be the most practical way forward as this would free up experienced crews and twenty-five surplus aircraft to reinforce the four remaining Mk XIII squadrons until March while what few Mk XXXs came off the production line and went to form a new unit in the meantime. To understand this, of two Fighter Command NF squadrons during this time that were assigned to the role of bomber escort, twelve aircraft were written off during September and October, the situation regarding replacement aircraft and crews had been difficult since Operation 'Overlord' during which time 'wastage' (to use a euphemism for casualties of the time) among night fighter crews had been quite high.

Five NF squadrons were on loan to Bomber Command for 'Bomber Support'. This did make sense as the shortage of Mosquitoes on the OTUs resulted in the scarcity of replacement night fighter crews. Other commands were in need of replacements, which had slowed up. No. 108 Squadron in Greece, Mediterranean Command, were overdue re-equipment; they were flying Beaufighters, but the demand for a night fighter service in that area was now regarded by AOC-in-C Mediterranean Allied Air Forces, Air Marshal Sir John Slessor, as virtually redundant. Therefore, as of January 1945, he confidently offered to disband this unit. This alone was an indication of the growing confidence among the Allies that the end, by the start of 1945, was very much predictable and in sight, thus the willingness to disband an operational flying squadron, albeit one that was seen as surplus in its specific role. In earlier times, the unit would simply be rerolled or split to form the cadre of additional squadrons and deployed somewhere they were needed.

Before the war had ended in Europe, Britain, already facing bankruptcy, had, through such opportunities as afforded the AOC-in-C MAAF, begun the process of dismantling its own war-driven outsized military complex, or at least made a tentative start by attempting some streamlining here and there and perhaps given the circumstances this was a case of the sooner the better. As of March 1945, with Allied forces moving against almost non-existent resistance in some parts of north-west Europe and speeding through parts of Germany, predicting the outcome of the second global conflict, in Europe at least, was no longer a high stakes game. The Government felt it could go further and in no way compromise military operations by disbanding more operational units. Thus, it was that 100 Group in Bomber Command and 2nd TAF were to disband; one NF30 Mosquito Squadron in 100 Group before the end of April, with one NF.30 Squadron and two Squadrons equipped with the Mk VI Mosquito in 2nd TAF to disband forthwith, allowing the NF.30 aircraft to replace a third Mk VI squadron. This would give 2nd TAF a night fighter force of no more than three NF.30 and a single Mk VI squadron. As few as the night fighter units were during the war, less than twenty years later, nearly all air defence interceptor squadrons would be all-weather and night capable. With the end of hostilities assured, the NF.30

was scheduled to be replaced from May with the Merlin-113 engined NF.36; at least, this was the plan but for technical problems with the Mk 113 engine. The aircraft could not be cleared for release to operations until such difficulties had been resolved, but despite the overall mass unit disbandment about to commence, the night fighter squadrons were, for all their limited numbers, due to expand. Meanwhile, many of the older NF Mosquitoes once replaced were headed to the OTUs.

2

Post-War to Cold War

Before the D-Day landings had even taken place, the British Chiefs of Staff, on 25 May 1944, had already approved and issued a paper outlining the threat of air attack to which the United Kingdom was likely to be exposed during the ten years following the defeat of Germany and proposed a policy that would govern the air defence of the country during that period. There were certainly a number of assumptions in place; firstly, they considered that the scale of attack likely would not be less than that mounted by Germany during the period 1940 to 1941. The language of the time was certainly far more direct; words were certainly not minced when produced in secret anyway: 'Even if our defences are strong the possibility of a sudden attack by a treacherous enemy cannot be entirely ruled out'.

Planning for the post-war world and its impact on national defence therefore occupied even more defence thinking. Before the war was comprehensively at an end, the new British Prime Minister, Clement Atlee, was setting about the task of seeking to determine the size, shape, and purpose of the post-war British defence requirements. There was much to consider: the threat of hegemony from Nazi Germany had disappeared, of this there was nothing more certain. In vain, as opponents of Hawkish attitudes today would like to think, the thinking almost seemed like an attempt to find someone or something to be worried about in military terms. On 24 July 1945, a Chiefs of Staff Committee meeting was convened to address, in a very much preliminary sense, the future shape of the air defence of Great Britain, during the decade ahead.

This committee had already been put on notice that the Prime Minister, still Churchill for another two days, did not feel it conducive to address what the Chiefs of Staff had to propose over the question of the air defence of post-war Britain as an individual matter as it formed only a part of the overall post-war layout. Yet still, as early as July 1945, the Defence Chiefs were considering how best to proceed with this matter specifically.

Among the more vexing questions occupying the service chiefs' thinking of the day were such matters as deployment areas for 5.5-inch guns. This specific point was to be addressed more by the War Office than the Air Ministry, but the former sought the latter's support when presenting proposals to the Ministry of Agriculture as such deployments required their co-operation. The War Office were not confident that they would get the land or even retain what they still had, from the war, for the placing of anti-aircraft guns. The Prime Minister's request for the 'whole post-war layout' to be addressed was taken to mean he expected the Chiefs of Staff Committee to take into consideration the whole matter of the post-war economy and wider national policy. The Defence Chiefs had already put forward a report on 7 July that outlined what they believed was going to shape the air defence of Great Britain in the decade ahead. Quite solid points based on what could only be guess work were placed in the report, such as the claim that we would be likely to obtain two years notice of a major war, but that a sudden attack at shorter notice could not be ruled out.

Their proposals were quite wide ranging, such as a non-regular reserve force that would be used to bring the regular forces to a reasonably expanded posture at short notice. This reserve was yet to be recruited and trained. Other matters were addressed, including town development, agriculture, and building schemes and how air defence factors should be taken into account. Also recommended was that immediate vital improvements and re-equipment of defences should not be deferred. A rather tall order considering the circumstances of the country at the time, the report went on to point out that a large proportion of 'the equipment installed in the air defences of this country is obsolescent'. It may be of note to consider that the three defence chiefs of the day were still those which had headed each of the three Armed Services during much of the war; 1st Sea Lord, Sir Andrew Cunningham; Chief of the Imperial General Staff, Lord Alan Brooke; and Chief of the Air Staff, Sir Charles Portal. The threat they perceived was very low but, in graduation of concern, placed focus on three different nations' air forces and what was expected in the given time scale:

1. No German Air Force
2. Only a relatively weak French Air Force
3. A strong Russian Air Force

Among the more recognisable elements involved, such as the fighter force and chain radar installations, reliance on these assets went without saying and the leaps and bounds forward in technology were focusing concerns to ensure that Fighter Command was properly equipped. As of 1945, even the highest-ranking military officer could not clearly state whether the future manned fighter type would be jet or rocket propelled, there was a not insignificant likelihood that the latter may yet prevail, or a mixed force of both. What was for sure with the current crop of piston-engine beasts was that the very best and cutting edge of them was to be relied upon initially. The longer term would demand development of the new-fangled jets and rockets. Despite this, there were the now seemingly quaint layers in the UK air defence system which were expected to still be there, such as the ack-ack guns and balloons; the brass hats of the era felt that barrage balloons (for all the expectations of developing and now proven technologies such as jet engines and radar) should be developed to reach higher and present a more lethal obstacle to an attacking enemy aircraft. It may seem somewhat ironic, but it was the diminishing effect of 'present types of guns' that drove this particular consideration, especially against low-level, high-speed future targets. Another oddity, if you will, was the anti-aircraft smoke apparatus that would be 'largely independent of man-power for its operation'.

It was of course expected that air bases, whatever the number required, would need modernising. Future requirements put forward would come with a degree of subjective comment to make the case and, as the PM had already more than hinted, would need to be place within a wider context, not just of the RAF overall or even the Armed Forces, but within the confines of the economy that no one was looking forward to remedying. The breakdown of the country in terms of defended areas was simple enough; there were two essential zones in air defence terms:

1. The Defended Area: This area covered the East and South coasts of the United Kingdom which (in the thinking of the time) is facing foreign territory, together with a limited depth inland from these coasts.
2. The Shadow Area: This area covers the rest of the United Kingdom outside the defended area.

Anti-aircraft rockets, as they were so referred, did not figure highly given their stage of development, but it was considered that this position should be regularly reviewed.

If there was one means of defence that was going to make its way to the fore it was the night fighter. Despite the developments using derivative airframes so far, the best still available to the RAF was undoubtedly the de Havilland Mosquito, but aircraft in this category were still not seen as pivotal. The day fighter still ruled the skies, the image of the dashing young fighter ace was still very much composed of the single-seat single engine thoroughbred racing car of the air, with guns of course. The night fighter was still regarded as the bomber become a fighter, and despite the inroads made, the image of the Bristol Blenheims and Beaufighters still filled budding fighter pilots' heads. The post-war era introduced a change of direction. As new aircraft continued to make their way off the drawing board and onto the prototype stage, they grew bigger, heavier, yet sleeker. With the first jet-powered fighters already in service, we had moved on from bomber designs being utilised as all-weather fighter types. The jet fighters that had originally been intended as day fighters were soon to be the platforms for the next generation of night fighter, utilising existing airframes rather than bombers, while the day when the production of the thoroughbred day fighter would disappear and the night fighter concept became the definitive intercept fighter was on its way.

In 1946, the Chiefs of Staff, at their 160th meeting to consider the basis for the future air defence of Great Britain, endorsed a number of assumptions, including that 'There will be no appreciable period of a warning of attack'. This was explained as needing to design UK air defence forces in such a way that they could expand rapidly and deploy in full strength on a war footing to meet any definable threat.

One development that the chiefs of staff were giving substantial consideration was the impact of National Service, effectively the post-war continuation of the wartime draft. Now formally recognised as a peacetime reinforcement of the armed services, and regardless of all the more demeaning stories about National Service life, it was actually welcomed as a remedy to the manpower shortage that loomed on the horizon. It may not have been the ideal but it was certainly something.

In this immediate post-war period, all three Armed Forces faced a significant shortage of skilled personnel, particularly those with knowledge and experience of such things as radar. Naturally, the kind of people needed were finding far better opportunities in civilian commercial companies. Given the short-term nature of National Service, the most effective application of drafted personnel was to staff other areas of air defence such as Anti-Aircraft Command.

Of paramount importance was the country's Fighter Command Control and Reporting system and the Royal Observer Corps. The chiefs concluded that twenty-six AAC Air Defence Units would be required and a need to man the whole of the control and reporting system on a four-watch roster basis. The ROC (Royal Observer Corps) had been reconstituted and allowed to recruit up to a personnel count of 28,000, this being the planned full wartime strength. At this early post-war stage, with the war against Nazi Germany still prominent in the minds of many, one of the principal protagonist nations involved with the defeat of the Third Reich, Russia, was already being regarded as likely to pose a future military threat and British military chiefs were already pondering uncertain factors in respect of Russian military capabilities. What was seen as credible was that Russia's willingness to embark upon a major conflict was limited only by the rehabilitation of Russia's military and industrial complex. This was deemed to be subject to a series of three 'five year plans', the first and second of which would end their respective cycles in 1951 and 1956. During these periods, the idea of a Russian threat of hegemony was unlikely, but in the years following, such a threat would become far more significant.

So, concerns about any kind of immediate air threat to the UK may have been dismissive, but work was proceeding with quite futuristic designs with a view to meeting rather stretching requirements of high performance, jet-powered day and night fighter designs. In 1947, the Air Ministry issued the following design specifications: F43/46 for a single seat highly manoeuvrable day fighter and a two-seat type to meet specification; F44/46, which had to be able to reach an altitude 45,000 feet in under ten minutes, among these were the first sketches of aircraft that would reach operational service, including the highly impressive first Mach 2-capable fighter, the English Electric Lightning; also included was the design for the last pure day fighter, the Hawker Hunter, which perhaps was the most sophisticated and powerful fighter to be mass produced. It was the last step before the Lightning, but as a day fighter, the last of its type. The scramble to meet F44/46 produced a couple of designs that would make it through to production and active service with both the RAF and the RN. Unlike the Hunter and Lightning, it would fail to leave anything like the lasting impression on aviation history, media, and enthusiast alike, with nothing like the valediction afforded the other two. It was de Havilland and Gloster who were responding specifically to F44/46.

In the meantime, despite the advent of the jet-fighter in the form of the Meteor and the Vampire, the best choice as a night fighter by the end of the 1940s was still the wartime-era prop-engine Mosquito. However, the design that survived had outstripped the competition and was a rather more popular airframe than not only the early wartime NF efforts, but those it competed with in other roles; it also surpassed its peers in maritime strike, reconnaissance, tactical bombing, and various off piste types of operational flying activities. The de Havilland Mosquito, perhaps the fastest, highest flying, and longest ranged fighter of the war, was truly multi-role, or certainly multi-adaptable to be more accurate—an all-round utility machine produced in the UK. In 1949, this meant the Mosquito NF.36 and NF.38, the latter being the ultimate version, were the RAF's mainstay of all-weather fighter operations. Like all the old warbirds, however, they were not long for the peacetime world, such as it was.

The Mosquito NF.38 had been ordered in 1945. Looking back to this time from 1949, the best that could be said by the air staff was that no doubt the outlook had been different. Now that the NF.38s were about to start delivery as the NF.36 replacement, they had been overtaken by developments in the interim. The Mosquito NF.36 was already well established in service and despite the NF.38 being the heir apparent, jets were already on order and the next step forward in what was turning into a rapid evolutionary development.

Now with the last Mosquito mark about to arrive, while 'far superior' jet night fighters were expected to begin arriving shortly after, the suggestion by the then Vice Chief of the Air Staff, Air Marshal Sir Basil Embry, was to hold onto the Mosquito 38s as war reserves, or failing that, scrap those being delivered. The RAF had sufficient NF.36s to last until the first of the jet-powered, radar-equipped fighters arrived. More to the point, the NF.38 was considered a poor aircraft; indeed, air council conclusions were that its performance was little worse or better than that of the NF.36.

Rather worryingly, the aircraft's AI9B radar was unreliable above an altitude of 25,000 feet. This was due to the fact that the radar did not have a pressurised aerial and did not have the ability to lock onto the target automatically. There was some mention of the NF.38s being used for training but as no dual-control examples existed, this was out of the question. Modifications were suggested, including upgrading the radar from the Mark 9B AI to the Mark 10. However, as of 1949, the thinking, quite rightly, was that they would be spending money on getting into service an unsatisfactory design that would be superseded in any case about a year to eighteen months down the road by the first jet all-weather designs. There were two designs waiting in the wings, so to speak; one of those designs was to be the de Havilland Vampire NF.10. Sir Basil Embry, by chance, got to be on hand to receive the first of the Vampire NF.10s. Immediately after practical trials, he contacted the CAS, Sir Arthur Tedder, to report his findings. Sir Arthur had told him that he expected the Vampire to have not much better performance than the Mosquito NF.36 and that he thought at the time that someone's arithmetic had been at fault when looking at the specified performance levels of the Vampire.

With regards to the performance comparisons between the two, it was found that the Vampire NF had, for the age, a respectable climb rate—about 13.8 minutes, including taxi time—to reach an altitude of 30,000 feet.

However, this was without drop tanks, which, on an operational scramble, would almost certainly be required. In this case, an additional seven minutes could be added onto the clean wing configuration. This rendered the aircraft's climb rate rather worse than the Mosquito's. In conventional flight, the Vampire was comfortably ahead in overall speed. Bearing in mind that the Vampire NF was a two-seater, therefore encumbered by a large heavy nose, which also carried the radar aerial and four 20-mm Hispano cannons, its performance was respectable. The fastest measured climb rate was from brake release to 10,000 feet in four minutes, after which the rate of ascent started to dissipate. Indeed, during the climb to 10,000 feet, the speed dropped off from 280 mph on unsticking to 245 mph. This compared favourably with the best single-seat fighter in service at the time—the Meteor IV had a top speed mach 0.78, considered to be good but at this speed, it could not fire its guns accurately, whereas it was expected the Vampire NF could. These figures also compared well with the nearest single-seat Vampire, the FB.5.

The Vampire NF's direct rival of the day was the Meteor NF.11. The layout of the Meteor required the radar operator to sit behind the pilot in a tandem operation, which in itself was better in terms of streamlining. In the NF Meteor's case, there was no room left for the guns once the radar had been incorporated in the nose. The natural position for them therefore was in the wing. This change was in process of being incorporated in 1949, but had not been completed successfully. The principal role of the night fighter, unlike during the Second World War when they operated alone, was to shepherd the single-seater fighters. Crucial to this was the ability to use the Gee Mk 2 radar system, which could be carried by the Vampire but only a miniaturised version could fit into the lengthened fatter nose of the Meteor NF. Again, the Meteor was behind the curve in this instance as the scaled down radar type had not yet been produced. All this pointed to the need to get the Vampire NF.10 into squadron service at the earliest opportunity, so reasoned Sir Basil Embry in a letter to Lord Tedder. To Sir Basil, the evidence in favour of proceeding with the Vampire night fighter variant was conclusive if only to guard against the likelihood of the Meteor failing in production and or performance.

In any case, it would put night all-weather fighter development and air defence control procedures ahead by a year to eighteen months.

Some months on and the start of 1950, Air Chief Marshal Sir John Slessor had taken over as CAS, by which time the air staff had decided on the purchase of 200 Meteor NF.11s. Sir Basil Embry still headed Fighter Command and was less than happy with the Meteor decision; he was now writing to Sir John to express his concerns with the Air Council decision and pointed out:

> Those who have flown modern aircraft and had practical experience of night fighting, are not altogether happy about this aeroplane. So much so that I'm convinced we should go for the 2-seater Vampire, not only as an insurance against the Meteor not coming up to scratch, but because I believe it may prove to be a far better night fighter and achieve a financial saving.

Sir Basil made further comparisons, acknowledging the good points of the Meteor—that it had a good climb rate and overall speed—but that it also had a list of shortcomings, such as the tandem-seating and the AIR (airborne intercept radar) operator's forward view, which he described as extremely limited. The concern here was that the AIR operator/navigator was of little use to the pilot in visual search or in solving the problem of identification. Another interesting point was that in the event of inter-communications failure, he would not be able to communicate with the pilot because he was sat in the back. These concerns would certainly be remedied by the side by side arrangement in the Vampire. Finally, there was much evidence to support the side by side seating arrangement over the tandem style, including assistance with navigation in the event of RT failure.

By now, Sir Basil felt confident also in stating that the Meteor was less stable, less manoeuvrable, and guns mounted in the wings afforded less concentration of fire power. He even went on to suggest that in order to compensate for a 'float' problem affecting the Meteor, that it may be prudent to lengthen all the runways throughout Fighter Command, at least. By now, the de Havilland Venom was also entering the picture and was regarded as the next step forward and already promising to be vastly superior to both the Meteor and the Vampire. The overall concern with the Venom, due to enter service in 1951–1952, was that production would be pushed back by the purchase of Meteors, which Sir Basil was deeply worried would prove to be a costly flop. At this stage, however, the Venom was only looking at going into production as a single-seat day/tactical fighter; orders for even the prototype two-seater NF version were yet to happen. Despite his misgivings, Sir Basil later said he neither wanted cancellation or even a reduction in the order of Meteors, but he merely wished to have the Vampire introduced to be used for experimental research, in house so to speak.

Interestingly, despite the concerns about the Meteor's tandem seating arrangement and its disadvantages compared with the Vampire and Venom seating arrangement, it became quite the norm. The latter concept became quite common as well over the following decades. The side by side seating arrangement was applied in some future designs: the F-111, the A-6 Intruder, and, more recently, the Russian-built SU-24 and SU-34, the latter seen lifting off runways in Syria recently to support the dog they have in that particular fight. Interestingly, the SU-34's cockpit, like the Vulcan, is accessed from below, just forward of the nose wheel housing, making it all the more of an oddity for a fighter. The US Navy and Marine Corps were also stepping ahead of the RAF at the beginning of the 1950s with their own first purpose built all-weather night fighters, the Douglas F3D Skyknight and the Demon (the Americans leave even us Brits in the shade when it comes to picking terrific names for military aircraft) were already in use during the Korean conflict from 1951. The Skyknight, for all the world, resembled a large twin-engine Jet Provost and with only modest greater performance didn't make much more of an impact on impact shooting down about six enemy aircraft over Korea. It was equipped with a rear facing warning radar in the tail section which had a range of 4 nautical miles and proved invaluable for providing timely notice to the pilot and radar intercept officer.

The Skyknight also employed the two side by side cockpit seating arrangement, supposedly allowing greater co-operation between the two crew. The list of tandem two-seat fighters and Strike Aircraft has many examples: F-4, Tornado, F-14, F-18F, Mirage IV, 2000D/N, Buccaneer, and (while only ever a prototype) TSR-2.

The first purpose-built night all-weather fighter to be accepted into RAF service also incorporated this design. On 13 April 1949, the Ministry of Supply issued instructions to the two primary bidders, de Havilland and Gloster, to start work on their respective designs. Gloster were ready to address the air staff requirement for a purpose designed high performance all-weather night fighter in 1951. Their proposed design had started out as a single-seater but the rear cockpit was quickly incorporated. It also possessed a variety of radical new features, which were to become quite common place: a delta wing; two engines but both buried in the fuselage (a feature that was hitherto typical only of single-engine aircraft); and the tail section mounted on top of the fin and given a swept leading edge with a moderate corresponding sweep along the trailing edge. This was the GA.5 that was aimed to possess the level of performance capable of meeting the challenge of intercepting fast targets at very high altitude and possessing very long range as far as the compromise over speed and climb performance allowed.

Competition came directly from the DH.110, being put together by de Havilland. This too could claim to be a first for the same reasons, but as events would prove, for the Fleet Air Arm of the Royal Navy rather than the Royal Air Force. For all the world, the latter looked more curious, with its own swept delta-like wings and twin-engine arrangement submerged in the main fuselage with air intakes forming a part of the wing chord and presenting as little disruption to the streamlining as possible. The twin-boom tail was already a feature of some past designs—the Lockheed P-38 Lightning and of course from the same stable as DH.110, the Vampire, and Venom, perhaps being the most prominent. However, the cockpit arrangement on the DH.110 bore more similarity to a tank, the pilot sat on top and off set to the left, this made room for the 'coal bunker' cockpit to the right but sunk into the forward fuselage with the limited window view blotted out rendering the observer/radar intercept officer's position somewhat disorientating. So, these two prototypes were the pioneer designs for the next step forward toward the next stage in British fighter evolution.

The first GA.5 prototype, WD804, took to the air on 26 November 1951, just as the Vampire and Meteor were in turn replacing the last in the line of de Havilland Mosquito NFs. WD804 amassed a total of sixty-four flying hours before being lost on 29 June 1952. A further prototype, WD808, made its maiden flight on 20 August 1952 and accrued nine and a half hours before being taken apart on 19 September 1952 for modifications.

By 1952, the Gloster GA5 was seen in general terms as indirect competition with DH.110 project being pursued by de Havilland. In September, the two bespoke all-weather fighter designs were to be paraded before potential clients, not to mention the general public, at the Farnborough air show. At the time, each of the British manufacturers, and quite a range of them there were, were out to field their futuristic propositions to equip not just the RAF and the Fleet Air Arm, but any possible overseas customers. Each of the firms, including Avro, English Electric, de Havilland, Gloster, Handley Page, Hawker, Supermarine, and Vickers, had something to show off in terms of the military market.

Much has been said since that what happened at Farnborough made up the RAF's mind to go with the Javelin, but it and the DH.110 (Sea Vixen), were already being pitched at the RAF and FAA respectively. In any case, whatever interest the RAF would have held in the DH.110 was not necessarily dashed once and for all following Farnborough 1952 as the first GA5 prototype had already been lost only two months earlier.

On 6 September 1952, at about 2.50 p.m., over Farnborough, the de Havilland DH.110, WG240, broke up mid-flight, showering wreckage, including one of the two engines, into the public enclosure. This was the second public day of the then annual Farnborough SBAC exhibition and flying display. The crew of the de Havilland prototype were typical of the frontiersmen of the age. The pilot, John Derry, was a veteran of the Second World War; he had served in the RAF and been awarded the DFC (Distinguished Flying Cross) on 28 June 1945. The citation read:

> This officer has participated in a large number of sorties as air gunner and later as pilot. He has at all times displayed great determination and spirit and his squadron has been of the highest order. In April 1945 he led his squadron in an attack against enemy gun positions. Despite intense opposition the attack was pressed home with great accuracy. The success of this operation was due in no small measure to Squadron Leader Derry's gallant and skilful leadership. This officer has set a fine example to all.

Derry was a typical test pilot of the 'empire of the clouds' era; his experience and background was forged in the heat of war, during which he had flown many prop engine types and was now a pioneer of jet development. Working under John 'Cats' Eyes' Cunningham DSO DFC, he was in the vanguard of pilots during the late 1940s who were already risking life and limb by stepping into such a vast area of unexplored, high-performance flying and all its increased demands. Jets such as would become synonymous with the Cold War and familiar to generations of aircrew in later years, had to be tamed first by men like John Derry and his contemporaries: Neville Duke (Hawker Hunter), Bill Waterton (Gloster GA5 Javelin), Roly Falk (Avro 698 Vulcan), and Roland 'Bee' Beaumont (English Electric P1 Lightning). John had initially been involved with the DH 108, a swept-wing, tailless aircraft, adapted from the Vampire.

Upon leaving the RAF at the end of the Second World War, he had been approved as a test pilot for the Ministry of Supply and assigned to Vickers Armstrong in December 1946. The following November, he joined de Havilland at Hatfield in Hertfordshire. John had also been medically examined, most recently on 4 July 1952 at RAF Henlow, and had been cleared as fully fit, receiving the service medical category grading A1 G1, this referring to the best rated standard for military service both in the air and on the ground. He was also the first British pilot to successfully exceed the speed of sound in an operational fighter aircraft.

John Derry had accrued 2,000 flying hours, including ninety-seven on the DH.110. His navigator, Mr A. M. (Tony) Richards, was a younger man in comparison, being only twenty-four years of age. Tony was not trained as aircrew and had no military training, but had flown with John Derry on nearly all test flights. His background was as a technician, described as a promising young man—a typical product of the de Havilland Aeronautical Technical School. At the age of seventeen, he started training in December 1944. By the end of his apprenticeship in 1948, he had become an associate fellow of the Royal Aeronautical Society and by 1952, he was assigned to the company's flight test section, where he had been engaged on general flight test observations and calculation. Not that it should have made any significant difference in his particular line, but he had only recently been assigned to the DH.110 project from trials work with the Heron Light Transport aircraft. Since his transfer, he had become the first British flight test observer to exceed the speed of sound.

On the day of the incident, the weather had been fine and the subsequent accident investigation ruled out any suggestion that it had any bearing at all. Just as with the Javelin, the Sea Vixen (DH.110) was billed as a subsonic or transonic fighter; however, that does not mean neither pointing straight down with the wind behind them could not breach the sound barrier. Furthermore, this was 1952 and demonstrations by aircraft (whether officially truly supersonic or not) smashing through the sound barrier at such events was something of a treat; indeed, a popular treat at RAF Battle of Britain displays in the early 1950s was the sonic 'boom' courtesy of an F-86 Sabre, the cutting-edge day fighter in the West's arsenal pre-Hunter. Naturally then, the DH.110's display included a supersonic dive as part of the rehearsed sequence. To give some idea of the scale and scope, a modern display by a Typhoon or F-16 in the finest weather would look for a ceiling of perhaps as much as 15,000 to 30,000 feet, depending on just how dramatic the final flourish will be. In 1952, John Derry needed to take his Sea Vixen prototype all the way up to 40,000 feet, then commence a dive toward the airfield, pulling out in the 'vicinity' in view of the spectators. On this particular occasion, two bangs associated with a supersonic dive, were heard. John Derry then pulled out of the dive and turned to make a fast pass along the runway. He then turned to the left into a tight circuit at low height and high speed. While rolling out of this steep turn, about one and a half miles north-west from the public enclosure, in transition from straightening out then into the roll, the aircraft broke up in mid-air. The wreckage trail extended 1.5 miles on the reciprocal heading, south-east toward the crowd line. Derry and Richards made no attempt to abandon the aircraft and were consequently killed. The engine fell into the public enclosure, killing twenty-nine spectators.

Sonic booms were still to be outlawed and the early fifties was the era when prototype and experimental jets capable of exceeding the sound barrier, even if it required nudging the nose into a slightly depressed angle in order to achieve this. One thing we can be sure of, no one was going to register a complaint, certainly not officially. So, it was then that the best of the best: Bill Waterton (GA5), John Derry (DH.110 until his tragic death at Farnborough), Neville Duke (Hunter), and Roly Falk (Avro 698)—he who rolled and looped the Vulcan—were on hand to impress. However, given the propensity for hidden faults and imperfections in every new aircraft design, especially during the envelope stretching age of the 1950s, the number of instances where a prototype or in-service aircraft came to a messy end were far too uncomfortably numerous to be dismissed as within any acceptable range, by twenty-first century standards. The Gloster GA5 was typically ambitious in design, like the Avro 698, which would become the Vulcan, GA5 was a delta-wing, a completely new concept but seemingly popular with designers looking to push the edge of the envelope as the saying goes. So, the delta wing was pursued, largely because of the options, and quite a few there were—for instance, the swept leading edge could do nothing but lesson drag and enable acceleration.

On 29 June, Bill Waterton was flying the first prototype GA5, WD804. At 3,000 feet, the control column started to vibrate; he found that he had lost elevator control leaving free movement with no resistance at all when pushed fore and aft. He was able to control the aircraft using the trim on the trailing edge of the elevator and managed to get the aircraft up to 10,000 feet this way. After carrying out a number of trials here, he decided to try and land at Boscombe Down. As the trials had demonstrated that the controls worked better at higher speed, he came in fast toward the runway and bounced heavily on landing. After the jet had bounced a number of times along the runway, the undercarriage collapsed and a small fire started. Before coming to a halt, the aircraft's port wing sheared and the starboard undercarriage ripped through the wing. Later Javelin models had an all-moving tail section. What had happened was the elevators had come apart from the tail section at 3,000 feet; one was later retrieved. Bill Waterton suffered some light injury. he was Gloster's chief test pilot at the time. It was said of Bill that he had demonstrated 'not only great courage but great confidence in the aircraft itself', this due to his decision to stay with it and attempt a wheels-down landing. Five prototypes were built, each to trial specific elements; they were, in order of first flight:

WD804 F/F 26 June 1951
WD808 F/F 21 August 1952
WD827 F/F 07 May 1953
WT830 F/F 14 January 1954
WT836 F/F 20 July 1954

The second prototype, WD808, was also lost when it entered an unrecoverable 'super stall'.

Flying of WD808 had resumed on 12 January 1953. Tragically, WD808 was lost five months later, on 11 June 1953, along with the pilot, Fleet Air Arm Officer Lt Peter Lawrence, who sacrificed his life staying with the stricken aircraft for as long as it took to correct its position in order to bring the aircraft down without risking harm to life, limb, or real estate. The aircraft was so low at the point of ejection that his chute failed to open on time; Lawrence was just 400 feet up when he ejected. Recorded data found that the aircraft was unstuck from the runway after a distance of 400 yards and at a speed of 110 knots, with flaps up. With flaps at 28 degrees, this was improved to 300 yards and 90 knots. Between them, 804 and 808 notched up a total of 104 flying hours for 166 flights.

The third prototype, WT827, first flew on 3 March 1953 and by the time it was retired, it had accrued 225 flights and 142 hours and thirty minutes total flying time. A further three prototypes were built by Gloster. The last, XD158, the prototype Mark 2, took to the air for the first time on 31 October 1955.

However, matters were moving apace rapidly, with prototypes still being used to develop and test the product. The first production Mark 1, XH544, had already made its maiden flight on 22 July 1954, flown by test pilot Dickie Martin. XH544, although not a prototype, was needed for trial and evaluation; the operational debut, or to use a modern phrase, IOC (initial operational capability) was still almost two years away, a date which could have been much better set further back still.

Altogether, they had completed 470 hours of test flying by 29 February 1956. By this stage, the aircraft could have done with an extra two years or so gestating. The first fifty-six production aircraft astonishingly had to be used for further trials with three of them being handed over to A & AEE at Boscombe Down, a not unusual figure in itself.

The third production aircraft was lost on 21 October 1954, again with the loss of the pilot. During high speed trials at low altitude, the port lower undercarriage door tore away, leaving slight damage to the rib on the stub tailplane, which resulted in the tail actuator jamming at 540 knots. On this particular flight, the aircraft accelerated to 550 knots at 3,000 feet. The acceleration occurred quite rapidly with the engines running at 8,200 rpm. At the maximum number, 8,600 rpm, the aircraft was still accelerating but more slowly, at which point the run was broken to avoid cloud. At higher altitude between Mach numbers of 0.87 and 0.88, the aircraft was described as a satisfactory gun platform. Above this, the aircraft was unsteady but controllable, sufficient for the pilot to traverse the aircraft with intent—in other words, heavy forces were encountered, but the pilot remained in control. The loss of the undercarriage door was unnoticed during the flight.

In the ongoing testing of equipment for the night all-weather fighter role, one young chap, Jock Sneddon, a Meteor pilot of that early pioneering post-war era, was testing the latest Gee nav/ref equipment for night fighters when he and his navigator, Ed Lewis, got lost testing the kit's reliability for referencing. They found themselves, after a period of time airborne, overhead a location that did not concur with the information supplied by the GEE set. The story was related by Jock Sneddon to Barry Mayner back in 1963. Barry was a navigator on 29 Sqn at Leuchars at the time, and told me the story when I met him a couple of years back over assistance with *Northern 'Q'*. He has been good enough to recount it here:

> In the mid 1950s, Fighter Command Meteor 11 and Vampire NF.10 were fitted with GEE Mk3 a new receiver to fit in AW Fighters. As the primary nav aid, this system used a new receiver and indicator box which was much smaller than previous GEE equipment. One major change was veeder counters which showed a numerical display of the GEE fix. It was very quick and fixes could be plotted on the GEE CHART very rapidly.
>
> Jock and Ed got airborne to do a cross-country from Tangmere in a 29 Sqn-NF.11 in 1954.
>
> The route was flown above cloud until they tried to contact base to recover. They were unable to talk to Tangmere so elected to descend below cloud to make a no-radio recovery. When they broke out of cloud and visual with the ground, nothing was recognisable. After a few minutes, they realised they were over France and so turned onto

Meteor NF.11 of 151 Squadron in 1953, one of the RAF's last utility night all-weather fighters of the 1950s. (*Barry G. Mayner*)

north, expecting to quickly reach the Channel coast. Sometime later, they were over the sea at low level and short of fuel. Eventually, they fixed themselves visually south of base to the west of Tangmere. Somewhere over the water a few miles from Littlehampton, they were about to run out of fuel. So, Jock climbed to a height suitable for baling out (NO BANGSEAT DAYS); Ed informed his captain that he was wearing his best uniform and shoes with no intention of climbing over the side. Jock elected to ditch the aircraft, despite the Pilots Notes advice not to attempt to ditch a Meteor.

The ditching was successful and Jock got out of his cockpit and, with his dinghy, he swam as fast as possible away, inflated his dinghy, and climbed in. He then started looking for his navigator. He saw Ed walking along the wing of a floating NF.11, carrying his dinghy pack. Ed inflated his dinghy on top of the wing, climbed into it, completely dry, and proceeded to launch into the sea. They were rescued by a fishing boat and the A/C sank. Later, at the Board of Inquiry, Ed insisted that he had taken fixes every five minutes and had plotted them on his chart and navigated around the planned route. Jock was given a Red Endorsement in his Log Book.

Some weeks later, a fishing boat saw the Meteor on the seabed and reported the find. The Gee box was recovered and sent off for investigation. A serious defect was discovered in a large resister on a circuit board, which would have caused an insidious progressive error of the Gee readout. Jock was summoned to HQ Fighter Command for an interview with Air Marshal Sam Patch (AOC 11 Group at the time). Jock's Red Endorsement was replaced with a Green Endorsement. He then related the circumstances of the ditching to Sam Patch. Jock found himself attached to Handling Squadron Boscombe Down to help write ditching notes for the Meteor NF.11. Jock and Ed were young first tourists at a time when the RAF was expanding into a large force of jet aircraft at the start of the Cold War.

There were many incidents we can look back at and smile. This was not the last adventure this crew experienced. They were crewed together on 29 Sqn Javelin Mk 9s in the early sixties. They kept me laughing on many occasions recounting stories. Jock taught me a great deal about air to air gunnery, and was fun to fly with. Jock was on 85 Sqn flying Venoms when the Mk 1 Bone Dome was introduced; his helmet was painted red with the 85 Squadron hexagon motif and red and black chequers. That Bone Dome remained with him until he finished flying but that was his Lightning story from Coltishall.

Gloster were working on a number of projects in order to meet the demands of two new operational requirements (ORs). OR 309 required an aircraft able to intercept and engage an enemy aircraft as far out from UK shores as the extent of control and reporting technology would permit. OR 234 set the task of finding an aircraft to act as a long-range bomber escort and GA5 was to be considered as a candidate.

3
Cold War Night Fighter

In 1954, ministers examined the defence programme in light of the detonation of the hydrogen bomb. At that time, Fighter Command was expecting by 1956 to have twelve squadrons already equipped with the Gloster Javelin, totalling 264 aircraft, with twenty-four day-fighter squadrons, totalling 528 aircraft, of which twelve units would be equipped with Supermarine's chief competitor to the Hunter, the Swift. The remaining units would be operating four squadrons with Sapphire-engined Hunter F2s and F5s, with eight squadrons operating the Hunter F6. This allowed for a U. E. (unit establishment) of twenty-two aircraft per squadron. Following the 1954 defence review, it was decided, on recommendation from the air defence committee, to have a smaller fighter force composed as follows: eighteen all-weather squadrons (288 aircraft) and eighteen day fighter squadrons (288 aircraft).

In 1955, before the first operational Javelins were delivered to the RAF, investigation was already underway at the RAE, in company with Gloster, to develop a truly supersonic version employing a thin-wing design. In a report from Sir Arnold Hall, he described the term 'thin wing' as a misnomer because it did not have a thin wing by the standards of the day and that in order to give the aircraft a fair supersonic performance, the wing would have to be thinned down by 4 to 5 per cent. This would actually increase the weight of the aircraft by about 5,000 to 6,000 lb, a loss of height (all quite counter-intuitive) but an increase in speed to about Mach 2.0; to improve upon this would have meant virtually starting over again with a new aircraft design.

So simply put, the RAF could have either a really fast fighter with a weapon system designed for stern chase attacks, or a much slower fighter with a weapon system designed for head-on collision course acquisition, or near head-on attacks.

The weapon system such as it was followed what Sir Archibald Sinclair described as a mother and child concept. This relied upon the weapon itself to have supersonic performance but not necessarily the aircraft itself. This idea negated the need for a supersonic airframe, provided the weapons system worked fine. This was what Sir Archibald had to say to the Deputy Chief of Air Staff, Air Marshal Sir Thomas Pike. The Javelin had been built around the AR.18 radar, which was a comparatively large and heavy set, but one which would have a good long range. With this in mind, Sir Thomas came away encouraged about the prospect of the Javelin in service, especially given that it would be propped up, by the tandem arrival in service of the F.23 (English Electric Lightning). It would appear that the Javelin promised not all that much of a leap forwards and upwards; expectations, officially, were as follows:

> The Javelin, which has been developed as an all-weather fighter, will in its original form be somewhat lacking in speed, but its sophisticated weapons system will be a compensating asset. It is capable of further development. It will be in production in 1955; the developed form, known as the thin winged Javelin, is capable of collision course attack, and should be ready for production by 1959.

The Ministry of Supply's paper raised and discounted the possibility of 50 per cent improvement in the speed of the thin-wing Javelin. The air ministry was aware of Gloster's claims, but had not had time to evaluate anything. There were indeed doubts about Gloster's capacity to live up to any promises, but the improvement they were claiming could, it was argued, put the thin-wing Javelin in the same class as some of the new, quite advanced American fighters. If the aircraft could carry collision-course missiles then its ability to provide a reasonable degree of protection against any supersonic bomber designs the Soviet Union may have been developing was recognised. It would not, however, be available until 1961. Further, it was described as having no development potential beyond that and would be quite expensive to develop and produce. While the English Electric P1 was already at the prototype stage, there was a need for something else, at least to provide some degree of insurance if nothing else. To meet this requirement, the Air Staff wanted an American fighter, if possible. As a general election was expected in 1955, any decision to buy a new American fighter design would have to wait until after the election had rendered its outcome. In the meantime, postponing the thin-wing Javelin until then was not appealing, certainly not if, in the end, the Air Staff were after all impressed with Gloster's claim following evaluation. On the other hand, money has always been such a weight around the necks of those charged with making such decisions that fear of taking a disastrous and scandalous step financially often has resulted in doing just that anyway. No better example exists today than the UK's *Queen Elizabeth*-class aircraft carrier programme. Therefore, the expectation was that a degree of risk would be incurred and that a supersonic all-weather fighter other than the P1 would need to be pursued and that the risk would have to continue because the Javelin about to enter service was less than adequate.

One favoured alternative was being developed by Avro in Canada. The CF-105 Arrow was suggested as a thin-wing Javelin alternative and could be ready as soon as 1960, if we could somehow get the aircraft fitted with 'free' supplies of an American electronics system. Earlier, this proposition was advanced on the grounds that it could be available in 1962. This was dependent on the Canadian Government giving satisfactory assurances that they would provide certain levels of design and material assistance, a matter for which they were as of May 1956 yet to be approached. For their part, the Americans would prefer to provide material aid in the form of equipment of their own design and manufacture, including whole aircraft. Casting further doubt, the RAF's Central Fighter Establishment had gained the impression that, from the Americans at least, the Canadians were trying to push the CF-105 to the point of being an advance on anything the Americans had to offer, but with no indication of success.

The Air Staff were making the case for US all-weather fighters, claiming:

> An efficient Fighter Command is an indispensable factor in our contribution to the allied deterrent to war ... it is essential that we should provide the best measure of defence for our own nuclear bases and for similar US bases in this country in order to ensure that they can launch the necessary counter attacks. Furthermore, the more efficient the allied air defence the greater the proportion of his total resources which the aggressor must devote to developing the quality of his attacking force, and to increasing its size, and the longer he will take to do it.

Although Sandys' infamous 1957 Defence White Paper was still a couple of years away from publication, the Air Ministry was already resigned to the belief that to maintain fighters in the numbers they would like to have, especially with the introduction of aircraft and weapons that were increasingly costly to maintain, was unaffordable. It was already accepted that the numbers of fighters were going to have to be reduced. However, to make the best of the situation logically would mean devoting all available resources to the all-weather fighter force. This in turn meant all-weather fighters would need to be of the highest quality. Further, the position at the time was, 'We do not believe that guided weapons suitable for UK conditions can make a substantial contribution to UK defence before 1965.'

On top of this scenario, a suitable successor to the Javelin was seen as unlikely before 1963 or even 1965. Also, the Javelin's performance was, as the first aircraft formed the first operational squadron at RAF Odiham, inadequate against a supersonic bomber such as the Russians may have in service after 1960. Even before that time, its performance was considered only marginal against the best of the current threat. The only option seen at the time that could be delivered in time was a high-performance US fighter with air-to-air guided missiles and adequate spares. The balance of spares payments at the time precluded purchase of what was provisionally 300 to 400 aircraft, which meant having to explore the possibility of US assistance in their acquisition.

Under Basic Force Mk 2, the all-weather fighter force in Fighter Command was planned to increase to twelve squadrons (264 UE) by the middle of 1955 and continue at this level beyond 1957. In addition, were four AWF Squadrons (64 UE) in the 2nd Tactical Air Force, expected to retain beyond 1957. Also, a further two squadrons in MEAF with an establishment of just sixteen aircraft was to be reduced by a squadron by the middle of 1955. The big plan, *circa* 1955, was that by 1958, the RAF would field an all-weather fighter force of 336 jets that, if not by this time, would ultimately be all Gloster GA5 Javelins. Ambitiously, the more specific aim was that they would all be Javelin FAW.2s, a clear indication that the likelihood of going through nine variants in three years to reach the definitive mark was not being entertained, fitted with AI18 radar and capable of delivering the Red Dean missile, unless another type capable of doing the job just as well (but cheaper) could be found. As the FAW.2 was not expected before the end of 1958, the back fill or interim fighter was to be the Javelin FAW.1. It was clear that everyone expected the Mark 2 aircraft to arrive as a much more capable and definitive aircraft than the premature version it turned out to be. Not only that, it was in the end nothing but an alternative model to the Mark 1. Problems that would culminate in the variety of models never got ironed out in time. Considerable difficulties were already surfacing one headache was the radar for the Mark 1. About 145 APQ-43 AIR sets had so far been ordered, which in itself fell far short of the operational requirements envisaged. There were a total of four radar sets considered for use: the AI.17 (least favoured by Fighter Command), the AI.18, the AI.19, and the APQ-43 (also known as AI.22)—the latter being an American design.

The definitive plan was to retrofit all Javelins with the AI.18, including those (Mark 2s) equipped with the APQ-43. The AI.18 was seen as the best radar and therefore chosen over the three other options: the AI.17, the AI.19, and the APQ-43. Much of what was expected was falling short, the FAW.1 should have carried Blue Jay missiles from the start, the FAW2 should, of course, have carried the Blue Jay, as it turned out neither would be armed with anything but cannons and serve as interim aircraft only, but the desire to get a missile armed, or potentially missile armed, all-weather fighter into service was facing a priority for airframes to be made available whatever the availability of realistic equipment, intercept radars were available from the start, but no missiles.

Ultimately no Javelins carried Blue Jays, neither the AR.17 nor the APQ-43-equipped aircraft would be capable of carrying it. As time pressed on, revised planning expected that the first aircraft to be delivered would be modified retrospectively to carry missiles, even if not necessarily Blue Jays.

By May 1955, the arrival in service of the first Javelins was starting to look unlikely to make the original planned in-service date without a list of defects and other unresolved problems and so, reluctantly, early production and delivery, it was already suggested, should be stretched. The suggestion came from the Ministry of Supply so that fewer aircraft would be built before the technical faults were ironed out. A desirable side effect of this was the expectation of getting more aircraft in service with the higher-thrust SA7 engine. The original target of December 1955 for getting seventy-eight aircraft in service had been revised in April to a figure of fifty-nine.

A letter was sent from Air Chief Marshal Sir John Baker, on 21 May 1955, to Air Marshal Sir Thomas Pike. It was in response to the request the previous month to slow down the production rate of the Javelin until development problems could be resolved. This request had been agreed and the matter was to be addressed by slowing production down by eighteen months and, as had been suggested, using the opportunity to equip more aircraft in the long run with the SA7 engine instead of the SA6. This amounted to about 100 aircraft, but there would be eighty fewer aircraft delivered by September 1956. This was as far as the Air Ministry could possibly go without incurring redundancy charges. It also put an end to the idea of just a single interim (FAW.1) and a definitive (FAW.2) variant. The process of entry into service and development was going to arrive at many variants of the Javelin in the pipeline with the RAF now facing the process of evaluating the performance of each: those with the SA6, those with the SA7 alongside those with additional fuel, also those aircraft with strengthened undercarriage. Furthermore, a comparison was made of performance between the different Javelin variants being proposed to enter service and the different configurations. Sir John Baker was, on the other hand, confident that between Gloster and the RAE, they could iron out current troubles with low and high-speed flight handling.

Acceptance of this new plan principally allowed the firm and the agency time to resolve the major defects. It would, of course, delay the formation of the first Javelin squadron in Fighter Command and the first one for 2nd TAF by a further three months. A further suggestion was to hold off until September 1957 before forming the first squadron in Fighter Command, if this wasn't stretching matters a tad rather far, the proposal further recommended holding off the first Germany based squadron formation until June 1958.

On the up side, bearing in mind the desire to get uprated engine Javelins in service soonest, it was expected that this would allow the re-equipment of two Meteor NF.11 squadrons in 2nd TAF with SA7-engined Javelins instead of with the expected SA6. The later conversion period would extend the out of service dates of the Meteor NF.11 and the NF.12/14 by six and three months respectively, also deferring the run-down of the Venom NF.2 and NF.3 squadrons in Fighter Command by three months.

Venom NF3, starting up at Leuchars, along with the Meteor NF.14, the last stage before the Javelin. (*Barry G. Mayner*)

Always keen to see the bright side, even in private, the author of the proposals pointed out that while his report was regrettable, he still expected the defects with the Javelin to be eradicated and the fallow period would give the RAF a somewhat improved capability (expected with the quicker widespread number of aircraft with SA7 engines), albeit later and over a slightly longer term. However, the actual phrase used by the Secretary of State for Air, Lord De L'Isle, was 'of the assumption that the present defects in the Javelin will be eradicated'. Still, the plan was approved by the Minister for Supply, who was Selwyn Lloyd at the time of the proposal, but now as of 21 May, was Reginald Maudling. This then meant that the RAF were still going to get the same number of Javelins by March 1958, the caveat from Air Chief Marshal Sir John Baker, who was Controller of Aircraft, was 'should we still want them'. This may have been a subtle hint of what was coming around the corner, but whatever the thinking at the Ministry of Defence, there was not even a hint at present about any radical changes in the foreseeable future. A new Defence Minister had indeed just been appointed: Mr Selwyn Lloyd.

By June 1955, AOC-in-C Fighter Command was getting impatient and expressed the view that he would like to get the first squadron of Javelins formed as soon as possible 'providing the aircraft weren't too dangerous to fly', he was prepared to accept them in almost any form. Following on from this, he would like the second squadron as quickly as possible but with the various buffeting faults so far encountered to be resolved. From the third squadron onwards, all fitted with SA7 engines, by delaying the order, he expected to get the improved AI.18 radar instead of the much inferior AI.17. This was not the position of the DCAS (Deputy Chief of the Air Staff), Sir Thomas Pike, who was now also inclined to advise the CAS to accept the Ministry of Supply proposals for cutting back production and go for quality over quantity. His concern was that both numbers and capable aircraft were important but that introducing larger numbers of Javelins which were less than worthy of being sent into combat would inevitably become public knowledge and the criticism would be very difficult to dismiss. He drew comparisons with the Hawker Hunter when it entered service; any critical observations made by the press were easy enough to explain because from the start, they knew they had a good aircraft. With the Javelin, this 'might be different'. The Air Staff were also looking at offsetting redundancy costs through reduced and slowed down orders by modification charges to bring the early marks of Javelin up to an 'operational standard'. This was the situation now as of 8 June 1955.

As it was to materialise just the same, all Javelins entering service did so with the SA6 engine until the arrival of the Mark 7 in 1958. This amounted to about ten squadrons, although such was the state of flux that at least two of these disbanded during the same time while six operational marks and a trainer version equipped the remaining squadrons, but more of this in the next chapter.

Whatever the headaches generated by the fighter, there was serious consideration afforded to the idea of a bomber version of the Javelin in 1955. Under Air Staff requirement OR 328 and described as a decision to develop a tactical version of a special weapon, there was a desire to define a detailed operational requirement for a suitable aircraft to deliver a tactical weapon. Whichever aircraft was used, it was expected to be in service by 1959. The design used would need to possess a level of performance sufficient to allow it to not simply evade, but which would have 'the greatest possible immunity from contemporary defences and with an ability to deliver effectively the weapons concerned, at the greatest possible ranges'. To meet these requirements, the Air Staff had determined that of all options available, the Javelin could best suit the provision of 'best possible performance, particularly in range and speed'. The reference to a 'special weapon' suggested a nuclear warhead-equipped bomb. It was also hoped that the aircraft would deliver a suitable weapon from high altitudes using blind bombing techniques within the range of friendly ground radar stations. The more specific requirement was for a 'developed version of the Javelin fighter, as defined in the Air Staff standard of preparation reference C.53281/53 dated August 1954'. By low level, the Air Staff target was a mean height of 500 feet or less above the ground or 1,000 feet above mean sea level, for most of a sortie. Typical range would be around 1,000 nautical miles from the launch base. It was expected that such an aircraft, were it to happen, would operate from larger airfields, but no examples are given. However, the fitting of a braking parachute was considered acceptable. Alas, the plan for the bomber version did not advance much beyond the stage of requiring the best of every conceivable performance consideration, as asked on paper. The crew would be accommodated in a pressurised cabin with standard low differential pressure characteristics. There is no suggestion that the Javelin bomber was a direct contender against the TSR-2, but it is hard to imagine any other driving reason.

This being the age it was, there was no end of contenders on the blocks facing difficulties, both real and imagined. The F.153.D was another contender to fulfil the remit given the Javelin. It was criticised because it would not have supersonic performance. Sir John Baker asked the RAE to evaluate and assess whether the F.153.D would be the best choice of all-weather fighter by 1960. The DRAE believed that there were certainly difficulties in designing an aircraft that could reach 50,000 feet, boast supersonic performance, and carry the necessary equipment, which would be quit bulky and heavy, while carrying the Red Dean air-to-air missile and not requiring close control from the ground. The F.153.D was being compared with the American Convair F-102 Delta Dagger, which was on the point of entering service with the USAF. The British design was an inferior aircraft in general respects but was expected to carry the AR.18 radar, which was superior despite certain short comings including a blind spot which appeared as a very small cone in front of the target.

While the Javelin, yet to start line production, was being assessed against other likely contenders, the Belgian Air Force, looking to re-equip with a more formidable and capable mount started looking seriously at the Javelin as a replacement for their own Meteor NF.11s. In the end, Britain's increasing inability, usually through lack of Government resolve when their assistance was called upon to command the attention of overseas buyers failed to convince the Belgians, or anyone else on this occasion and the Belgians selected the Canadian CF-100 Canuck instead. It may well have been another case of too little too late. Exports of British designed and built military hardware, in particular aircraft, were already slipping and sliding away downhill, more was to come with the TSR-2 and the Lightning, but as of 1955, the Belgians already had an idea of just what specification of all-weather fighter they were looking for; the earliest version of the Javelin that would come close to meeting expectations was the Mark 7. The RAF were not of course due to see their first Mark 7s before 1958. The Belgians instead were offered, albeit as an opening commitment, twelve Mark 1 aircraft. This offer was declined. The production of Javelins would continue to be troublesome. A planned target for delivery had a total number delivered figure of 611 Mark 1 and 2 aircraft, variously powered with either the SA6 (8,000-lb thrust) and the SA7 (11,000-lb thrust). By March 1958, this order, of course, still assumed that all else regarding the aircraft would have reached a definitive point by September 1956 when the first of the uprated engine equipped airframes would roll off the assembly line, instead of having to produce five more versions the last of which, the Mk 7, eventually introduced the SA7 engine. These were superseded again in 1959 with the arrival of the Mk 8 and 9 beasts. Each new mark introduced another refinement: the Mk 2, the Westinghouse APQ-43 (AI.22) radar (the AI-18 never happened); the Mk 3 was the two-stick trainer (for pilots essentially, it was not radar equipped); the Mk 4, an all moving tail piece; the Mk 5, additional fuel capacity in the main plane (wings); the Mk 6, the improvements of the Mk 5 but with APQ-43 (the Mk 4 had the AI.17), and the Mk 7, essentially the Mk 5 with the more powerful Sapphires and the ability to carry Firestreak.

By the start of October 1955, tentative proposals put the Javelin order at 470. Some 400 of these had already been confirmed; of the possible follow on order for another

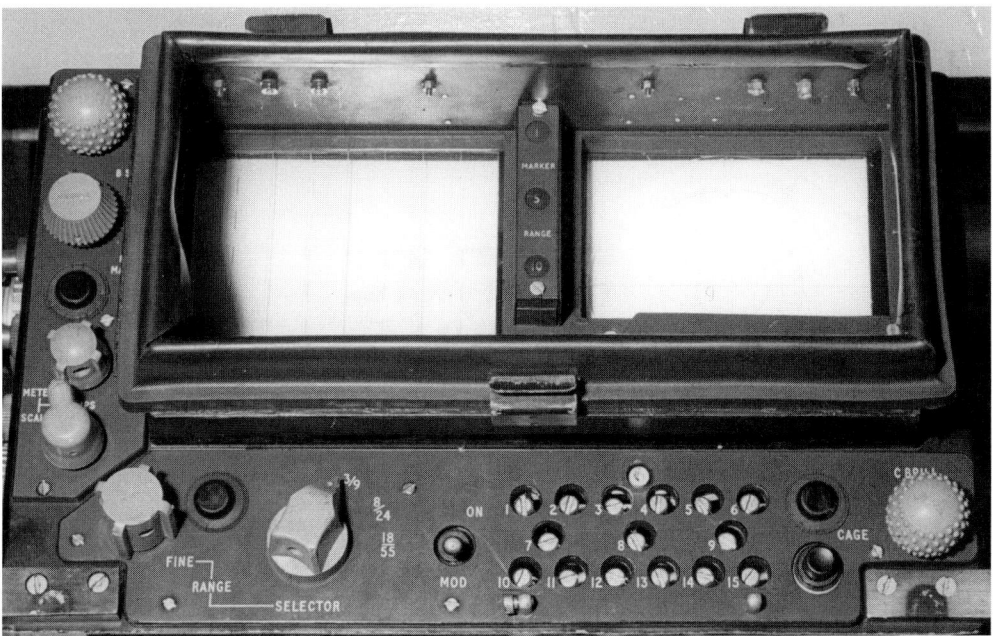

AI.17B Air Intercept Radar as used in FAW.1, 4, 5, 7 and 9. (*Barry G. Mayner*)

seventy, of these twenty had been earmarked for the Belgian Air Force in the meantime until a proper evaluation could be carried out. Uncertainties persisted over the Javelin's acceptance as an operational aircraft. Despite all, the first aircraft were due to enter service and in preparation, the RAF station selected to train the RAF's Javelin crews, Leeming, was having its runway lengthened to accommodate the heaviest and most powerful fighter to enter the RAF's inventory to date. In the meantime, the designated OCU, No. 228, was detached on 'Bolthole' to RAF North Luffenham, near Stamford in Leicestershire. Such was the overlap that the OCU, when back at Leeming, had a mobile conversion flight put together with the responsibility for going to the operational stations where Javelin squadrons were in the process of forming and providing what help they could. Whatever importance was put by the idea of a dedicated operational conversion unit for each aircraft type not just entering service but remaining through operational service as late as the 1960s, the first operational squadrons of some new types began working up with the new aircraft before the OCU was properly formed and functioning, ready to take its first course of students. Not just the Javelin but the Canberra and Hunter represented the RAF's new state of the art front line, save for the incoming 'V' bombers. They had a far more managed lead in to initial operational capability and the respective OCUs were up and running first as the 'V' jets represented such a radical advance. Otherwise, in 1955, OCUs for new types, typically, were still following the first operational squadrons rather than the other way around. All had a high incidence of accidents during the early stages of their operational deployment, the most shocking perhaps being that of Hawker Hunter, with just over thirty-four 'major' accidents for 10,000 flying hours. The Javelin, it was expected, would at least have a low rate of serious accidents per 10,000 hours because it had been so long in development and while not as savage as the Hunter's results, losses of Javelins in the years ahead were quite severe; only in relative terms could they be seen as moderate. Air Marshal Hubert Patch, the Air Defence Commander, stated on 28 March 1956:

> Our bitter experience with Venoms, Swifts, Hunters and now Javelins has shown clearly that the present system for introducing new fighter types into the service is unsatisfactory. I consider that there are too many steps between the aircraft industry and the user of the aircraft, which makes for unnecessary delays. I strongly recommend that the policy governing the participation of my Command in the development of new fighter aircraft be reviewed with the aim of starting the tactical evaluation as soon as possible.

By the time 1956 arrived, the Swift had been removed as an interceptor, from the order of battle on the grounds of unsuitability. This was seen as good news for the Javelin as this development could only point to ever greater store naturally being placed by all-weather aircraft and now plans had been altered to favour their number with a straight forward even balance. NATO had been told by Fighter Command that the need for all-weather fighters in greater ratio was for the greater good of course, but the overall number of fighters was being reduced through economic considerations which were being driven by Government priorities, needless to say. Further economic

XA552, having seemingly suffered an undercarriage malfunction. (*Barry G. Mayner*)

pressure by this time had meant that the day fighter force was to be cut to 192 aircraft divided into sixteen smaller squadrons between September 1957 and June 1958.

A note about the Hunter: the Mark 2 and 5 versions were powered by the same Armstrong Siddeley Sapphire turbojets as the Javelin. These were considered inferior in performance to the Avon-engined F6 and less versatile. They were viewed as incapable of the ground-attack role, something that the Avon-engined Hunter F6 was adept at with a derivative model, the FGA9, being delivered from 1959. As such, Sapphire-engined Hunters could not be assigned to war reinforcement roles overseas for which a ground-attack capability was required.

4
Service Debut

In 1956, the Air Defence Commander, Air Marshal Sir Hubert Patch, described the Javelin's introduction into service in less than glowing terms, worried about operational effectiveness and continuity suffering from what he described as dislocation caused by retrospective modifications, the nature of which could not be over emphasised. He also feared a similar premature birth affecting the F.23 or English Electric P1 Lightning in time to come.

In February 1956, the Gloster Javelin made its operational debut with No. 46 Squadron at RAF Odiham in Hampshire. This being pre-Sandys White Paper days still meant a large fighter force based along the east coast and a ring of fighter stations—Biggin Hill, Odiham, Tangmere, North Weald, and Duxford—arranged around the Greater London metropolis, largely owing their existence to the air defence arrangements of the last war but all to disappear over the forthcoming five years. Indecision over which airborne intercept radar to continue with meant essentially every new variant resulted in two new marks entering service at some stage or other almost simultaneously; the actual order of arrival into service was out of numerical service as well. The Mark 1, which equipped 46 Squadron, carried the British-built intercept radar. The next, shortly to follow, was the FAW.4 with 141 Squadron at Horsham St Faith in February 1957. Very shortly to follow was the Mark 2, introduced in fewer numbers, carrying the American radar, APQ-43 or AI.22 to use the UK term. Beyond this, both versions were burdened by the same flaws and drawbacks. Both had under-powered engines, neither was missile armed and neither had the internal fuel capacity of later marks much less the availability of in-flight refuelling. However, this was the RAF's first purpose-built all-weather fighter and could give the sleek Hunters and Swifts a good run as far as speed and ceiling were concerned.

The Javelin's arrival, however hastened, was seen as a significant improvement to the fighter force at the start of 1956, the much looked forward to thin-winged Javelin was confined to the bin though. The first sixteen jets were expected by March with the re-equipping of further squadrons expected to resume about six months on from then owing to what was described as 'unaccountable deficiencies'. The other main improvement required a touching faith on the part of the Air Staff; this was understood to be the increase in fighter numbers from thirty-four to thirty-six

First of the Flat Irons, 46 Squadron in formation *c*. 1956. (*Barry G. Mayner*)

squadrons. What was coming around the corner would render a shock of some magnitude to the kind of mindset that regarded these numbers as some kind of *status quo*. Following the 1954 Defence Review, the plan did authorise an establishment of thirty-six air defence fighter units split evenly into eighteen day fighter squadrons and eighteen night all-weather ones. The latter were expected to see a significant increase in the order of battle, growing from fourteen squadrons. On the fair-weather side of things, the Mark 6 Hunter was also due to begin replacing the earlier marks from the third quarter of the year. While a subject of a joint study at the time, the number of airfields the air defence commander, Air Marshal Hubert Patch, required was set at eighteen based on the number of squadrons planned, of which he was resigned to coping with just seventeen:

> I am forced to accept an extensive runway resurfacing programme starting early in 1956 to satisfy the operating requirements of the Thin Wing Javelin (now cancelled) and future breeds of fighters … it will result in considerable turbulence and possibly a loss of efficiency amongst those squadrons deployed to alternative bases whilst runway works services are in progress. Nevertheless, it is important to start this work as quickly as possible so that my airfields are developed to an adequate criteria by the critical period of 1958.

After 46 Squadron at Odiham finished equipping with the FAW.1, the first marker in the Javelin production history was reached; this was significant for the simple reason that it represented the end of the Mark 1 production line; just forty FAW.1s all told for 46 Squadron and later 87 Squadron (they received 46 Sqn's hand-me-downs) in Germany and to various other organizations: Rolls Royce, AFDS (Air Fighter Development Squadron), and A & AEE for trials and evaluation. The FAW.2, equipped with the

XA627 'B' one of 46 Squadron's FAW.1s. (*Ian White*)

46 Squadron FAW.1 in climb, *c.* 1956. (*Ian White*)

APQ-43 radar, represented a smaller batch, just thirty-one aircraft with some of these being used to replace 46 Squadron's Mark 1s. The rest went to form 89 Squadron at Stradishall, which, due to reshuffling, brought about by the fighter squadron cull inspired by Duncan Sandys, was re-numbered as 85. The overseas commands—Near East and Far East—would not begin receiving permanently based Javelins until 60 Squadron received Mark 9s in 1961 at RAF Tengah.

By that stage, several of the squadrons formed were being disbanded, essentially to re-equip with Bloodhound missiles, in keeping with the Sandys plan up to that point.

As 1956 progressed, it was clear that the RAF's brand new operational steed was at least providing a much-improved cutting edge; the Hunter was clearly unsuited as a night fighter, carrying only a range measuring radar set, certainly not even the most basic target acquisition AIR equipment. As such, its future lay in the field of close air support and tactical reconnaissance.

On the down side, the Javelin displayed, not unexpectedly, a farrago of teething problems: malfunctioning of airbrakes and defects with the rotax double-cartridge firings on the Sapphire engines resulting in single cartridge starts as a precautionary measure, the cartridges in use were considered to be the cause, and further defects regarding excessive nose-wheel shimmy had been encountered and was being investigated by Gloster. All these problems required urgent remedial action.

A little-known point here: at the time the Javelin was entering squadron service with the RAF, and in addition to the assets of Fighter Command, UK airspace was further defended by an element of the United States Air Force. The US 3rd Air Force's UK component, the 49th Air Division, was equipped essentially for the tactical and medium range strike role and was so equipped, at the time, with Republican F-84F Thunderstreaks and B-45 Tornados. A further element consisted of three squadrons of F-86D Sabres, for air defence duties with a UE each of twenty-five aircraft. These units did not fall under the operational command of the 3rd Air Force but under that of Fighter Command, as the 406th Fighter Interceptor Wing, and so were a part of Fighter Command's overall order of battle. However, administrative and logistics control continued to be exercised by the 3rd USAF. Three units, 512th Squadron, located at Bentwaters under 12 Group together with the 513th and 514th Squadrons, under 11 Group, both based at Manston. The F-86D, nicknamed 'Sabre Dog', was equipped with the heaviest fighter-launched air defence weaponry available to UK air defence at the time. Mighty Mouse rockets were unguided but hefty at 2.75 inch or 70-mm calibre. Also known as FFAR (Folding Fin Aerial Rocket), this at least was a significant step ahead of the 20-mm and 30-mm cannons arming British fighters of the day. The weapon was deployed on board the F-86D in a pack of twenty-four in a retractable deep tray, which were spewed forward when fired; while this was a fairly destructive package, it was disappointingly inaccurate. Intended as an air defence weapon, Mighty Mouse was far better suited to the role of ground-attack for which it was eventually more predominantly used by other aircraft, including the CF-100 Canuck.

The Americans were carrying out their own assessment of the Javelin as it was American dollars that were being ploughed into production and they were keen to know that this was not money being wasted on an inadequate design. Their report revealed some criticism that had to be addressed. Next, the RAF and the Ministry of Supply had to come to an arrangement to propose a list of modifications that would be agreeable to the Americans in order for them to proceed with paying out dollars for another country's fighter, chief ally or not.

Throughout the Javelin's development, the Air Staff pressed for improvements to the stall and spin characteristics. By the time of the US evaluation report being issued, June 1956, the aircraft was already being delivered as the Mark 1. The upshot was that the aircraft could not have these issues properly addressed without a major redesign of the airframe, so the Air Staff had to accept that the Javelin, meant to be the seminal future 'beats all' fighter design, must not be taken beyond the stall warning; this itself was regarded as affording adequate safety precautions. At the same time, an artificial stall warning was being developed in order to improve manoeuvrability and handling capabilities, this was to enable pilots to use more available g in the buffet zone while manoeuvring, yet still avoid reaching stall condition. It is the stall factor that bedevilled the Flat Iron so often. The artificial stall warning device was essential in all marks of Javelin after the Mark 1. The Mark 4, the version evaluated by the Americans, was not to be modified to carry the Blue Jay missile because they were not expected to survive that long on the front line.

Their assessment was sufficiently critical to prompt an indication at least that they may decline the request to pay for any Javelin marks prior to the FAW.7 and 8 at

FAW.1 XA556 at RAF Valley where it served on the Guided Weapons Training Squadron from 1959 to 1962 for trials on the Firestreak missile. (*Barry G. Mayner*)

all, which met the original specification OR.227 issued on 10 November 1953. The ministry of supply in response contended that the Americans were mistaken, that they had evaluated the FAW4 and based this on the specifications for OR.227 which related only to the FAW.7 and FAW.8. The MOS responded, claiming that the earlier model FAW.4 was built according to specification F.4/48, issue 2, released on 23 July 1952. Further, given the pressure for the Javelin to enter service, the only suggestion was that unsatisfactory Javelins were all there was unless they were prepared to extend the time for execution of the offshore contract, which covered this arrangement. This was the state of affairs as of 5 July 1956, seven months after the first squadron formed. The Air Defence Commander, Air Marshal Hubert 'Sam' Patch, described not just the Javelin's entry into service but that of its predecessors—Venom, Swift, and Hunter—as all presenting a bitter experience and stated that we could not allow the same situation to arise with the F.23, this being the English Electric Lightning, the first prototype model, P1A, which had already flown two years earlier.

Further, he cited a study of the USAF system of procurement of aircraft as likely to reveal support for his viewpoint. What never seems to have taken hold in the history of British Ministry of Defence procurement practices and what Air Marshal Patch also clearly advised was the insertion of a heavy penalty clause into contracts that just might ensure a more realistic effort on the part of the manufacturers to provide aircraft on time, complete with all required modifications and fully equipped and able to meet agreed performance standards. The balance between day and all-weather fighters was also now seen as something of a handicap. That there was such a thing as a day fighter at all was to follow the analogy of persisting with muskets in place of some rifles; the logic simply was that to have 50 per cent of the fighter force unusable under the conditions mostly likely to be favoured by a potential enemy for a crucial initial air attack, was frankly, illogical. Not only that, but a part of Patch's concern was that in 1956, half the day fighters were still Meteors. Their replacement by Hunters was seen as a great step forward as far as meeting the high-altitude threat during the day was concerned but this was negated by gun firing restrictions on the Hunter and poor serviceability resulting from under manning, lack of spares and a variety of modifications. An interesting note, Patch also remarked that the Hunter was unable to shoot down a balloon without risking severe airframe damage; indeed some years later, Hunters operating in close air support out in Aden in some cases had to limit their available four Aden cannons to two operating in order to preserve the airframe. Yet all these problems would be addressed with the full deployment of the Javelin and looking further ahead by at least 1962, the English Electric Lightning, the time that the entire fighter force would be all-weather rather than the point by which the Lightning would enter service.

Flight simulators for both the Hunter and the Javelin, at this stage, were still not in service. An array of new equipment had to be introduced in conjunction with the arrival of higher performance fighter and bomber aircraft, specifically, recovery systems and let down aids to cope with the fast approach and limited endurance of the 'modern jet fighter'. There was still a shortfall in the number of GCA (Ground Control Approach) systems at the airfields that needed them; ILS (Instrument Landing

Javelin FAW.4, XA631, at Moreton Valance about 1956 before being delivered to Boscombe Down, later serving with 72 and 87 Squadrons. (*Barry G. Mayner*)

System), BABS (Blind Approach 6 System), and Rebecca 8 were already available but the installation of these systems was gathering pace slowly. The simulators were of particular importance as the new aircraft were leading inevitably toward fewer peacetime flying hours for the crews.

The year 1956 was something of a crossroads for Fighter Command, the very *raison d'être* of air defence and just how it should be affected was being scrutinised ever more closely, the results of which would present quite a culture shock to the RAF the following year. For now, the air defence committee had been instructed to consider only what would be and was required to defend the new V-bomber force against a surprise attack. Something of a dilemma was now looming: the fighter force, if it was to be sustained at the planned size, already accommodated a degree of contraction but consummate with an increase in the ratio of all-weather fighters and what was already being suggested—guided weapons (SAMs). The concept of the day fighter was certainly coming to an end and the Hunter F6 would be the last one in the RAF deployed on the front line and would be gone from the air defence tapestry of the UK by the middle of 1963. What was not expected was the radical plan to be announced by Mr Duncan Sandys waiting just around the corner.

Meanwhile, a degree of fanfare had accompanied the first operational Javelins on 46 Squadron at RAF Odiham. Movietone News were there to record the squadron shortly after forming in order to bring the RAF's fantastic new toy to public attention. The Mark 1 Javelin powered with the SA6 engines and armed just with four 30-mm Aden cannons had a short operational history ahead. By August 1957, the unit that introduced the Javelin was re-equipping with the Mark 2 variant already, although their second-hand Mark 1s found a new home in Germany. By October 1958, 46 Squadron were operating the Mark 6 when they disbanded. That this one squadron went through three marks of such a sophisticated fighter in just over two-and-a-half years defines just how erratic and in turmoil both the country's air defences and the Javelin programme itself were. Squadrons still to re-equip with the Javelin when 46 Squadron disbanded would themselves disband again after a similarly short history with the type.

The majority of the squadrons re-equipping with the Flat Iron maintained the lineage, having previously operated a previous generation night fighter variant. A couple of Hunter squadrons also converted; both indeed survive to this day: No. 3 Squadron became the first unit operational with the Eurofighter Typhoon and 41 Squadron is today the reserve number plate for the 'Fast Jet & Weapons Operational Evaluation Unit'. So unsettled was the deployment of Javelins during this period that the first disbanded as early as January 1958 and the last to form did so as late as July 1961. With the Mark 2 entering service by the late summer of 1957, the Mark 4 was already being delivered. The Mark 2 differed from the first simply by being fitted with the APQ-43 radar. The Mark 4 was the same as the Mark 1 but with an all-moving fin. Next would come the FAW.5, also during 1957; this introduced additional fuel capacity compared to the FAW.4. The Mark 6 applied all these updates to the FAW.2. Each variant brought a fresh upgrade or improvement, but in this piecemeal fashion all the way to the FAW.9, the first of which were delivered in 1959.

With just one Javelin squadron fully formed by January 1957 (46 Squadron at RAF Odiham), public interest into how matters were progressing, for better or worse, was being expressed by the BBC—chiefly, how many squadrons had formed and how many more could be expected. The FAW.4 was next up to the plate with a service release issued only in the previous December. The next to form then was 141 (White Lions) Squadron at RAF Horsham St Faith in Norfolk, with said version. At the end of May, Horsham was selected to close with immediate effect courtesy of the bombshell Sandys announcement. No. 141 Squadron were saved momentarily by being moved to Coltishall only to disband, or rather be renumbered 41 Squadron, given the latter unit's greater seniority. No. 141 Squadron's great moment with the Javelin was to mount a diamond flypast together with 46 Squadron's Mark 1s before HM Queen

First and second generation Javelin FAW.4 and Venom NF3 from 141 Squadron during transition stage. (*Barry G. Mayner*)

Elizabeth II on 4 June 1957 at RAF Leuchars in Fife. Meanwhile, back in January, the BBC air correspondent was told that the first Mark 4 unit would form between February and March, with a second beginning to form immediately afterwards and be fully equipped by April, and that a steady build-up of the Javelin force would continue from there. That there would be more than a shed full of marks of Javelin was also public knowledge at the time. One of the questions asked by the BBC correspondent was 'Has there been any delay or trouble in getting the Javelin into service?' The response was emphatically no, production was phased to take in as many aircraft as possible of later marks:

> So, next question: 'When will the later marks appear in service?'
> Answer: 'The next squadron to form will be equipped with Javelin 4s.'
> The first Mark 2 aircraft, and the first with APQ-43 radar, went to replace the Mark 1s of 46 Squadron in August.

The new fighter provided a substantial leap in performance over its immediate 'all-weather' predecessors: the Meteor NF and Venom NF. A simple comparison shows the contrast. The best performing of the outgoing radar-equipped fighters, the Meteor NF.12, could reach a speed of 504 knots at 10,000 feet, reach a ceiling of 40,000 feet, and could reach an altitude of 30,000 feet inside twelve minutes. The stark comparison allows the Javelin FAW.1 to shine, somewhat, being able to reach 540 knots at 40,000 feet, reach a ceiling of 52,500 feet, and reach 45,000 feet inside ten minutes. The Flat Iron to be fair was not breaking any records in the grand scheme

FAW.4, XA632, used for Firestreak trials. (*Ian White*)

of things. The Americans were introducing such sleek and formidable beasts as the F-100 Super Sabre, F-101 Voodoo, and F-102 Delta Dagger at the same time. Yet the Javelin represented a phenomenal leap ahead from its immediate predecessors. Much was different about the Javelin to set it apart from its immediate predecessors; gone was the straight wing of the prop-driven design influence, which still featured among the first-generation jet fighters until the arrival of the early swept wings of the F-86 and MiG-15, as well as the introduction of the fin-mounted swept tail section and the shear size of the thing.

The number of Javelins already on order by July 1957 was 400 altogether, of all Marks and with varying abilities. Previous suggestions that the Marks 5 and 6 should carry Firestreak and should be reheat capable were shelved. The Mark 8 would be fitted with reheat and carry Firestreak just as the Mark 9, or as it was at the time, the Mark 7 with a decision as to whether it should have reheat still to be made. The Mark 5s were destined for service with the OCU and it was hoped would be gone by December 1958. This would be before the introduction of Firestreak. The Mark 7, next to be delivered, had auto-pilot trouble and problems with the fuselage and until these could be resolved then there would have been no knowing the effect they would have on performance. On the other hand, the RAF desperately wanted the Mark 7 in service, with or without reheat, to replace the remaining Meteors and Venoms. This was of particular importance as far as the CAS, Sir Dermot Boyle, was concerned as without the Mark 7s, there would not be enough Javelins to rearm Fighter Command to the extent required, there would be a much unwelcome shortfall, (Sandys wanted missile defence as soon as possible and it would not do to leave him with an excuse to proceed with greater haste), and strongly urged the immediate issue of them without delay, even if they arrived without reheat. While plans for the virtual wholesale dismantling of the fighter force were taking shape, the development of the Javelin continued forward at a brisk pace. The decision to fit the Mark 7 Javelin with reheat was concluded in September 1957, the cost of upgrading the engines being set at £3.25 million.

There was of course some delay inevitably with arriving at this decision under the circumstances. The Mark 7 was the latest version and 141 airframes were expected. Some 104 of these were determined to be delivered with the reheat fitted Sapphire SA7R, leaving thirty-seven to be delivered to the RAF with the non-reheated SA7s. This was based on production of SA7Rs beginning in August 1957. Due to some delays, the production of the first augmented Sapphire engines was not expected until the early months of 1958. In the meantime, production of the non-reheat Sapphire 7 engines had continued and it was expected that no more than twenty reheated engines would be available; therefore, they would be able to equip just ten aircraft coming off the production line. This programme would not itself start until August 1958. Thus, the bulk of the uprated aircraft would need to be refitted retrospectively. Altogether, a force of four squadrons was envisaged with the more powerful engines. A further concern was that not all the Mark 7 Javelins were modified to carry the new Firestreak air-to-air missile. The lack of this capability was seen as a considerable drawback, especially as it was also proposed that modified aircraft were to be withdrawn from

FAW.4, XG644, in a rare aerobatic pose. (*Ian White*)

the frontline to be issued to the OCU to make up a demand for training, there being insufficient numbers of the earlier Mark 5s for this purpose.

Being brand new and a seminal first design to meet the specific requirements of all-weather interception, it would normally be expected that the Javelin would be out and about during the RAF's annual showcase extravaganza in September. It came to be known as the 'silly season' given that the Battle of Britain 'At Home' day followed back to back with the Farnborough Show each year. This euphemism was used both light-heartedly and at times with more than a hint of bitter frustration by some RAF commanders when September loomed on the calendar. Farnborough was not an RAF-organised event, but it was the main event for the UK aerospace industry and therefore heavily attended by the Junior Service in the 'forge ahead' years of the British Aviation Industry, put together with the then highly numerous Battle of Britain 'At Home' spread across the country, and so occupied a large chunk of the RAF's home based ORBAT (a shortened phrase derived from 'Order of Battle' or battle order, referring to a military force's availability of active units, equipment, and personnel). As such, September 1957 should have been the time when the Flat Iron should have enjoyed significant public prominence; alas, already, concerns about its reliability in terms of low-level aerobatics ensured that its appearances would not be particularly robust.

Due to delays in deciding whether to proceed with reheated engines for the Mark 7, orders for more were being reviewed and already, 46 Squadron were handing their Mark 1 jets to 87 Squadron in order to receive the Mark 2, which had the more reliable American APQ-43 (AI.22 in UK parlance) radar.

The Javelin was now progressing through its turbulent variant by variant introduction into Fighter Command. The Central Fighter Establishment were busy evaluating the next version in line. By August 1957, they were able to issue a report on the Mark 5 Javelin, which showed little promise of retaining quite the same level of performance of the Mark 4, let alone any improvements. For a kick-off, the take-off acceleration and climbing speed was described as noticeably longer. In strong turbulence at ground level, instrument flying was described as most difficult and unpleasant. A typical distance to un-stick was 1,000 yards with a 15-knot headwind component; this was with ventral tanks. The average climb, not attempting to break any records, was billed as taking twenty minutes and twenty-four seconds over a distance of 155 nautical miles to reach an altitude of 45,000 feet. These trials were carried out using full internal fuel and ammunition. In clean configuration, the Mark 5 took eighteen minutes and forty-eight seconds to reach 48,000 feet, again not a full rate of climb. By contrast, the Mark 4 made the same climb in sixteen minutes and twenty-three seconds. However, the Mark 5's patrol capability was described as acceptable. Flying a patrol at 45,000 feet posed no undue strain on the pilot.

It was further noted that the elevators at low speeds were not very effective and that a bounce or stall near the ground could cause the aircraft to porpoise. Failures with the Sapphire engines were becoming quite common, insofar as turbine blades becoming detached from turbine discs then chewing and smashing into the engine casing and causing major secondary damage to the fuel system. The proposal from Gloster was to fit a steel shield around the turbine area to contain broken blades within the affected engine. In the meantime, the short-term remedy was to reduce the maximum permissible engine RPM and limit the maximum jet pipe temperature to 595 degrees Celsius.

One thing the Javelin represented was an increase in the volume of jet noise. Even after the arrival of jets in the 1940s, it was not until the arrival of jets of the calibre of the Javelin that a substantial increase in disturbance to the local environment became a sudden new phenomenon wherever they pitched up.

Both civilian and military jet aircraft of the era were powered by standard turbojet designs, as opposed to the 'turbofan' engines. The latter design diverged in two different paths and never the twain shall meet: high-bypass engines for long distance cruise which conveniently lend themselves to less harsh sounding relatively quiet fan engines for commercial use, then the low-bypass high velocity military engines designed for high energy performance resulting in the higher more aggressive noise levels more commonly associated with turbo jets. However, in 1959, everything was a pure jet, whether the Pratt & Whitney engines of the Boeing 707s keeping the locals around Heathrow and Prestwick awake at night or the Avons, Sapphires, and Olympus engines of the RAF's Hunters, Javelins, and V-force. A report appeared in *The Times* in August 1959 when RAF West Malling re-opened after runway resurfacing and lengthening in preparation to receive the Javelins of 85 Squadron in the process of moving from Stradishall.

Of course, the principal prerequisite of the introduction of a front line military aircraft type has often followed the formation of a unit equipped with the type in question so that all proposed aircrew to fill the slots on the operational squadrons get to know the aircraft and its fundamental quirks and peculiarities before being sent to the war ready unit, equipped with a proven proficiency, if only rudimentary, on the given aircraft type. The demand for operational squadrons was given priority and thus the first RAF units to be equipped were squadrons made up of the first service personnel to have trained up with the manufacturer. The demand to get the Javelin into service was another case of getting one or more operational units up and running before the OCU was ready to start the first conversion course. As of March 1956, the new OCU, No. 228, had yet to receive its first Javelin let alone produce even a limited operational crew of a pilot and navigator, while 46 Squadron were a month into getting to grips with their first delivery of FAW.1s down at Odiham in Hampshire. Meanwhile, the OCU up at Leeming in Yorkshire was fully equipped with Meteor NF.11, Meteor T.7, Vampire T.11, and Prentice T1. Indeed, they were still running Meteor all-night, all-weather courses, the last to complete being course No. 172. Immediately after, No. 228 OCU deployed, temporarily, to North Luffenham while work at Leeming got under way resurfacing the runway. Nothing really began to take shape with regards to the Javelin until November. The OCU returned to Leeming this month with sixteen Vickers Valettas added to the inventory. There was also a newly installed Javelin cockpit trainer. Work was still being carried out on the airfield and runway to make ready for the eventual arrival of 228's principal new charges and, quite unusually, work was also carried out on the construction of a GCI (ground control intercept) station and a ground training centre. With effect from 1 January 1957, 228 OCU were organised into two wings: Flying Basic and Advanced.

The previous December, the mobile unit (Javelin mobile training unit) formed under 228 OCU. This outfit, with its own working AI .17 radar, had spent December to January training staff navigators before heading out to bases where the Javelin was already present or expected in order to provide some form of pre-requisite training prior to the arrival of the beast itself and some formal training and assessment of those who already had hands on experience. February thereafter marked the resumption of flying training at Leeming since the OCU returned to the airfield. By May 1957, the JMTU had completed its first deployment since February with the AI.17 set as the principal requirement was to get the Javelin training programme on track. On this occasion, at RAF Horsham St Faith, today Norwich Airport, while here, they helped convert Nos 141 and 23 Squadrons to the Javelin. As they were busying themselves about this task and preparing to head up to RAF Turnhouse near Edinburgh to begin converting Javelin crews for 151 Squadron (detached to Turnhouse from Leuchars due to runway and airfield work up there), the dark shadow of Duncan Sandys' Defence White Paper was being cast across Fighter Command and fighter units overseas.

A statement to Parliament by the Defence Minister spoke of a new age of a pilotless air force, at least in the realms of pure air defence and strategic strike, which was now looking forward to an all missile future—'Rockets Galore'. So, with this ominous situation at the back of everyone's minds and not knowing just how long for and how many squadrons would indeed be converted onto the Javelin (which was already being rushed into service ahead of much needed modifications), the future was less than reassuring. Yet for the JMTU and 228 OCU, it was business as usual.

In June, JMTU headed off up to Scotland while the home-based team started getting to grips with the AI.17 in place of the AI.10 upon which they had been training courses up until now, meaning no training was carried out on 'Basic Wing' this month, Courses 187 and 188 were completed with advanced wing following a two week plus delay due to further repair work on the main runway. With the first two operational Javelin squadrons fully functioning the first Javelins for the OCU were received in July 1957, these were Mark 5s with nine on strength by the end of month. The Valetta T4 was still the platform of choice for initial basic training on the radar, essentially for the navigators. Other types were retained also, so five different aircraft ranging from the Avro Anson to the Gloster Javelin, including two marks of Meteor, now equipped the unit. As if the unit's hands were not full enough, due to the demands of the prestige of the British Aerospace Industry, and even with so many Javelin units only formed to varying degrees, the then annual SBAC air show at Farnborough placed a heavy demand on the Armed Forces this year, particularly to show off all the cutting edge new stuff, for which 228 OCU and others were heavily engaged in producing in number, despite the fact that they were still in the process of training staff/instructor crews. Such as it was, a large detachment of the unit's Javelins was to take part in a flypast at Farnborough, while the JMTU, still in business, were off to Brüggen in Germany next to assist with the putting together of 87 Sqn.

Toward the end of 1957, 228 OCU had taken delivery of an additional seven Javelin FAW.5s. Of the total of sixteen, they were required to provide eight jets to go to Tangmere with supporting ground crew from 27 August until 9 September to

FAW.5, XA663, seen here in 1958 while serving on the OCU at Leeming. (*Barry G. Mayner*)

Shortly after reforming at Turnhouse, 151 Squadron returned to their home station at Leuchars. They are seen here on the Leuchars Flightline, 1957–1958. (*Barry G. Mayner*)

take part in the Farnborough SBAC show. Then, just five days later, on 14 September, aircraft from the OCU alone were sent to no fewer than seven RAF stations for their Battle of Britain air shows. These stations ranged from Kinloss in Inverness-shire to Valley in Anglesey and Chivenor in Devonshire and stations less far afield to Binbrook, North Luffenham, and Colerne.

September being the crazy month and fighters still prominent in numbers meant Fighter Command were still able to generate nine individual aerobatics pilots from the Hunter squadrons together with three aerobatics teams for the Battle of Britain 'At Home' day. The Javelin's presence was restricted to ten aircraft from Odiham, Coltishall. and Leeming, mostly from Leeming and one from West Raynham the latter for what was billed as individual aerobatics at St Eval and St Athan, although a subsequent intervention by a senior officer reviewing the arrangements ensured any such solo aerobatics or indeed anything involving robust performance handling at low level in public was suspended for the time being. The level of participation by Javelins given their operational number was slender.

The Farnborough show a week earlier was a different story. Twenty-seven Javelins were made available from 23, 141, and 46 Squadrons and 228 OCU to form part of a quite impressive flypast, which also included twenty-seven Hunters from 1, 34, and 41 Squadrons, but the most remarkable aspect of the RAF contribution to the SBAC show was the presence of 100 Canberras at contrail height.

The busy month of September saw 264 Squadron detached into Leeming from Middleton St George while that station had its main runway lengthened and strengthened in accordance with earlier plans based on a larger advanced fighter force than was now expected to materialised. While at Leeming, 264 was re-numbered 33. Also, the OCU's Valettas were largely seconded by command to take part in ferrying fighter squadron ground crews participating in NATO exercises 'Strikeback' and 'Counterpunch'. Of course, a large number of the base Javelins were involved with rehearsals for the SBAC show flypast. After September, JMTU were on their way back from Germany this time to Stradishall to assist in the conversion of 89 Squadron. Meanwhile, the very first official Javelin conversion course, No. 192, which would follow the definitive training syllabus all the way through from start to finish, was ready to begin training at the start of October. They were delayed about seven days due to weather and a lack of spares. As No. 192 sat down for their first introduction to their instructors, a Defence Ministry White Paper had already been issued, casting a dark shadow of deep uncertainty over the future of the RAF's whole *raison d'être*.

Javelin formation mass start up for flypast over Farnborough in September 1957. (*Barry G. Mayner*)

The Farnborough flypast formation line up to take off from Tangmere's main runway, September 1957 (*Barry G. Mayner*)

5

Duncan Sandys and the Javelin

After some delay in presenting the Defence White Paper, Duncan Sandys, appointed Defence Minister in January 1957, presented the paper and its contents to the Commons on 16 April 1957. He had reached his conclusions quickly and none of it was good news for any of the services. The paper heralded the end of National Service, which in turn presaged a reduction in the size of the Army through disbandments and amalgamations, taking it down to a strength of 165,000. This level of reduction was not actually reached for the first time until about 1980.

However, the fate of the RAF (while likewise not immediately reaching the proposed level of reduction) was about to meet with a radical policy change, which would impact particularly on Fighter Command and overseas-based fighter squadrons. The philosophy or rationale behind the looming bloodletting was the political belief, indeed conviction, that the manned fighter had had its day and was now obsolescent. It was believed that ground-launched missiles or guided weapons could not be evaded by either manned fighter or bomber and that nothing could stop the ballistic missile. In a sense, this was true, certainly of the ballistic missile. It overlooked a great deal in terms of the flexibility and versatility of military response, which could only be answered by manned aircraft assigned essentially to defensive and offensive roles.

The axe would swing and when it stopped, the RAF's UK air defence fighter force, in particular, would be reduced by about four-fifths over the next decade. By then, the replacement missile defence would be represented by a single squadron.

The impact of the radical shake up of the RAF's core elements through the proposed long term replacement of the manned fighting aircraft with unmanned, therefore much cheaper, fire-and-forget missiles was to have far greater impact on the RAF's front line than could be justified given the speed of the rundown of the squadrons and the slow build-up of the lower number of guided weapons units, both surface-to-air and surface-to-surface, which would then be run down itself with unseemly haste from the end of 1963.

For better or worse, this left the faintest shadow of the fighter force compared to where it was in 1957. Less than a year after the White Paper and in the middle of the Javelin's clumsy but progressing entry into service, the brakes were being applied to the number of Javelins ordered following the aforementioned review. However, as much of the impact of the changed outlook fell more widely on the Hunter squadrons, and with a variety of new types still under development with nearly all facing cancellation, the number of Javelins still to be delivered was not affected too severely. Sixteen of 220 aircraft yet to be delivered as of January 1958 were to be cancelled. George Ward MP wrote to the Secretary of State for Supply, Aubrey Jones MP:

> I like these changes and cuts no more than you do but they are inevitable within the limitations imposed on Air votes by our current Defence policy. Any alternative that I know of would seem to be equally distasteful to the industry, and certainly more unwelcome to the Service.

However, despite the sluggish start in 1956 and the subsequent policy change, the squadrons were, by the latter half of 1957, forming thick and fast, with an unprecedented number of variants over such a short period of time. By the end of 1957, seven squadrons were at various stages of operational work up with five different marks: FAW.1 (87/Brüggen), FAW.2 (46/Odiham and 89/Stradishall), FAW.4 (23/Coltishall and 141/Coltishall), FAW.5 (151/Leuchars), and FAW.6 (29/Acklington and 89/Stradishall)—not counting the two-stick trainer model, of course, the T3. The first unit, 46 Squadron, had already exchanged its original FAW.1s for Mark 2s after just eighteen months.

Meanwhile, the Ministry axe was already swinging away with No. 141 Squadron having worked up to a reasonable operational state for but a handful of months was already facing disbandment and was the first Javelin squadron to do so. Having formed on Javelins in February 1957, 141 disbanded scarcely a year later, on 1 February. It may seem odd that many Javelin squadrons were yet to form, but RAF tradition dictates that the oldest units must survive at the expense of more junior squadrons. The exceptions are squadrons with a particularly illustrious past, such as 617 'Dambusters'. Indeed, the upheaval of this era cannot be under estimated, 141 lived again from 1 April 1959 as a Bloodhound missile squadron before disbanding once and for all on 31 March 1964.

One of the overlooked problems about the air defence of the UK at the start of 1958, which the air staff were coping with amid the upheaval, concerned the concept of low-level air defence of the east coast. The problems were: the ordered significant reduction in fighter squadrons, but also the now appreciable growing threat to Western interests posed by the increasing possibility of air attack directed against the early warning system as a prelude to an airborne attack with nuclear weapons from the east, and that the defence of the RAF's east coast radar chain was in the hands of LAA (light anti-aircraft) regiments of the Territorial Army. The Air Ministry already viewed LAA as the least valuable component of the air defence system, given the disbandment of half of Fighter Command squadrons and all auxiliary squadrons in just the preceding sixteen months. For this last reason, Fighter Command and the War Office remained unconvinced that dismantling the Territorial LAA units would not have a significant impact on defence of the radar stations against low-level air attack, but that was as much because they regarded such attacks still as unlikely.

The Ministry, largely due to limitations of range, considered tactical aircraft as having only sufficient range to approach at high-level. As such, they would of course lose the ability to mount any kind of surprise attack on the UK radar screen, instead being intercepted by the new higher-performance fighters, such as the Javelin and the forthcoming P1 Lightning (no mention of missiles). More so, there was also no evidence that Soviet tactical attack air units were training to attack an enemy control and reporting screen. There was at least one Soviet aircraft that concentrated the minds of defence planners: the MiG-17 (NATO reporting name Fresco). Strangely enough, looking back from today, some may not rate it much, but this fighter was near supersonic—it was a direct upgrade from the Korean War-era MiG-15. The nearest bases to operate these at the time were 400 nautical miles from RAF Bawdsey, the most easterly located radar station in the country. This was seen as sufficient to prohibit any of the low-level sorties that the proponents of the LAA gun units were worried about. This then was deemed impossible unless the approach to and return were made at high altitude. The RAF came to the opposite conclusion: that the MiG-17 was indeed capable of low-level attacks, specifically against the east coast radar stations immediately prior to a nuclear strike by high-level bombers, naturally with the aim of disrupting the early warning control and reporting system.

So, at the heart of confronting this problem were Air Ministry concerns that the War Office's proposed retention of twenty Territorial LAA regiments was a lead-in to the provision of short-range surface-to-air guided missile units manned by the Army. This resulted in the usual inter-service, or rather, inter-departmental rivalry for which HM Forces are quite renowned. In this case though, the jostling was at the very top at ministerial portfolio level. The problem with Air Ministry attempts to prevent the army re-equipping all twenty regiments with missiles, at considerable expense, was the current climate, which pursued the very concept of surface-launched missiles as opposed to air-launched ones. With the air ministry still convinced that LAA could at least be dispensed with, a compromise was reached: two LAA Territorial regiments were to be retained, each of the two to defend the two control and reporting centres which covered the route in toward the V-bomber peace time bases.

Meanwhile, the high-altitude missile defence of UK airspace against the more strategic threat began this year with the first deployed Bloodhound missile squadron at RAF North Coates. The lack of faith in the all-missile defence though could be regarded as evident in the continued deployment of more Javelins, which continued to arrive in successive batches each made up of yet another 'improved variant' and by 1960, the first supersonic all-weather Lightning squadron, but the numbers of squadrons, already severely reduced over just the year before, continued to decline overall. So the principal reason for the Interceptor Force now was to defend the V-bomber Force. Everything depended on the V-bombers on dispersal getting airborne within the shortest time frame following the scramble order. Estimates of the time suggested that about a third of the V-force would be able to get airborne in time to avoid any damage and that all being well all V-aircraft could be airborne within fifty minutes. As it stood, RAF Fighter Command had, as of September 1958, fourteen airbases housing twenty-three operational squadrons that they could count on for assistance if pushed from Fleet Air Arm squadrons as available, which were deployed at the Royal Naval Air Stations at Brawdy, Lossiemouth, and Yeovilton.

Much of the defence review started to take effect from 1958, Fighter Command and RAF Germany were under orders to dismantle a large-scale list of their assets in order to fall into line with the proposed force size. Fighter pilots who were made redundant from the air defence role, if not from flying altogether, were 'in luck' the RAF were intent on re-training them and as many as possible. The disposal of surplus aircrew, by 31 March 1959 according to forecasts just over a year earlier, determined no fewer than 145 pilots and sixty-three navigators would end up without an operational posting, in addition to an existing surplus of 171 pilots and fifty-one navigators. Service wide, 800 pilots in total were surplus to requirements before an additional number expected by end March 1959. The process for dealing with this, other commands were contracting as well, was placing a strain on flying training where many were maintaining currency including many retraining for other roles or waiting for something to crop up. The RAF were keen to avoid a heavy impact upon moral and recruitment. This had been the case at the end of the war despite the obvious justification for general contraction. In all, compensation payments (redundancies) were unavoidable in some cases. Elsewhere, refresher flying and retraining rather tended to eat up the savings from sharply running down the Air Force plus some less prestigious yet vital postings such as to Maintenance Command, which now took on a surplus of unwanted aircraft. It was especially hard on the fifty-two NCO pilots and thirty NCO navigators for whom the future promised only posts within ground trades. Pilots in other commands who were already entitled to redundancy through service accrued would be replaced by pilots from Fighter Command retraining. Otherwise, volunteers were called for in order to minimise impact on morale. This was the backdrop to which the Javelin's build-up took place. Therefore, one can imagine the stiff selection required to get oneself onto the new type, despite its less than sparkling reputation.

As the 1950s drew to a close, the Air Ministry, in light of further reviews were now seeking to cancel original orders for Javelins as a result of both the pending arrival of the Lightning and the still continuing rundown of the fighter force. This now meant cancellations to orders placed only six months previously. Yet it was not just the need for further economies in defence spending, central to which was the idea of replacing manned fighters with missiles, but re-assessment of the operational life of the Javelin and the actual number needed to maintain the front line. It was not just an increase in orders from six months previous, which now had to be trimmed, but original orders going back several years partly as a result of the aircraft being delivered to the RAF much later than was foreseen.

The concerns about display flying in 1957 were better understood by 1959. When September came around again, a total of fourteen Javelins, most from RAF Waterbeach, were made available for individual flying displays at RAF stations across the UK on Battle of Britain 'At Home' day, seventeen out of thirty-two RAF stations, which included Gibraltar. On top of this, a number of formations for flying drills and flypasts were also to be made available.

Only two years in from the first operational Javelin squadron forming, the Air Ministry were already forecasting its demise in the very near future. The after-effects of the Sandys' review were still taking their toll by November 1958, by which point the CAS and Secretary of State for Air were both looking for further reductions in the RAF's fighter strength to continue forward beyond 1961.

The latest proposal was that up until April 1960, any further reductions would still be borne solely by remaining Hunter squadrons; it gives some idea of where the start point on unit disbandment was given that some squadrons would still be left flying Hunters in the day fighter role by 1960 despite the ruthless cuts. Thereafter, current plans were that a further six Hunter squadrons and one equipped with Javelins would need to disband before April the year after that. Any further losses sustained by Fighter Command beyond 1 April 1961 would then have to fall on the remaining Javelin units. Even so, the projected strength of Fighter Command's air assets by 1963 looked spectacularly handsome by any modern standards: 124 Javelins and 156 Lightnings. The Air Staff preferred to retain some Hunter squadrons at the expense of certainly the earlier Javelin squadrons. Of course, despite their recommendations, they were trying to retain what they could.

They proposed a reduction over the period 1959 to 1964 of eight squadrons down to twelve. The Chancellor of the Exchequer, not at all surprisingly, wanted to do the inverse and cut twelve squadrons or more down to a level of eight or less. Yet, by the start of the 1960s, the argument over the retention of Hunters versus Javelins was academic in any case. Even now, just four years into service from the initial delivery of the Javelin, they were both rendered comfortably obsolescent in the air defence role by the English Electric Lightning. Those squadrons not being converted to Lightnings were either going to disband or, fortuitously in the Hunter's case, be reassigned to either offensive close support or the fighter reconnaissance role. Nothing other than strictly all-weather air defence BVR interception was deemed worth risking the Flat Iron's talents on, certainly as primary role. The big fighter's closest rival and contemporary from the de Havilland stable, dismissed by the RAF even before the Farnborough tragedy in 1952, was doing well in the service of the Fleet Air Arm. Having met expectations when introduced to carrier service as the Sea Vixen FAW.1, the naval fighter had seen one further mark introduced, the FAW.2, which sported conformal over wing tanks extending from its twin-boom fin. More than this, the Vixen was capable of 'buddy-buddy' in-flight refuelling, tactical strike attack, and reconnaissance in addition to its bread and butter task of fleet air defence. There were some differences in the Javelin's favour, mostly marginal, particularly, the Javelin reached a slightly higher speed at altitude and could boast a comfortable greater margin in ceiling performance. However, the Sea Vixen was reliably more agile and versatile, so much so that two official aerobatics teams were formed: Fred's Five provided by the FAA Sea Vixen HQ Training Squadron, 766 and Simon's Circus, drawn from 892 Squadron. This meant that the fleet's albeit smaller number of Vixens remained in service with no reductions until the Labour Government's defence policy review in the 1960s put the Navy's air force on the road out with the 'nothing east of Suez' policy. Despite this, the Sea Vixen rendered satisfactory service until 1972, eventually handing over fully to a reduced number of McDonnell Douglas F-4 Phantoms. The latter managed a few years in Naval service before being transferred to the RAF following a temporary reprieve for the Navy's last angle-deck, Audacious-class aircraft carrier, HMS *Ark Royal*.

Of all things that the Javelin was being considered for at the time was anti-smuggling duties in Cyprus, but because of its low speed handling qualities it was thought more prudent by the CAS, Sir Dermot Boyle, in 1958, to be based in Cyprus. The resident fighter squadron was due to disband but the RAF still needed to meet a commitment for night anti-smuggling patrols, as the fighter cover from the end of 1958 was now going to be covered by rotating Javelin and Hunter squadrons from the UK. Hubert (Sam) Patch, still the AOC-in-C Fighter Command, advised that the Javelin deployments even at full strength would only be periodic rather than continuous and, with the Flat Iron's low speed handling qualities being what they were, suggested maintaining a flight of Meteor NFs would be better suited and in any case, as of October 1958, despite the identified requirement coming from somewhere, there had been no smuggling or night parachuting to date. This of course was a concern brought about by the then very real Cyprus emergency. The only objections ultimately were financial and so Sir Dermot Boyle suggested sending four Meteor NF aircraft to Cyprus not as a separate unit, but as an extension of the station flight at Akrotiri then only fuel would need to be paid for. The aircraft, spares, and trained and experienced crews were available as he expected the last Meteor NF unit to convert to Javelins shortly.

In 1959, curiously enough, it was the Minister of Defence who now stated that he did not advocate a further reduction in the size of the fighter force. What he was sceptical of was the argument for specifically defending the nuclear deterrent: the V-bomber bases. The Minister's position was that twelve squadrons of Lightnings, armed with both Red Top and AIR-2 Genie (nuclear tipped) air-to-air missiles, as was envisaged at the time, would suffice to meet the air defence needs of the United Kingdom. To defend the deterrent would mean retaining a further eight squadrons, which would be equipped with Javelins. The Minister's argument was that the need to concentrate on defending nuclear armed aircraft at other bases was pointless as it was inconceivable that the Russians would launch a surprise attack on Britain, 'unless they were confident that they could simultaneously eliminate all the strategic bases of the United States', the Secretary for Air had written the year previously, in a paper entitled 'Air Defence of the UK'.

> We must expect an increasing danger that the concept of confining war to Europe, and ultimately of 'Fortress America', will receive growing American support. For example, the Russians might calculate that a swift simultaneous attack on USAF Bases outside the USA and in the UK would greatly diminish the possible weight of allied attack on Soviet Russia that the United States, itself under direct threat, might be willing to bargain. Because of this and with the approval of the Minister of Defence, on the advice of the Chiefs of Staff, the target policy for Bomber Command planning covers a situation in which the United Kingdom might be forced to retaliate alone.

Javelin FAW.8, XH971, over Malta in 1959. No. 41 Squadron markings are well displayed on the fin. (*Barry G. Mayner*)

The Joint Intelligence Committee view was that if global war came, it was most likely to do so as the result of some miscalculation on Russia's part. Such a miscalculation could carry with it all the attributes of surprise and lack of provocation.

> It is the JIC view that should Russia deliberately plan to go to war she would take every step to avoid giving either political or military indications of her intention. As the Russians multiply their bomber bases there will be less need for re-deployment before attack, on a scale which could be detected.
>
> We cannot thus exclude the possibility of surprise attack on any hypothesis. If there were no active defence the Russians would only need to achieve surprise to succeed. Their planning would be immensely simplified; and the deterrent gravely weakened.

The Minister of Defence was prepared to place faith in the ability to disperse the V-force to the pre-planned dispersal airfields. However, a counter-argument to relying on this alone was that while the V-force could be scrambled a number of times while reacting to a series of feint attacks, this would in time exhaust the available number of bombers and crews available to react within the maximum period, which would then be followed by a genuine attack, which hence forth could destroy the bombers on the ground, certainly if there were no or insufficient air defence fighters to protect it. A further argument for the manned fighter, and perhaps most crucial of all, is that an interceptor alert force as opposed to a missile defence force would be a vital tool in avoiding an immediate precipitation of 'shoot first, ask questions later' while political consultations were in play.

Much of the RAF's nuclear deterrent and how it planned to defend it in the event of a pre-emptive strike was a work in progress toward the end of the 1950s, the V-force and the all-weather fighter force were gathering pace together. The fighter force was developing along more retrospective lines but a firm idea of how it all would look, by the end of 1965, was in planning. Even with the destruction wrought by Duncan Sandys taken into consideration, Fighter Command planned for an optimistic future, certainly compared with how things actually turned out by 1965.

Crucial to the RAF's ability to defend its nuclear retaliatory capability was the availability of fighters armed with guided missiles. Any expectation that this would be remedied with the arrival of the first Javelins had been misplaced for sure. The first RAF squadron to become effectively missile armed for air-to-air use was 25 Squadron, with the Javelin FAW.7, by the end of 1958. No. 25 were at RAF Waterbeach by then and getting to grips with the infrared homing Firestreak. From here on, the missile-armed Javelins started arriving in significant numbers. In 1959, No. 23 formed on the FAW.7 at Horsham St Faith, No. 41 at Wattisham on FAW.8s, likewise No. 85 at West Malling, and No. 64 (FAW.7s) at Duxford. All or most were already flying earlier Javelins, so the transition to using missiles was relatively simple. As the introduction to each unit of either FAW.7 or FAW.8 aircraft took place, 64 Squadron at RAF Duxford were expecting to be the first to receive the ultimate variant, the FAW.9, or as it was still being referred to in 1958, the FAW.7 (R). Thereafter, all would be on the move again in 1960: No. 25 were to move to West Raynham, No. 23 to Coltishall after re-equipping in 1959, and No. 41 were to move to West Malling when facilities for them would be available there. The year 1959 saw the JMTU wind up after converting their last squadron, No. 72 at Leconfield. The remaining squadrons to form would do so directly at Leeming with the OCU.

Meanwhile, No. 64 at Duxford were already slated to pitch up at Binbrook, still referred to as Lincoln 'X' during 1960, a move which actually took place in 1961 when the RAF abandoned Duxford once and for all. No. 64 moved briefly to Waterbeach before heading to Binbrook in 1962. During 1960, a further two squadrons were to re-equip with the FAW.9: No. 33 at Middleton St George and, as originally planned but then abandoned, No. 72 at Leconfield. As the Javelin force reached its zenith, any idea of its being around for too much longer was not something that the RAF cared to look forward to too much and by 1961, just five years after the first squadron was raised, the OCU was ordered to disband. The reason for this was the expectation that Javelin squadrons would from here onwards quickly fold, those units equipped with gun only armed aircraft first. Up to this time point, No. 228 OCU had used an interesting mix of types to provide the best balance of training for Javelin crews.

During the annual formal inspection at RAF Leeming in April 1961, Air-Vice Marshal Harold Maguire announced to all the assembled station and unit personnel on parade that the task of 228 OCU would be complete that coming August and that RAF Leeming would be assigned to a new role. It came as no surprise that much of the flying task was already run down. It would not be too long before the RAF had to re-instate the OCU, next time up at Leuchars in Fife, for Leeming was to begin a new life as the home of No. 3 Flying Training School. The last Javelin course, No.

Widely regarded as the 'hotship' mark, 64 Squadron FAW.7 was based at RAF Duxford in 1958–1961. Note the jet pipes are not fitted with the heavy afterburner nozzles seen on the Mk 8s and Mk 9s. (*Ian White*)

Instrument rating Squadron T3 pair, flypast with Lightning T4, from what was still known as the Lightning Conversion Squadron prior to becoming 226 OCU, on the occasion of the AOC's formal inspection of Middleton St George, 1963. (*The National Archives*)

229 (advanced), passed out on 13 August. There was one short course comprising eight pilots, No. 231, which completed on 31 July; the reserve squadron number, 137, applied to the OCU, disappeared the same day.

Peter Goodwin was on course 229. He was already an experienced fighter pilot with tours in the fighter/ground-attack role on 8 and 32 Squadrons under his belt. He had also been a test pilot in 1959 for Short and Harland at Llanbedr, test flying the Meteor U15 before they went aloft unmanned. Peter recollects OCU training:

> For the flying at Leeming, we would be vectored onto another Javelin. When the Nav had a good radar contact on the target I would call 'Judy'. The nav would take over the vectoring commentary until within gun range (800yds). There were no Firestreak missiles at Leeming, only on the squadrons. The commentary by the nav would be transmitted on a discreet frequency. A pilot instructor in another Javelin would have 'locked on' to me after take off following about 800 yards behind and would listen to my nav's commentary, also noting my reaction to the nav's commands.'
>
> Operational Javelins were equipped with a collimator, a 'Blip' which appeared on the gun sight when the nav locked on, the pilot then positioned the aircraft for either a guns or missile attack.

The OCU's final list of aircraft consisted of Mark 5 and Mark 3 Javelins together with Canberra T11s; the latter had made themselves useful during this last month by presenting themselves as targets for the Lightnings of 56, 74, and 111 Squadrons and the Bloodhound MEZ (missile engagement zone) controllers of 148 SAGW Wing (surface-to-air guided weapons wing) based at North Coates. Meanwhile, twenty staff flew continuation sorties on the three newly arrived Jet Provost T3s, so far delivered to No. 3 FTS. No. 228 OCU had been at Leeming since its original formation in 1947 from the merging of Nos 13 and 54 OTUs (operational training unit). From 11 January 1956, the unit had adopted No. 137 Squadron's identity for when operationally deployed. The original plan for the operational conversion units within Fighter Command was, in any case, to reduce rather prematurely. As circumstances prevailed, the need for a Hunter OCU was not expected to last beyond the end of 1960. The Javelin OCU was originally expected to become surplus during 1962 to 1963 and indeed disappeared during 1961, but would resume later. The future lay with the new OCU for the Lightning. The early plan here was to form the OCU in 1962 at Leuchars, alongside the training element of the Central Fighter Establishment, the Fighter Combat School.

By this time, the remaining Hunter squadrons were expected to be re-equipping themselves with the Lightning. Again, whatever the RAF were planning to occur just two to three years hence was being adjusted constantly due the overall trend toward fewer units and others being taken out of the equation to meet other requirements that arose unexpectedly. The famous Fighting Cocks of 43 Squadron, based at Leuchars, were originally to have become a Lightning squadron by the middle of 1961, but instead found themselves re-assigned to the dual air defence/close air support role with both Hunter F6 and FGA9 versions before being posted to Nicosia in Cyprus. Indeed, it was admitted at the time that much of the planning was theoretical good guess work resulting from lack of firmness in direction from on high.

The idea of Fighter Command fielding thirteen Lightning squadrons by the end of 1965, as forecast, was realistic enough if uncertain in 1958, showing just how easy it is for ministers to slash defence spending and spend what is left unwisely. The reality of 1965, had it been proposed just seven years earlier, would have shocked even those MPs least convinced of the merits of the country's air defence requirements. The Air Defence posture of the RAF over the British Isles by the end of 1965 comprised just four Lightning squadrons with a fifth just forming, together with a single Bloodhound missile unit. The only time the RAF Air Defence Fighter Force has been smaller has been the period from 2008 to the present.

The mounting Soviet long-range military flights, which started making increasingly regular trips around UK airspace from the mid-1960s through the rest of the Cold War, brought about a much-needed rethink. The process of rebuilding the air defence screen somewhat was long and slow due to the economic pressure and political heel-dragging, which while accepting the situation was far from good enough, continued to place far greater priority elsewhere. A five squadron interceptor force to defend all was frankly absurd given the scale of the potential depth of air attacks, which, in order to stand a realistic chance of repelling would need such an increase in assets as to seem utterly contentious were the case put before any but the most

Above and next two pages: Peter Goodwin's log entries covering his entire OCU conversion course at Leeming in 1961. (*Peter Goodwin*)

Page 1

Year 1961		AIRCRAFT		Pilot, or 1st Pilot	2nd Pilot, Pupil or Passenger	DUTY (Including Results and Remarks)		DAY		NIGHT		DAY	
Month	Date	Type	No.					Dual (1)	Pilot (2)	Dual (3)	Pilot (4)	Dual (5)	1st Pilot (6)
—	—	—	—	—	—	— Totals Brought Forward		130.45	754.00	6.35	15.30	76.05	262.0
				Summary For:-	June 1961	T	Javelin T Mk 3						
			Flt.Lt.	Unit:-	No.228 O.C.U.	Y	Javelin Mk 5					5.05	
			Sqn.Ldr.	Date:-	1st July 1961	P							9.10
				Signature:-	P.M. Goodwin	E							
							CERTIFIED 8 INSTRUMENT APPROACH						
Y	4	Javelin 5	690	Self	Flt.Lt. Galley	Trim u/s.							1.25
Y	5	Javelin 5	700	Self	Flt.Lt. Galley	Ex23. PIs. Ciné 1.							
Y	5	Javelin 5	703	Self	Flt.Lt. Galley	A1 u/s.							
Y	6	Javelin 5	691	Self	Flt.Lt. Galley	Ex24. PIs. A/GCA. Ciné 2							
Y	6	Javelin T3	396	Flt.Lt. Smith	Self	Ex25A/30. A/GCA							
Y	6	Javelin 5	714	Self	Flt.Lt. Galley	Ex28 A/GCA							
Y	10	Javelin 5	693	Self	Flt.Lt. Galley	Ex27 N/C u/s.							
Y	11	Javelin 5	693	Self	Flt.Lt. Galley	Ex27 PIs A/GCA Ciné 3							
Y	12	Javelin 5	688	Self	Flt.Lt. Galley	Ex31. PIs. A/GCA							
Y	13	Javelin 5	691	Self	Flt.Lt. Galley	Ex29 X-C A/GCA							
Y	17	Javelin 5	695	Self	Flt.Lt. Galley	Ex34 A/GCA							
Y	17	Javelin 5	695	Self	Flt.Lt. Galley	Ex32 A/GCA							
Y	18	Javelin 5	653	Self	Flt.Lt. Owens	Ex39A Ciné 4.							1.35
Y	19	Javelin 5	700	Self	Flt.Lt. Galley	Ex40 Ciné 5.							1.30
Y	19	Javelin 5	703	Self	Flt.Lt. Galley	Ex33 DNCO							
Y	19	Javelin 5	693	Self	Flt.Lt. Galley	Ex33							
Y	20	Javelin 5	695	Self	Flt.Lt. Galley	Ex43							1.35
				GRAND TOTAL [Cols. (1) to (10)] 1301 Hrs. - 15 Mins		Totals Carried Forward		130.45	754.00	6.35	15.30	76.05	277.4

No. 228 O.C.U.

WET DINGHY DRILL

This is to certify that F/O R.G. is operationally proficient in Wet Drill, and has attained the "Three Standard" laid down in Fighter Command Staff Instruction No. K/2.

Date 21st July 1961
(V.E. Thomas)
Wing Commander
O.C. Advanced

Page 2

Year 1961		AIRCRAFT		Pilot, or 1st Pilot	2nd Pilot, Pupil or Passenger	DUTY (Including Results and Remarks)		SINGLE-ENGINE AIRCRAFT					
								DAY		NIGHT		DAY	
Month	Date	Type	No.					Dual (1)	Pilot (2)	Dual (3)	Pilot (4)	Dual (5)	1st Pilot (6)
—	—	—	—	—	—	— Totals Brought Forward		130.45	754.00	6.35	15.30	76.05	277.40
Y	20	Javelin 5	714	Self	Flt.Lt. Galley	35T DNCO(R). A/GCA.							
Y	20	Javelin 5	695	Self	Flt.Lt. Galley	Ex 35T A/GCA (43).							
Y	21	Javelin 5	695	Self	Flt.Lt. Galley	Ex46 A/GCA Ciné 6.							1.25
Y	24	Javelin 5	691	Self	Flt.Lt. Galley	Ex46 Ciné 6.							1.35
Y	24	Javelin 5	643	Self	Flt.Lt. Galley	Ex41 (S.E.)							
Y	25	Javelin 5	714	Self	Flt.Lt. Galley	Ex47 A/GCA							1.35
Y	25	Javelin 5	714	Self	Flt.Lt. Galley	Ex42							
Y	26	Javelin 5	702	Self	Flt.Lt. Galley	Ex44.							
Y	27	Javelin 5	703	Self	Flt.Lt. Galley	Ex50.							1.30
Y	27	Javelin 5	691	Self	Flt.Lt. Galley	Ex48							
Y	31	Javelin 5	700	Self	Flt.Lt. Galley	Ex50.							1.30
Y	31	Javelin 5	691	Self	Flt.Lt. Galley	Ex49.							
				Summary For:-	July 1961	T	Javelin T3						
			Flt.Lt.	Unit:-	No.228 O.C.U.	Y	Javelin Mk 5					23.15	
			Sqn.Ldr.	Date:-	1st August 1961	P							
				Signature:-	P.M. Goodwin	E							
							CERTIFIED 20 INSTRUMENT APPROACH						
G	1	Javelin 5	700	Self	Flt.Lt. Galley	Tgt. + H.O. Ciné 7.							1.35
G	2	Javelin 5	703	Self	Flt.Lt. Galley	Ex 36.							1.25
G	2	Javelin 5	646	Self	Flt.Lt. Galley	Ex52T. A/GCA							
G	3	Javelin 5	693	Self	Flt.Lt. Galley	Tgt. Ciné 7.							1.35
				GRAND TOTAL [Cols. (1) to (10)] 1324 Hrs. 35 Mins		Totals Carried Forward		130.45	754.00	6.35	15.30	76.05	289.50

Above: The last Javelin course to pass through the OCU at Leeming. Peter Goodwin is seated to the far right with arms folded. (*Peter Goodwin*)

Above and opposite page: The monthly magazine of RAF Leeming had a very good artist known only by his signature initials. Here are four of his contemporary sketches depicting the Javelin era at the base; *Leeming Life* was required reading even at the most inconvenient of times going by this scene. The final scene depicts the handover of fighters to Flying Training Command, the departure of 228 OCU, and the arrival of 3 Flying Training School, for reflecting, for all the world, the style of the late *Daily Express* cartoonist Giles. (*The National Archives*)

sympathetic listener. So, all in all, despite its shortcomings, the Javelin perhaps could and should certainly have been retained in sufficient numbers as part of the fighter contribution to the UKADR (United Kingdom Air Defence Region), at least it would provide something of a stop-gap until something else came down pipeline, but due to the hitherto policy on surface-launched missiles, which had been all but completely withdrawn, there was in effect, nothing. The best hope would now lay with the McDonnell Douglas F-4 Phantom II, which the Government by the end of 1965 was pursuing, but more as a Hunter close support and reconnaissance replacement and for the Navy's Sea Vixens. Further unexpected cancellations, particularly to the Fleet Air Arm's front line and elsewhere meant that the Phantom would have to be relied on to do more as far as the RAF was concerned.

The air defence rethink considered some unexpected suggestions. Aldergrove in Northern Ireland was seen as a possible all-weather interceptor base; this was a nod towards the growing concern that the Soviet Union was closing to the point of being able to deploy long-range high-performance bombers, mentioned earlier, which could transit from bases in the far north to an IP (initial point) west of the British Isles before turning in bound for an attack, but such aircraft did not materialise until such concerns had slipped from the minds of politician and military officer alike. Again, for operational priorities as well as economic reasons, the Aldergrove proposal was abandoned.

6

The Javelin Operational

Before initial operational capability came in February 1956 with the arrival of XA570 (the first production Javelin FAW.1, at 46 Squadron), the squadron was despatching aircrew to Gloster for two-day courses on the Javelin's systems 'and a good time was had by all'. This was in the December prior and it was hoped they could attend again during January before they took receipt of their own aircraft at Odiham. They also made ready eight of their Meteor NF.12s and 14s, which were on their way to join 72 Squadron at Church Fenton, who were in the process of transitioning from the day fighter to the night fighter role.

The remaining Meteor NF.11s were used to provide cross-country training and cine-gun exercises while the opportunity to get to grips with the Javelin properly loomed. Indeed, they took delivery of a further eight Meteor NF.11s.

As of 29 February 1956, the squadron had a number of trials to complete; in addition, officers and staff from various firms associated with the Javelin had all arrived and a number of the squadron's navigators were detached away to Boscombe Down where they were being introduced to the AI.17 radar sets. Much flying was being carried out on the Meteor NF.11s in the interim and by the middle of March, the squadron had a total of six Mark 1 Javelins but the serviceability level was described as 'appallingly low'; as a result of this, the pilot conversion process had slowed to a crawl. The problem being with the electrical system and the Rotex starters, the former was being addressed with the introduction of a modification designed to minimise the chance of double generator failure, but not yet incorporated, the latter was to be alleviated with the introduction of a modified auxiliary gear box but at the time it could only be hoped it would resolve the problem. The length of time between flights by Javelins was slowing up the process.

More operationally focused flying training (to engage GCI, radar, and weapons) was introduced. An AI.17 simulator arrived in a caravan on 7 March and two days later, the navigators were getting to grips with it. By the end of March, all aircrew had gained some experience while the AIR fitters were able to practice with it for two days of the week.

The next step involved intensive flying trials. In May, the squadron had taken receipt of fifteen Javelins of which eight were earmarked for phase 'B' of the trials;

the rest were assigned to continue with normal flying practice and despite the initial lack of progress, all pilots had completed the initial syllabus stages and were as far as possible regarded as having successfully converted to type including one new pilot, Flying Officer A. E. Warner, who had only just arrived on 7 May 1956. Conversion of the navigators was progressing fully. This latter element was, of course, essential to the whole operational point of the Javelin getting airborne in the first place. Therefore, AI exercises and air tests now formed the bulk of flying, although there was a four-ship formation put together to join a flypast with twelve Hunters for the AOC's visit on 15 May by Air Vice-Marshal Victor Bowling CB CBE.

Night flying was now increased to four nights a week as GCI controllers could now start getting to grips with the particularities of the Javelin under close radar control. This was highlighting many problems for the aircrews and the controllers but that was for now largely the point—to expose the bug bears and write the procedures accordingly once successfully adjusted. A lot of GCI exercises were now being conducted at altitudes above 40,000 feet and night flying was becoming the norm rather than the exception. With fifteen Javelins taken on strength so recently and conversion training now continuing satisfactorily, tragedy struck with two of the jets being destroyed, one flown by the CO, Wing Commander F. E. W. Birchfield CBE AFC and his navigator, Flying Officer R. Chambers, who were both lost while flying XH570 on 15 June, incidentally the first aircraft delivered. Four days later, XA624, flown by Flying Officer A. Warner belly-flopped on the airfield. Following an undercarriage retraction, the aircraft was determined to have sustained category 3 damage.

Wing Commander Harold E. White DFC AFC took command of 46 Squadron from 19 June. He came straight from commanding Flying Wing at RAF Leeming. To meet the required time frame for trials and meeting operational effectiveness, flying operations were now conducted daily from 8.30 a.m. through to 2.30 a.m. the next morning, usually in pairs at thirty-minute intervals. Every type of operational procedure was put to the test and satisfactorily completed in eight weeks.

Due to the formation of 46 Squadron and indeed some other units pre-empting the fully functioning OCU on 13 February 1957, Wg Cdr White and Flt Lt R.A. Franks, a Nav/Rad, attended a conference at 81 Group HQ in order to advise on the task of Javelin flying training to be followed by 228 OCU once it reformed. On 20 February, Mr M. Chase, an Air Ministry photographer, was flown in the rear seat of a Javelin of 46 Squadron so he could photograph another one silhouetted against the back drop of London while lit-up at night. Two days later, 46 Squadron were visited by AOC-in-C Fighter Command, Air Chief Marshal Sir Thomas Pike KCB CBE DFC. He was accompanied by the Permanent Under Secretary of State for Air, Sir Maurice Dean KCMG CB, with his private secretary, Mr J. D. Bryars. After a briefing on the Javelin, they were each taken up for trip in the beast.

The honour of being the second squadron to step up to the plate and deploy the Flat Iron was bestowed on 141 Squadron, who were the first to receive the FAW.4. Hot on their heels came 151 Squadron, who were moved from their Leuchars home to Turnhouse while the latter had its runway resurfaced. The FAW.2 still managed to beat the FAW.4 into service; the first production example, XA768, off the assembly line, so to speak, made its maiden flight on 25 April 1956. This meant the more highly regarded AI.22, or APQ-43 radar set, was headed for the frontline and 46 Squadron at Odiham, where the first Mark 2 Javelins started arriving on 27 June, just eight days after official clearance. A grand total of thirty FAW.2s were built and delivered to all of three squadrons: 46, 85, and 89. The FAW.4, introducing the all moving fin, first flew on 7 December 1956. The next month, 141 Squadron started discarding its Venom NF.3s and taking receipt of the Mark 4 Javelin up at RAF Horsham St Faith where they were ensconced while their parent base, Coltishall, was having its runway resurfaced. They were declared operational on 19 May.

No. 141 Squadron were still at Horsham St Faith on 25 May when a small incident mushroomed into something more dramatic: one of their aircraft, XA732, was taxiing out, when the front attachment of one of the two 'Bosom tanks' under the fuselage came free and started dragging along the ground; this eventually burst into flames. 'You're on fire' was shouted over the R/T but without the preamble of a callsign. The crew eventually realised the situation and scrambled to safety over the nose cone. This was not the end of the drama: aircraft returning from an exercise found the airfield in complete chaos and with Coltishall closed for runway resurfacing, they had to head off elsewhere. Some Hunters flew to West Raynham where a further sixteen aircraft were trying to land. Once on land, the principal hazard was avoiding other aircraft that had been queueing to land and had run out of fuel while taxying.

No. 141 Squadron's first task after being declared operational was to send five crews to Turnhouse to participate in exercise 'Vigilant', during which they succeeded in claiming eighty-three aircraft destroyed and two damaged from thirty-one sorties between 25 and 28 May.

No. 41 Squadron Javelin FAW.5 XA667 overhead what appears to be the dispersal positions of its airbase. (*Barry G. Mayner*)

Sqn Ldr G. I. Chapman and Flt Lt F. F. Sanderson, from Training Unit Headquarters Fighter Command, flew with the squadron during the first two days of the exercise, then went over to Stradishall for the remainder. A preliminary try-out exercise came next, the purpose of which was to familiarise the crews with scramble procedures and broadcast control. Next came preparation for a flypast at Leuchars for HM Queen Elizabeth II who would be presenting new colours to 43 Squadron. For this, the four crews deployed to Turnhouse again, this time from 1 to 4 June for rehearsals prior to the event on 4 June 1957. Intensive air-to-air firing was carried out between 14 and 22 August. Then, on 27 August, the big event of the year was to dispatch nine of their Javelins to RAF Tangmere along with similar consignments from 23 and 46 Squadrons and 228 OCU, all to provide the chunky flypast at the Farnborough air show. Such was the demand that all flying was restricted other than flypast practices to minimise maintenance problems. The Javelins managed to make their appointment over Farnborough on five days; two were missed due to the weather. On 12 September, 141 Squadron sent twelve jets to Geilenkirchen to participate in Operation Counterpunch, where they responded to seventy-seven scrambles and claimed 103 kills, including Canberras, F-84Fs, and various marks of Meteor, B-45s, and a Valiant.

Their mount, the FAW.4, was the first version to be produced in any kind of realistic numbers, eventually equipping six squadrons. No. 23 Squadron shortly followed 141 Squadron, converting to the Javelin, also nominally based at Coltishall. When these two became operational, they were able to take up the new battle flight or 'Fabulous/Flinders' commitment. With the growing concern that the Soviet Air Force could reach the frontier of UK air space, Fabulous was as high a state of readiness that NATO fighters now incorporated as part of the routine. Known as battle flight by RAF crews stationed in West Germany, the requirement was to have fuelled and armed fighter aircraft, usually two, with the pilots and crews already strapped into their cockpits, awaiting the order to scramble, which would come through a Telebrief scrambler.

In 1962, NATO simplified procedures to a similar practice followed today. We have all seen the pictures of RAF Typhoons shadowing Russian military aircraft. They will have responded to a scramble order while waiting 'suited and booted' in an annex adjoining the facility containing their charge, whether a Typhoon or Tornado (or going further back, a Phantom, Lightning, or even a Javelin). The readiness states have always remained high but no one has to sit in the cockpit waiting anymore. The two-stick trainer (T-Bird), the Javelin T3, first took to the air on 6 January 1958. Not surprisingly, the first posting for these aircraft was straight to the by now functioning OCU at Leeming later that year. A total of twenty-eight of these were built, two more than the operational FAW.2.

Alas, 31 January 1958 arrived and 141 Squadron's days as a front line RAF fighter unit were at an end. The squadron disbanded this day and immediately rebadged as 41 Squadron. No. 141 Squadron were to fly again as a Bloodhound surface-to-air missile squadron based at Dunholme Lodge.

The T3s were to all intents and purposes non-operational: they had no radar, so were no good for training navigators hence the reason the Javelin OCU during both its incantations had various larger types (Valettas and Canberras) on strength equipped

T3 prototype, WT841. (*Peter R. March*)

with the AI.17 for navigation training. The T3 had a larger cockpit canopy with a raised rear seat for better instructor–pupil monitoring. The aircraft was armed with the 30-mm Hispano cannons for gunnery practice, but with no radar, it remained of limited use as a fighter if push came to shove.

During the latter end of 1957, the Javelin gave the RAF some sign of promise when aircraft of 87 Squadron were involved in Operation Beware. Two Javelins flown by Wg Cdr E.O. Crew together with Sqn Ldr J. Walton in one aircraft and Sqn Ldr 'Dicky' Martin and Flt Lt R Williams in the other, intercepted Canberras about 100 miles from the coast and surprised a formation of F-100 Super Sabres *en route*. These particular mentions in despatches were afforded to the Mark 1s and thus it was their great moment for now, but the later variants were now on their way.

Elsewhere, 151 Squadron, for the time equipped with FAW.5s, were involved; 151 were still at Turnhouse getting used to their new significantly more challenging mount when they were detached away from 16 to 24 September on exercise to Sola in Norway. They took eight Javelin FAW.5s with them on Exercise Strike Back. The airfield itself had four active runways. The main runway running north to south was 3,000 yards long but twice the regulation width of a British runway. Conversely, the ORP (operational readiness platform) at either end was narrower. Also, the Javelin crews would be dealing with civilian air traffic controllers. An aspect of Norwegian military life that could prove a little awkward, embarrassing, and (given the right circumstances) amusing was that the Norwegians had, by 1957, long since abandoned the custom of separate messing facilities for officers, senior NCOs, and junior ranks, still maintained by HM Forces to this day and something that everyone accepts as part and parcel of perks and benefits of career progression. Considering that being accepted for a commission for any junior rank or NCO is always a possibility, then that career progression has no limits. Yet, of course, for any element of Britain's armed forces in the rather more deferential era of the 1950s, with National Service to boot, to suggest that this was an insignificant and petty concern would be to misunderstand the culture completely. So, it was that British tastes (at least the more rarefied ones) were accommodated. Then again, due to the deployment taking more officers than NCOs, the officers were crammed in. In most cases, three officers shared a single room and one bunch certainly collectively drew the short straw as nine of them were bunked in a single room. The squadron's airmen were billeted with the ground crew from a Fleet Air Arm squadron, which was also participating in the same exercise. These chaps were all crowded into a disused dining room. Double-tiered bunks were placed in blocks of four with little space between them while the latrines and ablutions were under canvas. Eventually, a small billet was found on 17 September, which, together with a small classroom, alleviated matters just a tad.

Other problems were encountered. Norway (like many other Scandinavian countries then and now) has a particularly high cost of living and while everyone was paid LOA (local overseas allowance), this was found to be wholly inadequate. However, putting the domestic concerns aside, apart from the only two air wireless fitters on the detachment and one navigator going sick, the operational side of the exercise was quite successful. No. 151 Squadron impressed all in demonstrating their efficiency with the new aircraft, so much so that the exercise commander, USAF Major General Norman D. Sillin, expressed surprise at the speed at which the Javelins got airborne and managed to intercept Bomber Command Vickers Valiants at 48,000 feet, especially using the GCI (ground control intercept) equipment available.

No. 151 returned to Leuchars, their home base, from Turnhouse during 11–15 November.

By January 1958, 11 Group published some interesting figures regarding the rate of gun fire from the four different fighter types/marks in service:

Type	Rounds Fired	Stoppages	Rate
Hunter F5	3,282	4	821
Hunter F6	13,133	8	1,642
Javelins FAW.2/6	1,988	1	1,988
Meteor NF.12/14	7,718	10	772

Therefore, the Javelin appears to have been at the top in something else other than range, ceiling, and all-weather capability. In any case, the delivery of Javelins was now well under way. While the first of the many were getting used to their new mounts and impressing all into the bargain. In September 1957, 89 Squadron were still equipped with Venom NF.3 aircraft based at RAF Stradishall. Although a month yet before the unit's official reformation on Javelins, they received their first two jets (which at this still early stage were FAW.6s, XA 836s, and XA 820) on 30 September. The same

Above: No. 151 Squadron aircrew gathered in front of one of their charges. The pilot stood to the far left holds the squadron mascot, an owl *c.* 1961. (*RAF Museum Hendon*)

Below: Night flying briefing for 151 Squadron aircrew in October 1958 during Exercise Sunbeam. (*RAF Museum Hendon*)

No. 151 Squadron's FAW.5s on the Leuchars Flightline *c.* 1961. (*RAF Museum Hendon*)

day, a Blackburn B-101 Beverley transport (a huge behemoth of an aircraft) delivered the new Javelin flight simulator, which was installed in the squadron hangar. As was the procedure of the age (transition from one new type to another), the pattern was not to disband first and leave a period of time before re-establishing. Instead, 89 Squadron remained fully operational with the Venoms and took part in Operation Counterpunch as such. As 89 Squadron were being equipped with the Mark 6, parties of their navigators were sent to the Royal Radar Establishment at Malvern to get to grips with the AI.22 or APQ-43 equipment. During October, visitors from Gloster and Armstrong Siddeley explained and reassured 89 Squadron's crews of the merits of the Sapphire engine and gave a demonstration of its handling qualities. One of the visitors, Mr Leech of Armstrong, defied the new crews to cause a flame out by mishandling the throttles on the Sapphire during ground runs with several enthusiastic attempts to do so and, not as promised, without successfully reassuring everyone.

They devoted much of their time from the start to getting to grips with their new charge both on the ground and in the air. Some Venom flying took place on the first day of October, then the rest was devoted to classroom training while all flying ceased. Two weeks on, 89 Squadron disposed of all Venoms and spent the rest of October getting to grips with their new charge.

A new feature of the new second generation jets was the need for anti-g suits. The lectures being conducted included much to do with this essential new piece of aircrew kit. Before flying solo, each pilot had to complete three simulator sorties and successfully negotiate a question and answer session based on the official pilots' notes, requiring a 100 per cent pass mark.

Demonstration flying began on 22 October and by the end of the month, every pilot had at least flown in the back seat. Those who were able to go solo during the month expressed their delight at the aircraft's handling and well-appointed cockpit. Priority was given to training from the top down, so the station commander, OC ops, and the squadron CO went solo first, followed by the flight commanders. This was to ensure that the level of supervision was placed at the right end to pass on to the rest of the aircrew once the JMTU left. To spread the flying effort more evenly, 'A' and 'B' Flights flew on alternate days. The last Venom flight had been arranged for 13 October for the Royal Observer Corps Open Day; however, this had to be cancelled due to poor weather. On 15 and 17 October, nineteen Venoms were delivered to RAF Shawbury for disposal. One was left for maintenance training following a bird strike.

Before the end of the month, they had received eight aircraft: six FAW.6s and two FAW.2s. All of course had the AI.22 radar system in common. Indeed, due to the similarities in appearance, the FAW.6 jets were marked with letters from the first half of the alphabet while the FAW.2s started with the letter 'H'. The bosom tanks were removed during conversion.

By the end of November, all but three pilots had completed conversion, which was progressing smoothly, and the navigators were achieving 'lock on' during practice intercept sorties.

There were, of course, a number of aircraft going tech for various reasons, including: starter breaches, brake valve control, windscreen seals, and Gee box connector. A further Mk 2, XA806, arrived in January, giving them a total of eight Mk 6s and seven Mk 2s. Eleven from the total were grounded during the month, sometimes more than once, for some technical fault or another. No. 46 Squadron at Odiham also completed their re-equipment with the Mk 2.

On 9 January 1958, 89 Squadron's Javelins took part in Exercise Kingpin (ADEX), their first exercise since re-equipping. Of four aircraft scrambled, they intercepted two Valiants and a Vulcan. On 16 January, they took part in a 'Bomex' and claimed six Vulcans. Sqn Ldr G. H. Deacon was the most successful with three claims. At the latter end of the month, they took over the Halyard commitment. This was one of a number of coded references to the UK equivalent of the battle flight commitment in Germany and all of which would soon become QRA.

With conversion complete, most sorties were now practice interceptions at up to 40,000 feet. A period of intensive air-to-air firing was carried out in May, followed by two exercises. Another 'Bomex' required six aircraft to detach to Odiham, where night sorties were flown, resulting in eighteen of the attacking force being intercepted by the 89 Squadron jets. They claimed: five Vulcans, seven Valiants, five B-52s, and another unidentified bomber. Another Kingpin (ADEX) claimed eleven Canberras and a Valiant. Between exercises, there was air-to-air and air-to-sea firing at Lowestoft range and high and low training on the Trimingham range. Next on the agenda were rehearsals for the upcoming Queen's Birthday Flypast.

June 1958 provided the RAF with a high-profile opportunity to parade its new fighter in public at the Queen's Birthday Flypast. For this, a formation of sixteen was planned, drawing on aircraft from both 11 and 12 Groups. Three squadrons were to contribute: 23 and 41 Squadrons would provide six aircraft plus one reserve each, while four aircraft and two reserves would come from 89 Squadron. They would flypast at 350 knots at 1,000 feet.

No. 41 Squadron FAW.4 silhouetted against the evening sky, c. 1957. (*Barry G. Mayner*)

Group Captain D. G. Lyster DSO DFC AFC, Station Commander of RAF Stradishall, was to lead the formation with Squadron Leader D. J. Nicholson as his navigator.

When the Queen's Flypast was due on 12 June, the weather struck and it had to be cancelled despite the amount of careful planning, details of route and timings. Also, the formation flypast was practiced with success. Photographers from *Flight* magazine turned up to photograph the impressive line-up of twenty Javelins, resulting in the usual simplistic media reaction over 'All-Weather' fighters being grounded by the weather.

The next major exercise for 89 Squadron was at RAF Alhorn in Germany, where twelve of their Javelins took part in Exercise Goodplay, during which about seventy-five scrambles were made to intercept targets between 25,000 and 48,000 feet.

Following the disappointment of the Queen's Birthday Flypast, another more dramatic, if not quite as prestigious, opportunity loomed in September when forty-five Javelins were to flypast over Farnborough. These were to be drawn from 46, 89, and 151 Squadrons; a further three jets were required as airborne spares. Due to the high level of maintenance and availability required, the squadrons involved suspended routine flying during the lead up, rehearsals permitted of course. The forty-five Javelins were joined by forty-five Hunters overhead Farnborough each day. Again, the month known to the RAF as the 'silly season', for very good reason was here again, beginning with the Farnborough air show, then quickly followed by the Battle of Britain 'At Home' displays, in turn followed up usually by the ROC's annual events as

Javelin FAW.6 XA835 of 29 Squadron seen at Acklington. Meteor NF predecessor in the background, *c.* 1957. (*Barry G. Mayner*)

well. Wing Commander G. A. Martin, 89 Squadron's CO at the time, made his own feelings known by registering them in the Squadron ORB:

> Finally as a squadron commander and pilot, I have the unique experience of looking forward to the winter months, and the bad weather associated with them, in the fond hope that at least we shall be finished with these unproductive displays and fly-pasts and will be allowed to carry out operational training with somewhat less interference.

It may not be true say that all felt the same way, but many an ORB (Operational Record Book) has been annotated with remarks conveying a wish to avoid any extra-curricular activities such as air shows. Squadron commanders of the era struggled to maintain a full operational training programme in the run up and during the month of September, when nearly all were kept busy. This is now a long-gone feature in the RAF's annual calendar. Indeed, display flying throughout the year affects virtually no units in the present-day RAF.

Then again, Wing Commander Martin also regarded Exercise Halyard as interference. To place matters in perspective, his own unit on this occasion, by no means the only one affected of course, in addition to Farnborough, were called upon to provide a formation of four Javelins to fly over four other RAF stations on 20 September, with four more of his aircraft being assigned to be positioned at one of these four and another three stations as static exhibits. This was further compounded when on 19 September, he lost two of his aircrew: Flt Lt D. H. Kenney and Fg Off G. R. Lewis, who were rehearsing a solo display when their aircraft crashed during a low-speed run. Indeed, the squadron flew a total of seventy flypasts and flypast rehearsals during September 1958.

A further problem that baffled logic somewhat was the posting away of some of his personnel to No. 1 Squadron, who were flying Hunters, with personnel being posted in to his unit from same. None of the new arrivals had any Javelin experience and all had less than three months to serve.

During the latter end of October, 89 Squadron were honoured to provide a fighter escort of six aircraft led by Wg Cdr G. A. Martin, for Dr Heuss, the President of the Federal Republic of Germany, on the occasion of his state visit to the United Kingdom. The President flew in a Viscount aircraft and the Javelins formated on it over Koksijde (Coxyde or Coxhide) in Belgium at a height of 15,000 feet and escorted it to Cranbrook Beacon. This was successfully carried out despite appalling weather at the base. For his part in leading the escort, Wg Cdr Martin received the German *Verdeinstkreuz Einer Klass* (The Order of Merit of the Federal Republic of Germany). The following month, Fg Off David Downey, who provided some of the photographs seen here, joined from 85 Squadron. It would also appear that 13 November was the last day that 89 Squadron took to the air during another exercise 'Bomex'. There were four scrambles and only one Canberra was claimed 'due to bad GCI controlling'. However, they did intercept a B-66, of the USAF, not taking part in the exercise. The same month, 89 Squadron became 85 Squadron and Fg Off Downey was back on his old squadron again.

FAW.5 of 151 Squadron in static park at Leuchars' Battle of Britain day in 20 September 1958. (*Barry G. Mayner*)

FAW.6 of 29 Squadron in static park at Leuchars' Battle of Britain day in 20 September 1958. Note comparison with nosecone of the FAW.5. (*Barry G. Mayner*)

In August 1959, 85 Squadron were redeployed to RAF West Malling. They remained here until September 1960. During the early spring of the latter year, 85 Squadron began receiving their first FAW.8s. From here, they moved to West Raynham as a result of further contraction. This would be 85 Squadron's last station as an operational fighter squadron. Shortly after arriving at West Malling, they took part in Exercise Mandate. This was designed to test the ability of all-weather fighter crews to intercept incoming enemy aircraft with minimal input from the GCI, a process devised to address the likelihood of large raids crossing the North Sea against which close control would hamper rather than aid. Therefore, simple vectors toward incoming large formations would be transmitted the Javelin crews should they require little if any more assistance in finding the incoming raid. Mandate of course tested everyone, and by July 1959, this now found the Javelin force, in the UK at least, at its peak.

If there was one record the Javelin was in competition for, it would probably be the quite dubious honour for the most prominent number of accidents, often with tragic consequences. There were of course a number of survival stories, such as the collision between two Javelin FAW.6s of 29 Squadron. XA823, flown by Flt Lts D.

Newspaper cutting from August 1959, accompanied by a picture of an 85 Squadron Flat Iron touching down on arrival from Stradishall. The article highlights the concerns of locals about the forthcoming significant rise in noise levels. (*David Downey*)

J. Wyborn and J. S. Wilson collided with XA835, flown by Fg Off E. Wood and Flt Lt D. J. S. Clark. The incident occurred over the North Sea on 21 May 1960. All four ejected safely; Wyborn and Wilson came down in the sea just north-east of Scarborough while Wood and Clark came safely down along a stretch of the coast north-west of Hartlepool. Mid-air collisions were frighteningly common in the early stages of Javelin operations: two FAW.7s of 23 Squadron the previous year came into contact over Brundall in Norfolk during practice intercepts at night at 40,000 feet. The crew of XH775 managed to eject safely. However, those in the other jet, XH781—Flt Lt Christopher Brooksbank, aged twenty-nine, and his navigator, Sgt Graham Spriggs—were killed. Chris was following Flt Lt Stark, the pilot of the other aircraft, in a controlled descent from 40,000 to 26,000 feet when XH781 flew into the rear of XH775.

By 1961, the Javelin force had reached peak deployment, although it would not be settled for too long. We were also entering into that period unforeseen by Duncan Sandys where rapid response deployments of RAF fighter squadrons from the UK were becoming frequent due to the prevailing political climate. With Gary Powers being shot down the year before, tensions were growing. In the meantime, the Javelin force flying programme was full of exercises and training deployments.

No. 29 Squadron spent much of 1961 on routine deployments. From 9 February to 27 March, twelve of the squadron's Javelins were sent to Sylt in North Germany. In

The first FAW.2 destined for 89 Squadron having just arrived at RAF Stradishall, attracting a crowd mingling with the ground crew on 30 September 1957. (*The National Archives*)

XA 836 taxying in on arrival at Stradishall, 30 September 1957. (*The National Archives*)

XA836 taxying in at Stradishall on 30 September 1957. (*The National Archives*)

XA836, seen here a week or so later during a visit by ROC personnel, now sporting the colour bar of 89 Squadron on the fin. The jet's predecessor, a Meteor night fighter, sat further back awaiting its fate. (*The National Archives*)

August, they detached to Orland in Norway. The aircraft left in pairs, there being a specific reason for this—given the route to Orland, the nearest diversion airfields were: Gardemoen range 215 miles and Bodo range 245 miles respectively from the destination airfield (also, Sola, which is 345 miles distant from Gardemoen). With nowhere else to land in an emergency, the picked diversions posed problems. The terrain surrounding the approach to the diversions varied considerably with some highland peaks at 4,600 feet. Due to these problems, it was decided that two Javelins would be airborne at all times with one to lead the other in the event of R/T being lost. The last day of the deployment in Norway was 16 September. As this was the air show day at Leuchars, their return was included as part of the day's activities: first, a Britannia carrying 29 Squadron personnel on return entered into a display of low-level handling and then a short field landing demonstration. This may not have happened and the aircraft possibly diverted elsewhere as thirty minutes before the flying was due to begin, at 1.52 p.m., the wind was blowing at 90 degrees across the main runway and getting up to a strength of 68 knots. It had earlier in the day been measured at 15 to 35 knots. This placed the main runway out of safe use and six of the display items had already cancelled as a result. The short runway, which was being used at the time for refuelling aircraft, was quickly cleared and a revised flying display programme was arranged. With the time taken to do this, a rejigging of the proceedings was necessary and soon enough, a full afternoon of flying went ahead from 2.40 p.m. This of course required the crowd line to be realigned parallel to the cross runway. The televising of the display was cancelled as the relay station was wrecked by the strong winds, but the day was salvaged. Equipped now with the Mark 9 Javelin, 29 Squadron had the biggest and heaviest of the RAF's fighter type to enter service so far and made quite an impression.

The year 1961 brought two things to Fighter Command. The English Electric Lightning, which initially was re-equipping some of the Hunter squadrons while the Javelin force, having so recently reached its peak of deployed squadrons, was facing a number of disbandments still. At the end of February, 72 Squadron started a rundown of its crews; a slight hint of irony was marked by the ease at which they completed their preceding monthly flying programme due to some unseasonably good weather, but now those crews were being posted out with no replacements. Despite a disbandment dinner in Beverley near to their base at Leconfield, they were deployed lock, stock, and barrel to Leeming while airfield work services were carried out in preparation for the arrival of Lightnings. Despite the drawback, they still achieved 174 hours of flying in June when they were involved with three exercises: King Pin, Ciano, and Doris. No. 72 Squadron were not finally wound up until 31 July, but were officially disbanded on 29 June when Leconfield received its annual formal inspection by AOC-in-C of 11 Group, Air Vice-Marshal H. J. Maguire CB DSO OBE. No. 72 Squadron performed a flypast with eight aircraft over 11 Group Headquarters and RAF Leconfield. In January 1961, 64 Squadron were engaged in an in-flight refuelling trials programme now that they had the Mark 9 version complete with refuelling boom attachment. At the same time, they were also carrying out early training with Firestreak, which was now incorporated in practice intercepts.

Whatever the shortcomings of the Javelin, there is no doubt that in the hands of experienced RAF crews, it was proving itself worth its rations during training exercises. Meanwhile, back on the ground, 64 Squadron were introduced to a civilian boffin who gave an aerodynamics lecture on the Javelin with emphasis on the old chestnut subjects pertaining to the aircraft's notorious stall and spin characteristics; the ORB entry noted that the lecture was 'not entirely encouraging'.

About the same time, a number of 64 Squadron's crews went to the Martin-Baker factory for a lecture and tour. They got to see the seats and equipment being fitted and tested. The only comment here was made by a moustachioed ex-Glasgow policeman, who said 'I'm always impressed by Martin Bakers'. Through January 1961, 64 Squadron practiced 'dry' hook-ups with Valiants, which incorporated exercises involving PIs with Firestreaks carried. This progressed to 'wet' hook-ups where fuel was actually taken on board. Thirty-one of these trips were flown as cross-country sorties with flight times now extending to three-and-a-quarter hours. Amid the seeming development and progress, the CO, Wing Commander Mills, and Squadron Leader Macrostie gave the aircrew the benefit of the knowledge they had gleaned from a recent visit to CFE (Central Fighter Establishment) and it was not good news. Among various points that were hard to swallow, the most depressing was that the death knell (as many had been expecting) was sounded for the future of the two-seater all-weather fighter.

Tanker trials with Javelin FAW.9Rs of 64 while based at Duxford, queueing for the 90 Squadron Valiant's single drogue *c.* 1961. (*Barry G. Mayner*)

No. 64 Squadron FAW.9R XH766 exhibited in the static park at an airshow. (*Peter R. March*)

Wg Cdr Mills sensed, not unexpectedly, that many of his nav/rads felt this a mistake. One might ponder if only they could have seen past the current decade to the next, it may have sugared the pill somewhat. Furthermore, Mills could confirm that they would be moving in the months ahead to RAF Waterbeach, as RAF Duxford was soon to close. The squadron failed to reach their target of flying hours, essentially due to unserviceabilities, but IFR training progressed very well and navigation training was maintaining high standards. In March, Radio Compass and Rebecca (Rebecca was an early form of transponder working on VHF with a ground beacon) were installed in the Javelins in place of Gee navigation referencing equipment. To do this, the squadron had to accept lower than planned flying hours.

No. 64 Squadron were heavily engaged in tanker trials, typically lasting about five hours with up to twenty-eight sorties, none of which was counted as contributory to the allocation of hours for operational training. However, just the same, 64 Squadron almost completed their flying programme for February while a lot of ground-based work had been devoted to a planned deployment to Cyprus. Burgeoning problems there and in the Far East were placing an increasing demand on the RAF presence in these areas to provide what today is termed a show of force. Subsequently, as the first Javelins of 64 Squadron arrived in Akrotiri, they began their commitment straight away, placing two aircraft with crews on battle flight, still the current term in use. Much of the outbound flight were supported by tankers from Marham, hence the intense air-to-air refuelling exercises earlier.

In April, they practiced air-to-air refuelling for real in support of a deployment to Cyprus. By 13 July, a busy period ahead in particular beckoned as 64 Squadron bade farewell to Duxford and flew out to take up residence at Waterbeach. A crisis in the Middle East was developing with concerns that Iraq was showing some indication that it may be harbouring intensions to invade neighbouring Kuwait.

From July to August 1961, 23 (also operating FAW.9s) and 64 Squadrons were both drawn from to provide a detachment to fly out to Cyprus. This was in response to the threat from Iraq to invade Kuwait. The profile for the route was that rather than carry drop tanks, all twelve Javelins involved were to be FAW.9R fits and they would each carry four Firestreaks and 300 rounds of operational ammunition for the four Aden cannons. Also, as the op order stated, 'suitably in-flight refuelling qualified crews', which despite the recent training programme, was still something of a rarity.

A further move to Bahrain was anticipated under the circumstances. All commanded by the CO of 23 Squadron, most of the ground crew also came from the same squadron, although any further back up would come from 64 Squadron. As it turned out, each of the legs flown to Cyprus were made without any requirement for IFR. In this configuration, the aircraft were 3,500 lb overweight on take-off from Coltishall. Using 100 per cent cold power in the climb, the Javelins used up 3,650 lb of fuel to get to flight level 400 in sixteen minutes. Crews were briefed to fly as far as serviceability and crew fatigue would allow. The route officially went from Coltishall via: Orange, Pisa, then Luqa but the Javelin boys were briefed to regard Luqa as a planned as a night stopover, only if required.

The first six set out on 5 July and the remaining six on the following day. By the time they reached Nicosia, it was clear that to deploy further forward to Bahrain

FAW.6 of 29 Squadron on patrol breaking through the cloud. Note again the fountain pen nib faring between the jet exhausts, a typical feature of all Javelins powered by the SA6 engines except Mks 7, 8, and 9. (*Barry G. Mayner*)

FAW.9R of 64 Squadron, probably during tanker exercises in 1961. Note the Valiant with 'Chicks' in the distance. (*Ian White*)

would not be necessary. However, there was a of sense of tension when they arrived in Cyprus, such that the detachment was expected by HQ NEAF to share a twenty-four-hour CAP (combat air patrol), which, after some discussion, became one aircraft on standby but dismounted. This just was not possible at Nicosia, however desirable, owing to the intense heat. Another aircraft was posted at ten minutes readiness. During the day, this was shared with the Hunter FGA9s of 43 Squadron; however, at night, the entire duty naturally fell purely to the Javelin force. Sun canopies were used to try and maintain some small level of comfort for those crews at cockpit readiness, which could really swelter even with the occasional gust of wind, which only served to blow bits of the sun canopy away.

No. 43 Squadron were somewhat hampered in that they had a rather large number of new, therefore, non- or limited-operational pilots but with the presence of the Javelins now sharing the battle flight commitment, 43 Squadron were able to catch up on training. Eventually, the night state was ended to make more crews available for the day. This began on 7 July and remained the case through to the return to the UK. This was because HQ NEAF were more concerned with a threat from low-level attacks by MiG-17s and fair to moderate weather bombing by IL-28s of the Air Force of the UAR (United Arab Republic, a brief union between Egypt and Syria). Whatever their concerns the orders for the Javelin force made no sense. They were to adopt an unarmed shadow and identify profile if scrambled and, to ensure that was all that happened, Firestreaks were not mounted and the bolts removed from the Aden guns.

Also out of kilter was the base, which was more given to transport operations. The detachment commander observed that fighter operations and those of transport units did not mix. There was no ASP (aircraft servicing platform) or ORP (operational readiness platform) of any description. Regarding the comment about transport, Nicosia was at the time already predominantly a civilian airport, which it was feared could be given priority over any military use. Indeed, so much debris was strewn about the airfield that the Javelin with its low-positioned jet pipes, nearly sitting, would require a lot of sweeping up immediately following any scrambles.

Akrotiri had already been selected as the base for AW fighter operations in the future by this time—and indeed the present—but was so full of Canberras (four squadrons) and other air movements on top that there was no room for the Javelins or the Hunters until new hard standings and dispersals could be built. There was a plan to build an area for fighters at the west end of the main runway but the Javelin folk were unimpressed as in the event of a large-scale emergency or rise in tension, the runway would be under heavy use from the resident tactical bomber force, deployed V-bombers, and of course the AW fighters. Indeed, this deployment was fraught with problems: overheating of Firestreak nose sensors even with the red sheaths due to the lack of ground handling equipment at the base and it was decided that 30-mm ammunition, despite the non-armed QRA state, should be left in the magazines on board, then the shells began to weep in the extreme temperatures. The shells were left in Cyprus to be disposed of at the end of the deployment on 30 July.

August 1962 brought another move: 64 Squadron were given their marching orders again, this time to Binbrook. On 16 August, flying ceased so everyone could pack up and prepare for the move. The organisation of Fighter Command had changed since, now down to two operational groups instead of numbering four groups from the south-west, the UK was split in half, and now, 11 Group, which had identified the south-east since the Battle of Britain, now identified the north while the whole of the south of the UK was 12 Group's responsibility. So, for the Scarabs, the move to Binbrook on 22 August took them to 11 Group.

Within three weeks of arriving, they were requested to produce not one but two four-ship formation flying drill display teams for the Battle of Britain displays on Saturday 15 September. The two Flight Commanders—Sqn Ldr Lomas and Sqn Ldr R. J. P. Miers—led the two formations, Lomas to display over Ternhill and Wyton while Miers took his team to Benson and Gaydon. Both operated in what were described as 'fairly bad weather conditions' but each managed to make their respective appointments and arrive over each airfield in time. Again, such a level of effort towards display flying while still managing the rest of the commitments of an operational squadron is very much erased from the culture of the modern-day air staff.

Much welcome good news came in November regarding the facilities at Binbrook, with a new coffee bar nearing completion and a TV set installed for the benefit of the QRA crews. QRA had now replaced the old battle flight, Flinders and Halyard commitments, and no longer required crews at cockpit readiness. The new procedure allowed air and ground crews a degree of relaxation (ten minutes readiness nearby under roof, hence the TV). QRA as understood was now introduced NATO wide. No. 64 Squadron would eventually leave Binbrook for Tengah, being established there as of 1 April 1965. Due to the Malaysian/Indonesian situation, they would be on state. This required one crew at five minutes readiness and another at fifteen, occasionally increased to include a third at thirty minutes readiness. The training here, what could be managed under the circumstances, required low-level intercept sorties and cross-country training. On 1 and 10 May, 64 Squadron's Javelins were scrambled to intercept AURI Tu-16 Badgers and shadow them along what became known as the 'fence'. Aircraft were, in order to provide the level of air defence cover required, routinely deployed to Kuching and Labuan airbases in Borneo. From here, patrols along set routes with scrambles were common place.

No. 29 Squadron (now based at Leuchars) were engaged in numerous overseas deployments. In July 1962, an expected delivery from the USSR of Tu-16s to Egypt was expected courtesy of intelligence. That month, an operation was mounted by 29 Squadron in concert with their old Leuchars alumni 43 Squadron, now based at Akrotiri, together with some of the Canberras from the strike wing there. This involved the interception and monitoring in order to obtain information concerning the movement of 12 Tu-16 Badger long-range reconnaissance bombers from Bulgaria to the United Arab Republic. The first sorties flown on 6 and 7 July were unsuccessful. On 16 July, Javelins of 29 Squadron, operating from Akrotiri, on this occasion, intercepted a number Badgers and photographs were taken. It may seem insignificant to the casual observer, but this gleaned intelligence was then considered to be of great value. A report of this period describes the squadron deployment being contacted by phone from 280 Signals Unit at Troodos in Cyprus; 280 SU were at the time the long-range early warning RAF radar station covering the area that the British were responsible for in the Mediterranean. On 14 July, four Javelins were brought to two hours readiness in anticipation of intercepting and identifying two Tu-16 aircraft being delivered from Bulgaria to the United Arab Republic. The crews were briefed that they might need to reposition at El Adem in Libya. At 1 a.m. on 15 July, four Javelins were ordered off to their patrol positions then to recover to El Adem and awaited further orders. Should any Badgers be encountered they were to be referred to as 'Charlie'. At 1.45 a.m., the operation was postponed for twenty-four hours and a new briefing time of 1 a.m. on Monday 16 July was set. The profile was changed to two pairs of Javelins, one pair heading to patrol position 'Amber 10' and recovering to Akrotiri and the other to patrol 'Amber 1'. These were designated areas, the location of which carried a clue with regard to the respective recovery base the Amber 1 pair were to recover to El Adem. At 1.50 a.m. on Monday, one pair—missions 41 and 42—were brought to ten minutes readiness and at 4.25 a.m. were ordered to patrol a position 'Bravo' (32, 55N by 28, 55 E) at 5.15 a.m.

The two Javelins were airborne at 4.43 a.m. and commenced their patrol 10 nautical miles apart at 7.16 a.m. A radar contact was made by mission forty-one at

TU-16 Badger being delivered to Gamel Nasser's Air Force in 1962, perhaps the earliest intercept of such an aircraft by the RAF, in this case a Javelin of 29 Squadron over the Mediterranean. (*Barry G. Mayner*)

7.28 a.m. at 11 nautical miles, slightly displaced on the starboard (right hand) side. An interception on this target was made, which turned out to be a Tupolev Tu-16 reconnaissance bomber at flight level 330 (33,000ft) and travelling at a speed of Mach 0.78. Mission 41 then closed in from astern and 1 nautical mile to the left or port and using a handheld 35-mm camera, the crew were able to take several shots. Mission 41 moved under the Tu-16 and photographed the underside and the starboard side then, when moving back again the Soviet bomber, rocked its wings. Clearly interpreted as a warning, Mission 41 broke off to return and land at Akrotiri at 7.58 a.m.

The second pair—Missions 43 and 44—were briefed to go to position 'Alpha' (32, 20N by 26, 40 E) with instructions to orbit this position and then to recover to El Adem. The scramble order came at 6.50 a.m. and both were aloft at 6.58 a.m. and 7 a.m. respectively. They were approaching Amber 10 when they heard Mission 41 callout 'Tally Ho Charlie'. At this, Mission 44 started a radar sweep and found a contact in his 44 degrees bearing at a range of 35 nautical miles. This was another Tu-16 following a similar intercept pattern to that employed by Mission 41. These two Javelins shared the success of the day in gaining useful photo intelligence. Mission 42's radar went unserviceable and made no sightings. Mission 43 made contact with a target but was unable to identify it visually. Barry Mayner was with 29 Squadron and was among those scrambled to make the intercept:

> My first Russian was a Badger being delivered to Egypt on 16 July 1962. No. 29 Sqn—we were on detachment from Leuchars to Akrotiri. Four of our Javelins were scrambled to intercept on information provided by telephone calls from Sophia to London to Cyprus when the Badgers got airborne. We intercepted the stream of aircraft nearly 350 miles west of Akrotiri. Two of us managed to catch a Badger and take pictures.

Barry has quite a long association with the RAF's all-weather fighter force serving a number of tours on Javelins and Phantoms. In recent times, he and his family used to run a bed and breakfast in Guardbridge near RAF Leuchars, where he was stationed for many years, catering for many of those travelling from near and far to attend the air show each year.

The year 1961 brought further changes. No. 151 Squadron were next to bite the dust; the squadron were notified in January of that year that they would disband. September was the official stand down date, for which Major Hancock (USAF) led his squadron into the air for one final time over the north-east Fife coastline, which had been home since the unit first arrived with DH Vampire NF.10s in 1951. Much carried on through the year as though nothing had been said but by August, most of the squadron members had some idea of what lay ahead of them. In the final month, fifteen pilots and navigators had been told they would be going on to the FAW.9 and attended an introductory lecture on this version as a preamble to postings. The postings and other factors (such as leave and sickness) reduced the number of available pilots to eight by the start of September; this was reduced to six by the second week.

The official disbandment date was 19 September. Leading up to this, far more flying was devoted to formation flypast rehearsals, both for the disbandment flypast and, of course, being September, the annual 'At Home', which this year took place three days before the official disbandment. A total of twenty-two sorties were taken up with these practices.

After 19 September, all further flying was taken up with ferrying aircraft to 19 MU at St Athan; this task was complete by 28 September. Eleven of the squadron's aircrew were posted to neighbouring 29 Squadron effective from 25 September. Proving that all fighter pilots and navigators do not last forever, two of 151 Squadron's nav/rads—Flt Lt C. Robinson and Master Navigator Furniss—were respectively posted to the Blackburn Beverley and Armstrong Whitworth Argosy. Brian Henwood was on the Squadron at the time and recalls something of the north-east Fife social life at the time:

> I was a member of a successful cabaret which we put on in the crew room for a squadron anniversary. I do recall doing a striptease from flying kit to underpants. Also during that period we did a lot of rehearsing in Sqn Ldr Len Maynard's (NRL) office. One dismal Friday afternoon we rehearsed when there was no flying and come 5 o'clock Len decided that we should go to Kate's Bar in St Andrews for a small Happy Hour drink. On the Monday, however, the CO, Wg Cdr Bob Martin, received a complaint from the hotel about a noisy disruption. When asked who caused it he was advised that 'It was Brian Henwood and his mates'. I had to advise Len Maynard about this and he promptly announced himself to the CO as one of Brian Henwood's mates. Nothing more was heard of the matter.

No. 25 Squadron arrived at Leuchars from Waterbeach at the end of 1961. They had re-equipped at the beginning of the year, in January, having previously operated the Mark 7 Javelin. Their outgoing CO prior to arriving at Leuchars had not spoken highly of the move north of the border. Wing Commander John Walton simply noted, 'The Squadron regrettably had to re-deploy to Leuchars following the Cyprus detachment'. Quite what his cause for regret was he did not expand upon, but in any case, the squadron upon arrival was already under the command of his successor, Wing Commander P. G. K. Wilkinson.

They flew more or less directly from Cyprus to Leuchars, all arriving by 28 November this included a brief four-day stop at Waterbeach *en route*. Just the day after their arrival, they were engaged in intercepting V-bombers in Exercise Spellbound. The new CO had a more efficacious comment to make about Leuchars noting that 'the new home station of the Squadron, has done everything possible to help us to settle down, both domestically and operationally and by the end of the month full flying had re-commenced'.

In December 1961, the Leuchars wing were tasked quite separately. No. 25 Squadron were to remain at Leuchars, where snow and ice had prevented fourteen working days flying. The aircrew attended, perhaps as a result, no fewer than twenty-one lectures and demonstrations. The subjects included of all things; ejector seat training, intelligence on the Iraqi Air Force, aircraft recognition and the tactics and operation of Firestreak, while other officers were detached away on various courses including

No. 151 Squadron aircrew and officers celebrate, for want of a better description, being disbanded. In the background on the blackboard is the planned disbandment formation flypast in September 1961. (*RAF Museum Hendon*)

Major Hancock, USAF, CO of 151, leads his chaps out to their aircraft to conduct their final flight on 19 September 1961. (*RAF Museum Hendon*)

No. 151 Squadron seven-ship formation flypast. (*RAF Museum Hendon*)

Search and Rescue at Mountbatten and AWFLS at West Raynham. Meanwhile, they entertained the press and Scottish television on 5 December, even though the weather prevented any kind of flying.

As January 1962 arrived, 25 Squadron were able to make some inroads in the weather, which did not honestly show much sign of improving, but they managed to take part in three exercises with the V-force and co-operated with a number of 'Bomber Affiliations' whereby the V-bombers made themselves available as targets during their own training sorties for the Javelins to intercept. Having gotten rid of the snow and ice, the runway was now bedevilled by strong cross-winds and rain prohibiting night flying, but they did get airborne on occasion at night to intercept some 'embellished' targets—again V-bombers available for practice intercepts. To demonstrate the importance of good working personal equipment, 25 Squadron's crews were involved in Exercise Kingpin, specifically an air defence exercise, on 18 January. It was found that their pressure jerkins would not fit over their immersion suits and as a result, most of the squadron were limited to 42,000 feet. As a result, many targets they should have intercepted were allowed through because they nipped over the top at 43,000 feet or more. On 29 January, five of 25 Squadron's jets had to divert to Lossiemouth following another Spellbound exercise on account of the runway at Leuchars being blocked by eight Javelins visiting from 85 Squadron. The squadron were also involved with trials for V-bomber tail warning radars requiring them to carry out a number of sorties for that purpose.

While the weather remained bad, the CO took advantage of the situation to imbue a sense of worth in all squadron personnel, with a lecture on 25 Squadron's specific role in the event of hostilities. This included all technical and administration staff as well

Javelin four-ship from 25 Squadron *c.* 1962. (*Peter R. March*)

as aircrew. All, especially the ground crew, appeared to appreciate the greater insight into just how important their own individual role was and vital a contribution they would be making to the country should the balloon go up, to use an old expression (or, as became much more favoured in later years, 'when the shit hits the fan').

With improving weather in March, 25 Squadron were again involved with intercepting V-bombers high and fast with Victors and Vulcans in particular. Ciano exercises with jamming aircraft also consumed a chunk of the operational training schedule. Some ECM Valiants, just off the coast, were thrown into the mix here. Training also included AI (airborne intercept radar) training involving tail chases against violently evading targets; the renewed emphasis on this was considered to be a considerable improvement.

April is noted as a month in which a radical change took place in Fighter Command's commitment to provide aircraft at readiness for interception and investigation purposes. Essentially, this refers to the integration of Fighter Command as an assigned unit and component part of SACEUR's air defence force, and a re-appraisal of the readiness commitment. It was decided that a total of 3.5 per cent of the command's fighter force should be at constant readiness. This was to be split between the two remaining groups—11 and 12—who would each maintain their share: 11 covering the northern half of the country and 12 the south. This involved two aircraft at ten minutes readiness instead of just one at two minutes. In the north, 25 and 29 shared this commitment at Leuchars. Up until now, they had been detaching aircraft and crews to Middleton St George, with crews sitting in the cockpit for quite long periods. This was the much-dreaded Exercise 'Flinders' commitment.

As the year moved further along, concentration for 25 on countering ECM seemed to become quite the focus. Six aircraft deployed to Middleton St George for another Ciano exercise from 13 to 16 April. On this occasion, the problem of too many fighters to targets was encountered; attempted to avoid this arising backfired when scramble orders were staggered. The Flinders commitment had an adverse effect on the availability of air and ground crew and aircraft alike as now two jets were tied up in preparation to launch at the drop of a hat, twenty-four hours a day for the duration the responsibility was held. From the following month, 25 were expected to be away from Leuchars for a period of about twelve weeks. They were to deploy to Gütersloh in West Germany. Due to the length of the detachment, many decided to take their wives with them, even though this would have an impact on personal finances as the RAF would not pay an allowance for married quarters for those involved. Even so, the station commander and his staff at Gütersloh did what they could to help by making available as many spare married quarters as possible.

In order to find out what was going on, evidently the CO of 25 had to fly out to Gütersloh to 'spy out the lay of the land' as it were. When he returned, he briefed the squadron to expect to be maintained at a very high readiness state or 'state of preparedness' and although it was not confirmed or made clear, the presumption was the Berlin Corridor once again was concentrating everyone's minds.

On 26 May, seventeen Javelins of 25 Squadron arrived at Gütersloh and sure enough, the next eleven weeks were spent training for and being on hand to reinforce the RAF fighter force in West Germany for an expected renewal of tension over the Berlin Corridor. Training for this moved away from high level interception to medium and low level given the radical change of circumstances to those at Leuchars. While in Germany, the squadron operated from a dispersal position on the airfield.

Throughout 1962, 29 Squadron spent nearly half the year overseas on various deployments. In March, four aircraft were deployed to Middleton St George as part of a commitment to fulfil the Battle Flight.

No. 25 Squadron had a week's stand down on return before the Battle of Britain display on 15 September 1962, for which they provided a nine-ship formation display team to perform at Aldergrove as well as the home crowd.

The principal means of disseminating information to Fighter Command units by 1962 relied upon a variety of systems for getting fighters airborne in the quickest possible time; not just the early warning radar station was relied upon but other lesser known processes. The 'blind scramble' was to determine the arrival of the Soviet bomber raid against the UK and how it would approach. In the first instance, this was the use of forward-deployed radars and then what was referred to as 'Jim Crow' fighters. The latter were expected soon to be replaced by airborne early warning aircraft; at the time, this meant aircraft such as the Canberra equipped with AI and UHF or, to a lesser extent, by NATO fighters operating under agreed joint procedures.

To assess the operational effectiveness and capability of the typical Javelin squadron, Fighter Command's research branch were tasked with investigating this. The guinea pig used was 33 Squadron based at RAF Middleton St George from January to June 1962. During the latter three months of the study, 33 Squadron had 16.5 aircrews on

Above: No. 25 Squadron aircrew, *c.* 1962 at Leuchars, from left to right: Wg Cdr Pete Williamson (pilot/CO), Chris Cowper (pilot), Ivan Symonds (navigator), Jock Shields (navigator), Roy Evans (navigator with squadron mascot sub-species of owl unknown, but as Roy says, should have been a falcon as per 25 Squadron badge), Pete Deakin (pilot), Mike Harris (navigator), Fred Richardson (pilot), Hamish Cook (navigator), Mel Evans (navigator), possibly Chris Mawby (pilot), and Bob Rodgers (navigator). (*Barry G. Mayner*)

Right: 'Bomb Dump' at Leuchars and a chief technician inspects Firestreaks in store. This missile was used by Javelin, Sea Vixen, and Lightning fighters. (*Barry G. Mayner*)

effective strength on average out of a total of eighteen complete crews. Typically, they were divided into three flights of equal size. The study covered a typical four-week period, amounting to 160 working hours. Each found themselves on day or night flying duty on alternating weeks. Some 1,126 hours of flying was logged. The command task required 1,800; this was practically achieved during May and June.

Analysis of flying activity during week days during the four months of the period found that only 53 per cent of weekdays were 'normal' flying days. Day flying was carried out from Monday to Friday; they were not affected by other events such as exercises, bad weather, or preparation for detachment. Typically, most of the flying was distributed over the Monday to Thursday period, with much less on Friday, with night flying Monday to Thursday resulting in a long weekend. From late May, the squadron was required to provide one complete crew for QRA. The duty recently referred to as the 'Flinders' commitment and the pilot and navigator were based in the squadron crew room throughout. Data was obtained and calculated concerning the amount of time the chaps spent on leave, Bank Holidays, absence for medical reasons, courses, and on QRA duty, all of which were considered a drain on actual availability for squadron operations.

In addition, the study calculated the amount of time spent on flying related activities: for instance, the associated preparations, briefings, pre-flight checks, and debriefing.

Conclusions were that aircrew spent about one-quarter of their time away from the station; an appreciable amount of working time is taken up by the Flinders/QRA commitment; and after allowing for time spent on flying and flinders, about fifty to sixty hours was available for other duties. This amounted to two days per each of the weeks spent on the station.

The use of the term 'other duties' covers a variety of RAF sins, some good some not so good depending on your outlook, but a few examples, concerning officers and aircrew, would be: attendance at Courts of Enquiry; liaison visits to control and reporting radar stations (fighter crews more specifically); duty pilot; deputy OC flying; and various individually assigned duties such as inventories, officer in command airmen's accommodation block, or being in charge of the rugby club, theatre club.

The amount of time spent on all these duties was not calculated accurately but was believed to be small. That said, aircrew found attending to all these extracurricular matters rather taxing, not because of the amount of time taken but because of how they interfered with the otherwise relatively routine pattern of flying. An example given was unpredictability: if an aircraft was unserviceable, time was used up waiting for a serviceable one to be made available. The allocation of actual flying hours per individual was 200 per year. Not surprisingly, as the summer wore on, the amount of activity increased all around. In April, no one made more than a single day sortie with 15 during the day and 3 at night for the month. In May, seventy-two sorties were flown in one day. While 33 Squadron were being analysed in pursuit of aircrew wellbeing, others during the era were getting up to other things; most of the life of a Javelin squadron revolved around exercises and deployments.

Even so, what were considered normal days of flying departed considerably from the normal flying programme. The report also recorded the length of time each aircrew member spent off the base, finding this to be over a quarter in each case. On a high proportion of occasions, individual pilots and navigators flew just once during a flying period, day or night. A major factor contributing to the erratic departure from what was the expected level and distribution of flying was aircraft unserviceability, which was high: two-thirds of all flights gave rise to some defect or other, which, of course, added to the unusual pattern of flying. Among a list of recommendations for improving matters was the ambition for each available crew on duty on any given day to fly at least two flights during any given duty period; when that period was assigned to flying operations, this was expected to assist each crew member reach the Fighter Command target of 200 flying hours per year per individual. A further recommendation was the reduction in aircraft recovery time; indeed, waste was identified in the manner in which aircraft returned from routine sorties, the approach patterns and how long it took to get aircraft back on the ground again. One recommendation was to reduce the number of aircraft recovering at any one time. An increase in the number of aircraft available for use during the day would be improved by increasing the number of technical personnel on the night servicing party at the expense of the day team.

No. 33 Squadron's strength was sixteen Mark 9 Javelins, a T3, and a Meteor T.7, the latter almost certainly the squadron 'hack'. Hacks were commonplace on RAF fighter squadrons of the era. They were effectively run arounds for aircrew in order to nip off and collect someone and ferry from 'A' to 'B' and *vice versa* and was also ideal for running other errands. Among sickness, leave, courses, and stand down periods, one other activity was classed as a drain on operational effectiveness: that of the 'Flinders' commitment. This was coming to an end as the new procedure, brought in later the same year, 1962, the manner of maintaining a high state of readiness was brought into line with the new standard NATO procedure. This was the QRA (quick reaction alert) and allowed air and ground crews to remain *in situ* but stood down from constant cockpit readiness for this in the years ahead and in time for the Lightning, for which special QRA annex and sheds were to be constructed at one end of a small number of airfields.

There were still changes afoot with Fighter Command during 1962. Toward the end of the year, 33 Squadron were ordered to Geilenkirchen. They arrived with sixteen Javelins in two formations on 19 and 26 November. They then officially became 5 Squadron while the hitherto 5 Squadron disbanded. Only weeks before the polarised standoff between East and West relations deteriorated as far as they would throughout the history of that era, US Intelligence had detected an attempt by the USSR to station medium-range ballistic missiles in its most prominent client state in the western hemisphere: Cuba. This came to light when a Lockheed U2 high-altitude reconnaissance aircraft photographed what was identified as preparations for a launch site on 14 October 1962. The next two weeks brought the world to the closest it has ever been in history to Armageddon and while the world itself went about its business, the drama largely took place shielded from the press, which reported what snippets they could.

Whatever the degree to which Fighter Command braced for the worst, it would appear that operations were not unduly affected. Indeed, routine was the order of the

AOC's annual formal inspection at RAF Middleton St George on 8 May 1962 with a flypast by 33 Squadron overhead for the visit of Air Vice-Marshal G. T. B. Clayton DFC. (*RAF Museum Hendon*)

AOC inspects 33 Squadron on 8 May 1962. (*RAF Museum Hendon*)

Ground crew run towards their aircraft during a scramble for the visit of the Air Vice-Marshal G. T. B. Clayton DFC on 8 May 1962. (*The National Archives*)

Two Javelin T3s of the Jet Instrument Rating Squadron, this unit, spawned from the CFE, continued the responsibility for the evaluation of operational Javelin crews, the JIRS c. 1963. (*The National Archives*)

Peter Goodwin with XH768/E while on 25 Squadron during Cyprus detachment in October–November 1961. (*Peter Goodwin*)

Right: Belgian Air Force General F. J. Burniaux, C-in-C 2nd ATAF (2nd Allied Tactical Air Force) is given a guided tour of 11 Squadron's XH768 during a visit to RAF Geilenkirchen on 8 October 1964. (*The National Archives*)

Below: MPs visit to RAF Laarbruch and 5 Squadron, 26 June 1962, inspect the exhausts of a Javelin FAW.5. Note the clearly defined Fountain Pen nib style faring. (*The National Archives*)

day. No. 25 Squadron started the month with some standard bomber affiliation and daytime ECM exercises; they handed over QRA duties to 29 Squadron on 5 October.

However, even during what has gone down in history as the most critically tense period of the Cold War (when all hell could have broken loose, and not by half), the Northern 'Q' stood firm but unchallenged. The Early Warning Sector Operations Radar Station at Buchan scrambled the QRA aircraft at 5.25 p.m. on 23 October, but to no avail and the aircraft landed again forty-two minutes later. On top of this, 29 Squadron flew twelve Javelins to Wattisham on 17 October as part of Exercise Neuralgia or Cypex 3. From here, they flew eleven aircraft out to Akrotiri in Cyprus, one having returned unserviceable, a detachment of which for the junior officers would have made the pending Armageddon threatened by the Cuban Missile Crisis seem preferable.

Their accommodation was not just austere, it was Kennel class. Bearing in mind that this was Cyprus and with accommodation being at a premium, the privations were far from the grandeur and opulence normally associated with the privileges of HM Forces officer class—there were no curtains or shutters on the windows. Due to the nature of the deployment, the aircrew were required for periods at night and to sleep during daylight hours for short periods. Given the strong sunlight shafting through the windows and the unaccustomed heat, the pilots and navigators of the 20-ton transonic (supersonic in a shallow dive) Javelins were affected by fatigue, which could so easily have been avoided. Perhaps worse was the Spartan and sparse hygiene facilities: no ablutions facilities immediately to hand and the ones which were available in other billets looked like the baths and showers had never been cleaned. A broken door leading into an adjoining block allowed dust to be constantly blown in and in one case, a single wash hand basin was for the exclusive use of sixteen officers, five Pakistani tailors, a laundry worker, a barber, and three batmen. The only available showers were not working—one missing its rose sprinkler and the other had a blocked drain—while about sixty officers shared three baths, none of which were clean, one being used to store paint and another being used by the laundryman to soak dirty laundry. Among the recommendations for future detachments, the squadron commander listed, apart from the obvious adjustments such as working facilities which were also clean, were adequate drying facilities and that they should be for the use of no one else, save the personnel on detachment. It was not quite the stuff of the recruitment that was being relied on heavily at the time to attract recruits for all three services following the loss of the National Service intakes, but some may recognise the similarity in circumstances in relation to the then growing number of cheap summer package tours to sunnier climbs.

Nine of the aircraft returned at the end of the month, with two still staging along the return route on 31 October.

The crisis itself took place over the period 15 to 28 October. On 16 October, OC 25 Squadron led a formation of six Javelins on a flypast over Leith Docks and Princes Street in Edinburgh on the occasion of the state visit to Scotland of the King of Norway.

No. 25 Squadron were essentially non-effective by November but kept on at Leuchars prior to being properly disbanded and the aircraft being sent to join 11 Squadron, re-equipping with Mark 9s at the time.

Javelin FAW.9 Box-4 formation from 25 Squadron. (*Peter R. March*)

The CO remarked:

That from a Historical point of view it is most unfortunate that the decision had to be made to disband this squadron which has a considerably longer record of unbroken service than many of the All-weather Squadrons sill remaining in service. With regards to general efficiency, the squadron has flown more hours than any other mk 9 Javelin squadron in the service over the past two years, in fact, with the exception of one in-flight refuelling equipped Javelin squadron, we have flown over a thousand hours more than our nearest rivals. One is left with the impression that perhaps the reason for disbanding this squadron rather than another was to save as much money as possible on aircraft hours and fuel bills! However, we cannot help but feel, as Cordelia in Shakespeare's *King Lear*: 'We have seen the best of our times, machinations, hollowness, treachery, and all ruinous disorder, follow us disquietly to our graves'.

Roy Evans was still on 25 Squadron as the year drew to a close and the structure of Fighter Command and RAF Germany were being rearranged once again. While 33 Squadron were assigned to replace 5 Squadron then rebadge as 5 Squadron at Geilenkirchen, 25 Squadron were to do exactly the same in regard to 11 Squadron:

In December '62 we left for Geilenkirchen to re-equip No. 11 Sqn with our Mk 9s. Shortly after arrival, one of our pilots, Norman Glass & his regular nav/rad, also named Evans, stalled during a dogfight with a pair of Belgian F-84F fighters. After several minutes in an uncontrolled spin the navigator ejected, the stall-warners noise cancelled

Practice 'Demo' scramble on 13 September 1962 in preparation for the Battle of Britain 'At Home' day at Leuchars on 15 September 1962. George Beaton and Barry Mayner take the lead running for their aircraft during a demonstration scramble of four 29 Squadron aircraft. (*Barry G. Mayner*)

Four Javelins waiting for their crews at Leuchars during rehearsal for the open day scramble. (*Barry G. Mayner*)

out the news that Norman was trying to tell him that the spin was stopping & control was regained at 12,000 feet. The aircraft landed safely, minus rear canopy and ejector seat, this was the only recorded case of a Javelin being recovered and landed safely!

This illustrates the difference between multi-crew & single-seater, day boy mentality. In 1961 whilst I was on 25 at Waterbeach, under the leadership of 'Black' Jim Walton, a big annual Lanex exercise came up, my pilot Bob Kelly was sick with a cold, so he was appointed Ops Officer. I went off to sit in the crew-room and twiddle my thumbs as all available Javelins were already allocated to fit crews. After 10 minutes I was surprised to get a call from Bob, 'Get your kit on, an aircraft has just come up and you're to crew for the Wingco Flying, W/C A. Wright'. Although glad to get a trip, this didn't exactly fill me with Joy as the Wingco, a Battle of Britain chap, was a bit long in the tooth and of course not exactly versed in squadron SOPs (Standard Operating Procedures).

At Night Fighter OCU it is stressed that once an interception is set up, the Nav/Rad is God, the pilot does as commanded and remains to be responsible for the overall safety of the aircraft.

As most of our crews had already been scrambled up the lanes we climbed North East out over the North Sea towards a mass of contrails.

After 15 minutes we got to our allocated lane and I began interrogating all reciprocal echoes using IFF (Interrogation Friend or Foe). Eventually I found a promising target without any fighter in attendance 15 nautical miles away, 10 Degrees displaced to Port. Assessing this as four nautical miles displaced, I told the Wingco to prepare for a 230-degree hard turn to port at 12 nms. This was SOP and off we turned on time, descending slightly from 45,000 feet to maintain our attack speed of Mach 0.90. To my amazement after 60-70 degrees turn the aircraft suddenly steadied and reversed to a Starboard turn! 'What the hell are you doing?' I shouted at the driver, for the moment I forgot it was the wingco up front. 'Well,' said he 'I think it would be better that way!' I was furious, after all the effort to find a target and then get the attack messed up. I told him to steady up on a South West heading whilst I scanned again, and there was our unattended target at 10 nms. Ahead of us, going like stink!! I informed him of this bad news, told him our pigeons (heading and range to base) then left him to it; he was left in glorious isolation, and after we landed I whipped my canopy open, didn't wait for the crew-ladder to be put on, and after shutdown I jumped off the port wingtip and steamed into our Ops Room to where Bob plus Black Jim were waiting. 'The Idiot threw away a good chance by suddenly reversing,' I told them. 'Off you go for a coffee,' said Black Jim, 'leave W/C Wright to me!' Bob told me later that when Wingco Wright entered he started to say 'Very strange Jimmy, the sergeant wouldn't speak to me,' when BJ told him in no uncertain terms that if he ever flew in one of our Javs again and disobeyed his Nav/Rad., he wouldn't ever get another ride in a '25' aircraft! That my old mate was the way N/AW crews operated, and continued to successfully do so for the rest of my 8 years flying.

The year 1963 began with much in the way of change for the operational units operating out of Leuchars. No. 25 Squadron had disbanded before the new year as part of the further 'rationalisation' of the Fighter Force. On 11 January, 29 Squadron were officially notified that they were to replace 43 Squadron in Cyprus; this, for some reason, was expected to and indeed bring about a number of aircrew changes to the squadron. However, due to the contraction of the RAF Javelin force at this time, the need to shuffle people around and find staff for other vacant posts may have precipitated an unusual number of moves.

Sure enough, no fewer than fifteen of 29 Squadron's aircrew were posted prior to departure. Lt Col G. W. Eagle, USAF, on exchange tour was posted to fly the Mark 8 Javelin with 41 Squadron at Wattisham. Sqn Ldr George Beaton was to stay at Leuchars and would in due course become CO of the reformed Javelin OCU, following which he was to be posted to Kjelsås in Oslo as Sqn Ldr Air Ops. Three were to stay on to join 23 Squadron and one officer, Flt Lt Brian Carroll, would return to 23 Squadron, flying the Lightning—an aircraft in which he later established a record ceiling of 87,300 feet while flying a Mark 53 Lightning over Saudi Arabia. The squadron's two, by now rare breed, master navigators were not to be sent to the Middle East but to Bahrain and Aden. Their places were taken by a large chunk of ex-85 Squadron aircrew, which had just disbanded at West Raynham.

No. 29 Squadron were the second Javelin unit to be posted outside the European theatre when they were deployed, permanently, to Cyprus in March 1963. Barry Mayner was on 29 Squadron and flew with the CO out to Nicosia. He recalls the flight out there:

As for the move from Leuchars to Nicosia to take over the Air Defence force for Cyprus, I was the Boss's navigator on the move. We took 2 days for the move of 10 aircraft. The sorties as lead aircraft were: 26/27 February 1963.

1. Leuchars to Wattisham 50 mins
2. Wattisham to Orange (France) 1 hour 15 mins
3. Night Stop at Orange hosted by Flt Lt Louis St. Pierre of the RAF Support Unit Orange.
4. Orange to Decimomannu (Sardinia) 1hour 10 mins
5. Decimomannu to Luqa (Malta) 50 mins
6. Luqa to El Adem (Libya) 1 hour 10mins
7. El Adem to Nicosia 1 hour 10 mins

We took over the standby commitment from 43 Sqn (Hunter 9s) they deployed to Khormaksar (Aden) on 2 March four of the Squadron aircraft led By Sqn. Ldr Mike Waudby had deployed to Cyprus a few days earlier to get things sorted for the main party arrival, and to be able to take over from 43 Sqn.

Only one of our Javelins fell by the wayside it was left at Decimomannu to await an engine change, this was completed in remarkably quick time. Jock Sneddon and I flew (to pick up the stranded Javelin) in a Hastings of 70 Sqn on 12 March and flew the two legs back to Nicosia via El Adem on 13 March 1963.

Not long after the arrival of 29 Squadron at Nicosia, bad luck emerged from the shadows—indeed, you could even say a curse, as Barry Mayner further recalls:

Barry Mayner is introduced to the officer commanding RAF Nicosia. This section of 29 Squadron had just arrived from Leuchars on 27 February 1963. (*The National Archives*)

Javelin four-ship from 29 Squadron photographed by Barry Mayner in the fifth airborne spare. This is the 1962 Battle of Britain four-ship team rehearsing. (*Barry G. Mayner*)

In 1963 at Nicosia and Akrotiri, 29 Sqn lost three aircraft which were all coded 'C' our Senior Engineering Officer was Sqn Ldr. Vincent Victor Vocking, known as VIC.

The first loss was an aircraft on take-off at Nicosia, it suffered a compressor failure and fire. It was seen to come to a halt quite near the Squadron HQ. We were amazed to see the Nav, John Parsons, get out of his seat and ran towards the nose via the pilot's canopy, the pilot's head next appeared as he climbed on the radome and then hit the ground running. The pilot had a more sedate exit but once at ground level also ran away. The aircraft was a total loss.

The second 'C' loss involved Mike Waudby and Barry Mayner. We were leading a 4-ship on an air-to-air cine sortie, on the recovery to Nicosia we ran in for a run and break in close echelon. As 'C' touched down I heard and felt a loud bang on the left side of the aircraft.

Mike said 'Barry what have I done wrong,' by now I was broadcasting to the tower and the rest of the formation that we had burst a tyre. We left the runway at about 120 Knots, slowing down. The surface of the airfield was rock, sand and scrub with lots of large shallow holes in the surface, the GCA (Ground Control Approach) caravans were directly in front of us when we stopped, about 100 yards away. I left the aircraft really quickly and ran along the port wing. I was surprised to find the wingtip only inches above the ground. I turned around to hear the engines winding down (crash switch had activated) but Mike was still strapped in and he was looking down into his cockpit, I ran back to the aircraft and started shouting to him to get out, by now I had realised the main undercarriage legs were up. The ventral tanks were ripped to shreds and there was fuel around under the fuselage. After a few seconds my shouts got a response 'I am doing my shut down checks' came the reply. I then started swearing at him to try to get him out of the aircraft. The first vehicle to arrive at the scene was the Group Captain in his Standard Vanguard Estate, when he got out he heard me shouting and swearing 'GET OUT OF THE ******g COCKPIT'. The Groupie realised at once and joined me shouting! This seemed to work and Mike joined us in a dignified trot away from the scene. The Javelin emergency procedures prohibited raising the undercarriage at speed on the ground as the nose leg was likely to penetrate into the rear cockpit, that this did not happen was lucky for me. Somehow the nose wheel did not retract, or break off.

The third 'C' loss was at AKROTIRI, another uncontained engine compressor failure.

The crew left the aircraft (without the nav using the pilots head as a step) and ran away.

The aircraft was written off. That afternoon Viv Vocking came striding into the ops room and declared that none of his aircraft were ever going to be 'C' again.

Ernest George Percival Jeffries our CO, standing behind the desk said 'excuse me Victor but I was under the impression that the aircraft were mine' unabashed Victor said 'not until I give them to you to fly SIR!' A fair draw was my impression. We never did have a 'C' again while I was on the Squadron.

Later, in August that year, 29 Squadron took part in an exercise run by the Near East Operations Centre, calling for the deployment of six aircraft to Akrotiri from their then home base Nicosia. The purpose of this deployment was to assist the CFE with trial to establish the ability of Lightning aircraft to defend Cyprus against low, fast-flying aircraft. No. 29 Squadron played the part of the incoming aggressors. Altogether twenty-one sorties were flown, dummy attacks were made on the island as low as 100 feet at speeds of 450 knots over the sea. Evidently, this unusual sortie profile for the Javelin was enjoyed by all concerned, especially the younger pilots who had not had much opportunity to engage in this kind of flying before. The year 1963 also saw the further disbandment of the only two Javelin squadrons equipped with the Mark 8: 85 Squadron disbanded on 31 March, while 41 Squadron followed at the end of the year.

On 17 October 1963, the crew of a Javelin FAW.9 of 5 Squadron ejected at 27,000 feet. Flt Lts R. Boulton and L. P. Morley both landed safely (minus jet of course). They were two miles west of Zonhoven in West Germany. On 5 November, while on detachment at Orange (staging back from Cyprus) in France, two Javelin T3s ran into trouble similar to that which affected the 5 Squadron aircraft. Then on 7 November, an FAW.9 of 11 Squadron had to be abandoned by its crew over Belgium because of the same unique occurrence affecting the Javelin, which became known as 'centre-line closure'. This usually occurred while flying in cloud. To explain what it was all about, essentially, when the aircraft were operating at quite high throttle settings coupled with a significant drop in temperature, the sharp cooling effect caused the metal casing surrounding the compressor blades to shrink faster than the blades; consequently, those blades came into contact with the surrounding metal casing with the expected results. If the crew were lucky, the engine would just cease. The Javelin's Sapphire engines were especially prone to this.

A ban on flying in cloud was subsequently imposed. The problem was especially likely to occur if the aircraft had been flying in higher temperatures and then immediately flew through thickening cloud at higher altitude, the sudden lower pressure and drastically reduced temperature was a sure route to 'centre-line closure'. The two Javelin crews on this occasion survived, one ejected the other limped back to Orange with one engine still just about functioning. If the aircraft flew into cloud and met with imbedded storm clouds, cumulonimbus, then the ideal chances for this to happen were certainly met. By 26 November, the problem was being addressed by restricting just the T3s from flying through cloud but the FAW.8s and 9s (now the only other models in use) were permitted to enter cloud providing that a set procedure was followed.

Royal Air Force Germany were not happy with this and had passed their concerns to the Assistant Chief of Air Staff (ops). They were keen not to prejudice operational flying and put forward some suggestions of their own that did not compromise safety. A revised procedure was authorised but with the attendant note from ACAS that accidents due to centre-line closure were to be avoided at all costs. Before the new procedure SFI/59, the ACAS's office attempted to ascertain a level of cloud thickness up to which it would be safe for the aircraft to pass through without detrimental effect on the engine and were told any amount of cloud could contain super saturated and super cooled areas which the aircraft may pass through, indeed, the thickness of cloud bore no relation to the level of moisture therein. There was, nevertheless an optimum point where centre line closure could occur, as the aircraft climbed through

FAW.8s of 85 Squadron in stream take-off from West Raynham for the disbandment flypast in March 1963. (*Ed Durham*)

FAW.8 carrying Firestreaks with no unit markings. Note the apparent absence of the navigator. (*Ian White*)

20,000 to 25,000 feet. In the descent, the problem was much less likely to occur due to the lower power setting of the engines. The more definite restriction on the T3 was due to the SA6 engine being considered three or four times more likely to be affected.

To resolve the problem, the solution was to modify the compressor blades with an abrasive edge, which filed down when in contact with contracting engine casing. These modifications were made under the modification programme given the name 'Rockhide'.

During January 1964, other squadrons reported such instances (centre-line closure was particularly acute in Tropical climates where high temperature combined with wet conditions meaning heavy cloud from time to time) were refitted with the new Rockhide-modified Sapphires. No. 23 Squadron carried out a total of fifteen air tests, amounting to twelve hours and twenty minutes of flying time. Nevertheless, flying was achieved whenever possible and QRA was maintained. Through the previous December, low cloud for much of the month meant a good deal of training time was spent flying low-level PIs (practice intercepts). By the end of February, eight of 23 Squadron's Javelins had been successfully modified.

In any case, the Javelin was now fast being rendered obsolescent. Being subsonic with limited agility was not the kind of performance that a world-class air force would be entirely content with as a front line interceptor fighter in 1964.

What made the Mark 9 the ultimate Javelin? It had a comparable stablemate in the Mark 8. However, the FAW.8, like all the earlier marks, was not fitted with air-to-air refuelling and so the FAW.9 took the crown—it had all the bells and whistles but no truly significant gain in performance anywhere. The last marks were, aside from an AAR probe as different simply through the Mark 8 carrying the APQ-43/AI.22 while the Mark 9 had the more widely available AI.17. Beyond that, they were exactly the same version. Each airframe was powered by a Sapphire Mk 209 engine in the port nacelle and an Mk 210 in the starboard one. At sea level, the officially expected rate of dry thrust was 10,500 lb each. This was perhaps the guaranteed level of performance as the level of maximum thrust of both SA7 and SA7R engines in dry weather is often stated at 11,000 lb.

Modification 1660 introduced the Mk 211 and 212 respectively. This had brought the addition of a fuel de-icer to protect the low-pressure pump fuel filter. What is perhaps more common knowledge about the engines of the latter two marks of aircraft was the restrictions on the use of reheat. The output of the fuel pump was accordingly designed to allow excess fuel above that required for non-reheat use. Above an altitude of 20,000 feet, reheat provided a gross thrust 12 per cent greater than normal operating conditions. As you would expect, the level of thrust, with reheat, varied according to altitude at the point of selection. At 20,000 feet and a speed of Mach 0.85, the increase in thrust was determined at around 19 per cent. Reheat was attained simply by pushing the throttle levers through the gate but two switches in the throttle quadrant in turn operated two solenoid cocks in each fuel system when the associated throttle lever was moved beyond its normal full throttle position. There then was a 1.5-second delay before a pump pressure signal was fed to the nozzle control pressure switch and the nozzle of each jet pipe started to open. The hot streak accumulator was then discharged via non-return valves to the hot streak injectors, fitted one upstream and one downstream of the turbine. When reheat (afterburner) was cancelled, the accumulators immediately recharged for use. Reheat failure could occur where the reheat fuel would light, but the nozzle failed to open, in which case the micro-jet pressure switch energised the fuel cancellation relay, thus cutting off the reheat fuel supply.

Recommended climbing speed was determined to be 450 knots until coincident with Mach 0.85, then optimally maintained at 0.85 Mach until 40,000 feet with reheat, if required, not to be used below 20,000 feet.

The restriction on reheat use at lower altitudes was necessary as the fuel pump capacity was insufficient to maintain engine and reheat levels together at the full conditions. Reheat could still be selected but the engine speed, JPT (jet-pipe temperature), and reheat thrust would all fail to reach normal maximum performance conditions. At take-off with reheat selected, engine speed and JPT were initially low and dry thrust a few per cent lower than normal. The performance of the engine would continue to decline and sharply so until climb commenced; as the altitude increased, engine performance (including the impact of reheat) improved, with full performance levels reached at 20,000 feet.

Selecting reheat was simple enough and typical of such operation in most equipped aircraft. With the reheat master switches set to on, the throttles needed to be advanced passed the normal full travel position and thus, reheat was selected and deselected again once the throttles were moved back aft of the normal full travel position. Engine start-up was with a small cordite cartridge, which in turn would ignite AVPIN liquid fuel in the reaction chamber on the turbo-starter, the resulting pressure rise being passed to the starter turbine.

So much for the engine, but the airframe, while described as designed for the duties appropriate to an all-weather fighter faced some severe restrictions, intentional stalling, spinning, and aerobatics in the looping plane were prohibited.

If the aircraft was inadvertently stalled, resulting in a spin that could not be arrested before reaching 15,000 feet, then it had to be abandoned. Trials were carried out on the Mark 1 Javelin, which determined the following:

> If the nose is above the Horizon at high altitude then speed tends to fall off quickly, for which an artificial low speed warning was introduced. The natural stall warning in straight flight depended upon the rate at which speed was reduced, if speed was reduced rapidly, there may be no positive warning but if the reduction was slow, then gentle buffeting would become apparent at 140 knots, increasing until reaching a constant level at 125 knots then a general sloppiness of controls would be evident at 120 knots, wing heaviness became noticeable but could be controlled by aileron. Further reduction to 100 knots could bring about a gentle fore and aft pitching. Should speed fall to below 100 knots in the straight stall it would then continue to fall, extremely rapidly, to below 60 knots at which point the aircraft will yaw in one direction and roll out of control in the opposite direction. Any attempt to recover from this situation was not recommended

owing to such erratic behaviour, but the procedure should it be attempted was to; close the throttles, move the stick right back and centralise the ailerons and rudder. Allow the aircraft to make one turn of the spin and then follow the spin recovery procedure. This required first that the spin warning system be switched off so that communication between pilot and navigator was possible; with the control column fully back and aileron pushed fully in the direction of the spin. The control column was then to be pushed fully forward into the corner, this operated the auto-trimmer with the rudder centralised. The pilot/crew would be expected to see not one but two turns without any effect from the recovery actions but would have to be maintained until either the aircraft is successfully recovered or abandoned. The rate of spin was very slow but could easily reverse and the nose would also pitch up and down through as much as 70 degrees.

The maximum cleared altitude was 50,000 feet for the aircraft but 45,000 feet for crew using only standard flying clothing with an oxygen mask; full clearance to 50,000 feet was permitted if the pressure jerkin and anti-*g* trousers were worn. On the other hand, given that the Javelin made no claim to be in the league of many other all-weather interceptors that served during the 1960s, it did have a not too embarrassing level of performance in some respects as the following height and speed table shows:

Height band (ft)	Clean aircraft with empty ventral tanks	With full or partly full ventral tanks
S/L to 7,000 feet	535 knots	535 knots
7,000 to 20,000 feet	0.90 Mach	0.90 Mach
20,000 feet to 35,000 feet	0.95 Mach	0.95 Mach
Above 35,000 feet	1.08 Mach	0.95 Mach

Some 535 knots could be attained at low level using less than full power. At higher altitudes, the Javelin could go supersonic in a 40-degree dive at full throttle.

Clean below 20,000 feet, the aircraft had a respectable manoeuvrability at 5*g*; this deteriorated at higher speeds. All these figures for the FAW.9 changed again when the detachable in-flight refuelling probe was fitted, which had a less than efficacious affect.

When in the circuit, the aircraft's speed was restricted over the threshold of the runway to a minimum of 135 knots and a minimum height of 250 feet. While in the circuit, the speed was not to fall below 150 knots otherwise the minimum restriction was 170 knots—such was the threat of accidental stall. Concern about stalling was entirely justified here. The Javelin's tail elevators were cut off from the air flow by the huge delta wing if the angle of attack was too high.

Flying at lower speeds outside the circuit was acceptable at 200 knots; with sufficient airbrake deployed, the RPM could be maintained at above 75 per cent. Also, the hood could be open fully below 200 knots. Flying in bad weather

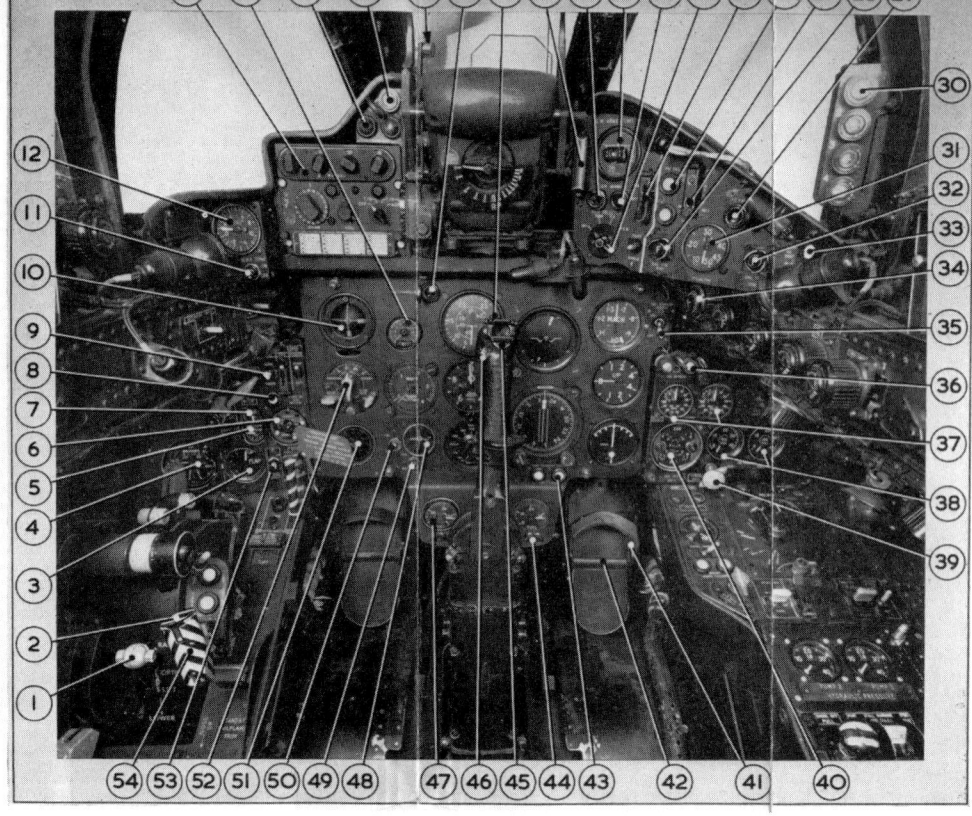

Above: The office: forward view of the cockpit of the FAW.9. (*Barry G. Mayner*)

Left: Legend for the above photo. (*Barry G. Mayner*)

Key to Fig. 2.—Front cockpit—forward view
1. Flaps control lever.
2. Clear wing jettison button at front of handle.
3. Flap position indicator.
4. Brake triple-pressure gauge.
5. Tailplane setting indicator.
6. Undercarriage position indicator.
7. Rudder trim indicator.
8. Stand-by trim neutral indicator.
9. Switch row, left to right:—
    Intercomm. normal/emergency selector switch.
    UHF main/stand-by set selector switch.
    UHF power normal/battery selector switch.
10. Zero-reader indicator.
11. UHF tone selector switch.
12. Accelerometer.
13. UHF control unit.
14. DME indicator.
15. Gun bay scavenge valve indicators (2).
16. Radio altimeter red limit light.
17. GW acquisition lights.
18. ILS marker indicator.
19. Gun/GW trigger safety catch.
20. Air louvre.
21. GW arming green light.
22. GW armed time indicator.
23. GW arming amber light.
24. Master armament selector switch.
25. GW arming selector switch.
26. No. 2 and No. 1 flight insts. inverter failure indicators (2).
27. Inverter emergency change-over switch.
28. Port engine fire extinguisher button and warning light.
29. Cockpit pressure failure warning light.
30. Hydraulic pump failure warning lights (4).
31. Cockpit pressure altimeter.
32. Starboard engine fire extinguisher button and warning light.
33. Fire warning lights test button.
34. Cockpit lighting dimmer switches (5).
35. Turn-and-slip stand-by supply switch.
36. Generator failure warning lights (2).
37. Engine speed per cent. RPM indicators (2).
38. Oil pressure gauges (2).
39. Parking brake control.
40. Dual jet pipe temperature gauge.
41. Brake pedal angle adjuster.
42. Brake pedal.
43. Fuel transfer air pressure warning indicators (2).
44. Leg-restraint cords stowages (2).
45. Tailplane trimmer switch.
46. Cine camera button.
47. Fuel contents gauges (2).
48. ILS indicator.
49. Max./min. sensitivity selector switch.
50. ILS/VP selector switch.
51. ADF compass indicator.
52. Zero-reader control unit.
53. Emergency lighting switch.
54. Ventral tanks jettison handle.

Gyron Junior engine XA552 used as a test bed for the Bristol 188. Specifically, the engines had reheat. (*Peter R. March*)

Prototype WD804, from which Gloster test pilot Bill Waterton had a narrow escape. (*Peter R. March*)

FAW.4 of 3 Squadron on the Geilenkirchen Flightline with a second Javelin making a low pass. Two F-86Ds or K Sabres from an unidentified NATO Air Force are also present. (*Keith Deal*)

FAW.4s of 3 Squadron start up on the Geilers flightline in 1959. (*Keith Deal*)

Javelin engines running, kicking dust up from the dry ground of the Pine Woods at the rear—a typical feature of many post-war NATO airbases, often providing natural screening from public view, the drawback being that it also provided intruders with somewhere to hide. (*Keith Deal*)

Javelin T3 of 3 Squadron apparently on the approach. T-Birds are routinely assigned to single-seat squadrons. The Javelin, a two-seater operationally, had a specific trainer version for pilot conversion and check-ride assessments. (*Keith Deal*)

No. 3 Squadron aircraft on the runway. (*Keith Deal*)

Scene outside 3 Squadron headquarters at Geilenkirchen *c.* 1959. (*Keith Deal*)

No. 3 Squadron's charges await their crew, cream foam extinguishers positioned to the rear of each jet. (*Keith Deal*)

Another smoky engine start on the Geilers flightline. (*Keith Deal*)

In the background, Javelin FAW.4, XA750, is taxying minutes before tragedy struck on 20 June 1959 in Norvenich. (*Keith Deal*)

Keith Deal posing with XA635 at the Norvenich Air Day on 20 June 1959. The jets in the background are F-84F Thunderstreaks of the Luftwaffe. The day was marred with tragedy with the loss of an aircraft and its crew. (*Keith Deal*)

Blast revetments at Geilenkirchen. (*Keith Deal*)

Jets of the All-Weather Combat School, an element of the Central Fighter Establishment (CFE), visiting Geilenkirchen from West Raynham to evaluate and provide further training for Javelin crews. They are identified by yellow letter codes just forward of the intake. (*Keith Deal*)

No. 41 Squadron FAW.4 visiting Geilenkirchen in 1959. (*Keith Deal*)

No. 25 Squadron FAW.9s take off from Waterbeach. Notice what appears to be a single missile on the starboard outer pylon on each. These are acquisition rounds, which are used in training to lock onto the target, but never leave the aircraft 1960–1961. (*Peter Goodwin*)

No. 25 Squadron FAW.9. (*Peter Goodwin*)

Javelin of 25 Squadron at low level over Cyprus in 1961. (*Peter Goodwin*)

No. 29 Squadron Javelin refuelling from KC-135, again during exercise 'Billy Boy' in April 1965. (*Barry G. Mayner*)

Javelin FAW.9R 'M' of 29 Squadron, almost certainly in transit overseas. (*Barry G. Mayner*)

No. 25 Squadron CO's aircraft bearing his initials. His jet is also distinguished in having a broader silver bar on the fin. This is possibly the Waterbeach flightline in 1961. (*Peter Goodwin*)

Javelin FAW.9s of 25 Squadron on the Leuchars flightline in 1962. Note the Balmullo Quarry in the background between the third and fourth fins in from the camera. It was here that a Lightning crashed six years later. (*Peter Goodwin*)

Spot the Javelin—the camouflage on this 25 Squadron Javelin works quite well as the aircraft flies over the west end of the main runway at Leuchars. (*Peter Goodwin*)

The same Javelin, better defined against background, this time over the Eden Estuary to the south. (*Peter Goodwin*)

Peter Goodwin's log book from July 1963. The Sgt Evans he flew with is the very same Roy Evans who has kindly contributed some anecdotal memories. *(Peter Goodwin)*

Further log entries by Peter, this time with his regular navigator. Note the times he flew in the rear cockpit was in a T3, to assist with evaluation of new pilots. *(Peter Goodwin)*

No. 23 Squadron FAW.9R at RNAS Lossiemouth in July 1963 for an air day. (*Richard Freial*)

XH886/F of 23 Squadron refuelled by Valiant BK1, XD816, from 214 Squadron *c.* 1963. (*Crown Copyright*)

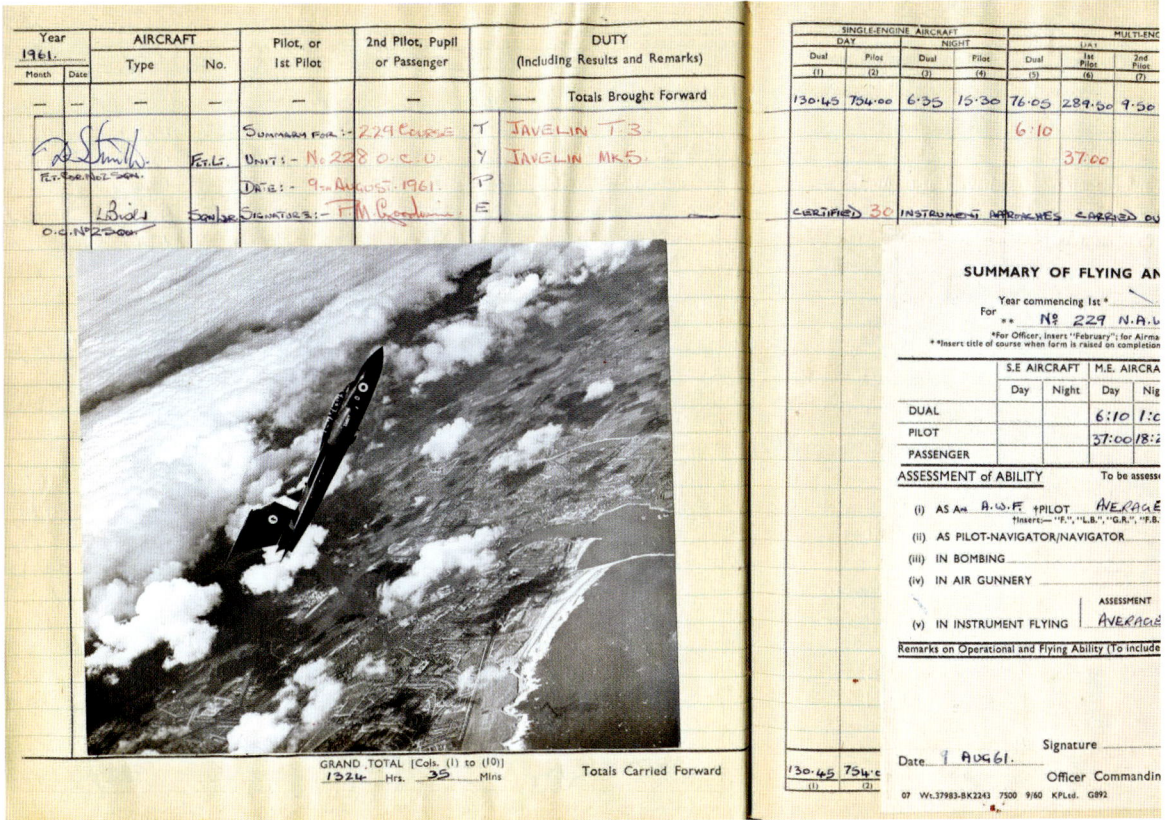

Further entries from Peter's log book. (*Peter Goodwin*)

The Javelins of 29 and 5 Squadrons on the flightline at RAF Luqa, Malta, for their part in the Independence Day celebrations on 21 September 1964. (*Barry G. Mayner*)

No. 29 Squadron's Flat Irons flypast over Malta on 21 September 1964. (*Barry G. Mayner*)

Above: The back office: navigator's forward view (rear cockpit of the FAW.9). (*Barry G. Mayner*)

Right: Legend for the above photo. (*Barry G. Mayner*)

Key to Fig. 4.—Rear cockpit—forward view

1. AI Mk. 17 on/off switch
2. Switch row, left to right:—
   FIS on/off switch.
   Gee on/off switch.
   Gee and IFF stand-by supply switch.
   AI and Gee DC supply circuit-breaker.
   AI inverter start switch.
   AI inverter stop switch.
3. Wire recorder switch.
4. Cockpit lighting dimmer switches (2).
5. Generator failure warning lights (2).
6. FIS indicator light (red).
7. Mk. 4B compass master indicator.
8. Hood-operating switch.
9. Flowmeter reset switch.
10. Fuel flowmeter.
11. AI Mk. 17 indicator.
12. AYF limit indicator lights (radio altimeter).
13. Airspeed indicator.
14. Altimeter.
15. AYF altimeter (radio altimeter).
16. First-aid outfit and asbestos gloves (stowed forward of item 17).
17. Gee indicator (Radio compass and Rebecca units. (Post Mods. 1294 and 1058).)
18. Crow-bar.
19. Hood jettison handle safety-pin and flag.
20. Hood jettison handle.
21. Oxygen regulator Mk. 21A.
22. Call light and push-button.
23. Ambient air temperature gauge.
24. Pencil stowages.
25. AI control unit.
26. Mk. 4B compass control unit.
27. Leg restraint cords (2) shown fitted to stowage.
28. Press-to-mute switch.
29. AI control unit (Type 901).
30. Vizor stowage.
31. FIS foot-operated switch.
32. Stowage for seat-pan firing handle safety-pin and disc.

(such as rain) did not hamper flying much. Forward visibility in rain was good and take-offs, approaches, and landings could be made with little difficulty. The figure of 200 knots was considered the optimum for the Javelin to be flown in particularly heavy weather, such as hail or heavy rain when damage to the radome could occur, if this situation should be unavoidable then 200 knots was the limit. Flying in severe turbulence was permitted between the best range and climbing speeds up to 40,000 feet. Armament for the Mark 9 was at its most potent among all Javelin models; this version was cleared to carry two or four guns (30 mm) together with as many as four Firestreak air-to-air missiles. The Javelin 9 was also cleared to refuel from both the Vickers Valiant and the Boeing KB-50J tanker aircraft. Later trials in 1965 with aircraft of 29 Squadron, during Exercise 'Billy Boy' cleared it to refuel from the Boeing KC-135.

Armament wise, the four Aden cannons in the wing were supplied by a total of 400 rounds of 30-mm ammunition and in the case of the Marks 7, 8, and 9, four Firestreak air-to-air missiles in addition. If necessary, the aircraft could be landed in an emergency with a maximum all-up weight officially determined to be 40,000 lb.

The following is transcribed from the Javelin FAW.9 pilots' notes:

Circuit and Landing Procedures; Normal approach thrust settings at 75 per cent RPM (approximately) when in the circuit, flaps varied speed from 170 down to 150 knots from up position to fully extended. This was recommended for instrument approaches with the undercarriage down;

Emergency Procedures—Engine and Fuel systems;

Engine failure on take-off;

Abandon take-off, proceed as follows;

i. Close the throttles and the HP cock and the failed engine.
ii. Transmit emergency call
iii. Jettison missiles if motors and/or warheads are fitted.
iv. Do not jettison ventrals
v. Lower full flap and extend the air brakes
vi. Follow barrier engagement drill;
1. Close the throttles and one HP cock
2. Transmit emergency call
3. Jettison missiles if motors and/or warheads are fitted
4. Do not jettison ventrals
5. Apply maximum brake
6. Lower full flap and extend the airbrakes
7. Keep the hood closed and ensure that harnesses are locked and tight

An open hood exposes the crew to risk of serious injury by the barrier top cable

8. Aim to engage the centre of the barrier in the gap between two sets of vertical ropes. Ensure that the nose-wheel is firmly on the ground and immediately before engaging the barrier, release the wheel brakes. At the moment of entry, duck the head forward. Allow the wheels to run over the bottom cable and then re-apply steady wheel braking.

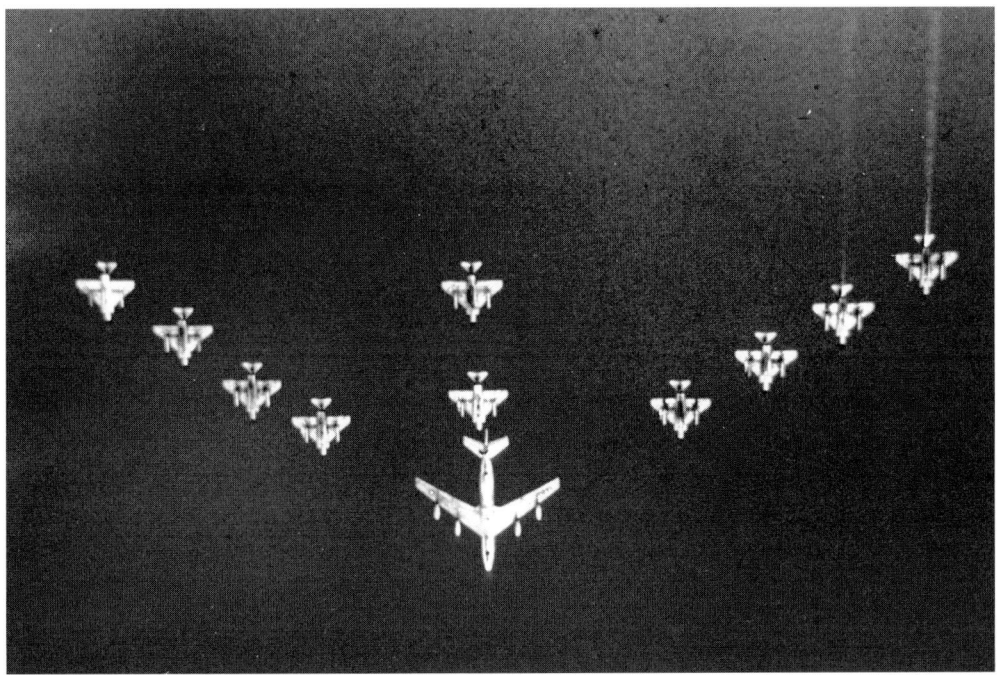
This photo was taken during exercise 'Billy Boy' and shows participating Javelins of 29 Squadron formatting on a KC-135 from the U.S. Air Force in April 1965.

No. 29 Squadron's FAW.9R, XH890, refuelling from a USAF KC-135 during exercise 'Billy Boy' from 26–30 April 1965. (*Barry G. Mayner*)

No. 29 Squadron Javelin refuelling from KC-135, again during exercise 'Billy Boy' in April 1965. (*Barry G. Mayner*)

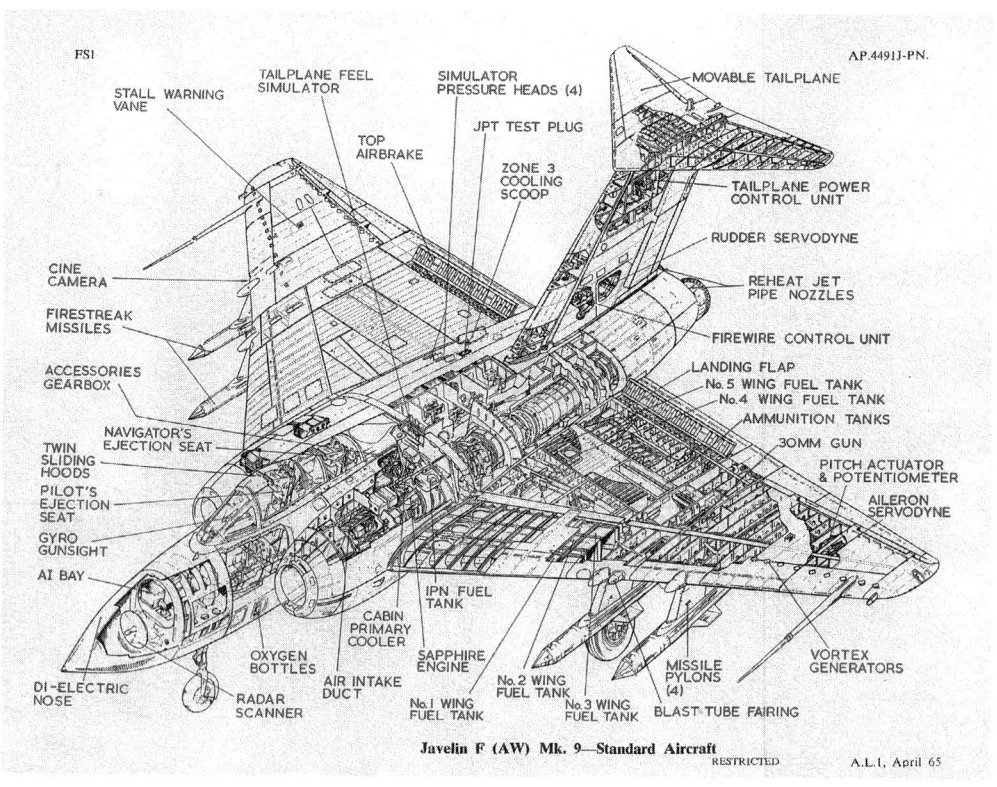

Plan diagram of Javelin FAW.9. (*Barry G. Mayner*)

9. Set the parking brake on when the aircraft comes to rest in order to prevent the aircraft rolling back and sustaining further damage.
10. Insert the ejection seat safety-pins
11. Vacate the aircraft as soon as possible

Aerobatics;

Note: Aerobatics in the looping plane are prohibited

a. All types of rolls are permitted. When in a steep climb the speed must be watched carefully and not allowed to reach a critical minimum

b. The maximum inverted flying time is 15 seconds

Descent;

a. To ensure clearance of icing and misting, set the windscreen de-misting control to HIGH two or three minutes before starting the descent

b. A rate of descent of approximately 5,000 feet/min is achieved at 250 knots, airbrakes out, throttles set to 75 per cent RPM when using two engines, to 88 per cent when on asymmetric power

c. For rapid descent, set throttles closed, airbrakes out and maintain 0.85mach/300 knots

d. For maximum rate of descent, set throttles closed, airbrakes out and maintain 0.9mach/400 knots. Some misting will occur

e. If maximum range is required on the descent, flame-out one engine, set the I.P. cock to transfer, close the other throttle and maintain 215 knots. If HIGH flow is selected on the windscreen de-misting control before starting the descent, misting of the windscreen will be minimised

Peter Goodwin flew as a member of the 11 Squadron 'aerobatics' team, actually one of several which formed occasionally, but bearing in mind the golden rule about looping the Javelin:

> In the aero display there was never much 'G' pulled, we were not allowed to do loops due to difficulty recovering from the stall should you 'Balls it up!' In a deep stall the tail plane is blanked off, if unable to recover, you should eject at 18,000 feet.

Peter also recalls the event involving Norman Glass's recovery following the rear seat ejection by Taff Evans, as he was on the airfield:

> Norman Glass attacked a German F-86 near Koln when he entered a high speed stall. The warning on the earpiece cut out the R/T between Norman and his Navigator, Taffy Evans, who then ejected. On his ejection, the aircraft recovered from the stall and returned to Geilers without him. I was on 'Battle Flight' and saw Mr Glass taxi in with the rear ejection tube sticking up in the air. Taffy was recovered ok!

Asymmetric Flying

For practicing asymmetric flying either engine could be shut down. Above 40,000 feet both booster pumps needed to be left on. Below 40,000 feet, one booster pump could be switched off. Ideally both booster pumps should be switched on, however, should the fuel feed not be even, the pump on the 'lower side' had to be switched off until balance was achieved.

If missiles were carried and one engine was shut down, the missiles on the associated side would eventually lose their heating supply. No hazard would endanger the aircraft but any attempt to launch a missile may result in the missile remaining dormant or, if it did fire, would not function as intended.

If a take-off has to be abandoned, the immediate drill is to close both throttles and the HP cock of the failed engine. Any missiles carried were jettisoned if motors or warheads were fitted, but not the ventral fuel tanks. Maximum braking was applied, including air brakes and flaps lowered.

When safely airborne, the undercarriage was to be raised; in the event of a failed engine, the HP and LP cocks together with the booster-pump were switched off.

In-flight refuelling probe, when carried, had speeds up to 450 knots or 0.92 Mach.

Pilot's notes on the Javelin FAW.9 state that Mach 1.08 is achievable above 35,000 feet. However, you would be hard pressed to find a Flat Iron driver who ever got beyond Mach 1 on the straight and level with the wind in his favour; with the slightest depression on the nose, it was a different story, as Peter Goodwin recalls:

> The Javelin had a good single engine performance, it could climb away with undercarriage and full flap down from 140 knots, but could not go supersonic, straight and level. We used to operate at around 40–45,000 feet max speed was about 0.92 mach+ or a bit, using reheat only when we had to; I.e. to close on anther aircraft, if you used it below 18,000 feet you slowed up! This was due to fuel being taken from the fuel for the engine. We did a great deal of flying at low level as well. If flying around 40,000 feet and you went into a slight dive, it went supersonic easily, with no trim changes. I can't recall the max speed I ever went, maybe 1.1 mach, it was almost unusual to go supersonic the way we operated, even if the Germans seemed not to mind the shock wave noise!

Despite the restrictions on aerobatics, it was a robust enough aircraft and could, when called upon to do so, provide a noisy demonstration of brute force, but appearances beyond formation flypasts were rare outside of the RAF Battle of Britain air displays, which in the Javelin's era were quite widespread. However, on at least one occasion, a single Javelin put on something of a surprise solo performance along the front of a small Scottish seaside town of Tobermory on the west coast.

In summer 1962, Roy Evans and his wife went to Tobermory on Mull:

> As it was advertised as 'The Sailing Centre of the Western Isles'. All okay if you had your own Yacht, which we didn't as I was a hard-worked, moderately paid SNCO Nav/Rad. However, after meeting a local schoolteacher in a local pub, he agreed to lend me

his old lugger to potter around in, an offer which I gratefully accepted. At the end of a fortnight, he refused to accept any payment; instead he said, 'if you ever get the chance, fly here and give us a show for my pupils'. I said that I would see what could be done. Normally on a N/AW squadron a crew would fly together whenever possible, but on 21 November 1962 my pilot had a cold so I flew in Javelin Mk 9 XH768 dubbed 'E', with another pilot, F/L Norman Glass for a normal HLPI (High Level Practice Interception) sortie. Our No.2 suffered a malfunction before take-off, & returned to dispersal to find another aircraft, whilst we got airborne to loiter at altitude & wait for them to join up. After 15 minutes we received the message that we were to do some local flying as No. 2 would not be coming! Norman asked me what we should do, so quick as a flash, knowing Norman was the kind of pilot who would be up for something different, I suggested a trip to Mull to beat up the Tobermory Bay, so that we proceeded to do. We headed to Oban, let down over the sea to 1,000 feet to get below cloud then proceeded on a North-West heading up the Sound of Mull. The cloud base remained at 1,000–1,500 feet and after 5 minutes we were able to turn left and enter Tobermory Bay. Now down to 500 feet we did a few wingovers in a tight left turn (No loops permitted in a Javelin), smacking the afterburners in & out a few times to increase the noise level a bit, after 5 minutes Norman decided we had woken the place up enough, so heading out of the bay we stood on our tail & made a near-vertical climb up through the cloud and once on top at +/- 8,000 feet we headed east to return to RAF Leuchars. A week after this I received a postcard of Mull from my teacher friend saying that he'd heard us, got his class of children outside to watch. Mostly everybody had enjoyed it, except for a few of the local greybeards, who had tried (luckily not successfully) to get our Registration numbers. He advised us not to return as next time they might have had better luck.

The year that the Javelin entered RAF Squadron service was a time of rapid development and there was no pretending that the first of the Flat Irons were not way short of the mark for what the specifications promised. Already, the RAF were looking to having a supersonic version capable of carrying either the Red Dean or Blue Jay nuclear warhead-armed air-to-air missile. Simply known as the thin-winged Javelin, this proposed design had a projected performance of Mach 1.1 at 65,000 feet. This was expected to be available by 1960, just four years away. In the meantime, the Javelin progressed, indeed rushed, through its it litany of versions, each bringing a little something new to the basic aircraft's features.

By the time the ultimate mark of the Javelin was operational, the aircraft that would replace it and the Hunter as the principal air defence interceptor for the Royal Air Force were already being delivered. However, the first English Electric Lightnings were not as one might have expected, given the relevant histories of both Javelin and Hunter: planned to take over from the Javelin at the earliest convenience, instead, the latter would be required to stand down first. The Lightning was introduced into service along the lines of two consignments of about two halves. The first half of the Lightning squadron build up, from 1960 to 1963, replaced the remaining Hunter fighter squadrons. So, the thoroughbred, 'the greyhound of the skies' as it was known for all its dash and charisma, of course lacked the Flat Iron's attributes; alas, all-weather capability was the priority. By mid-1963, Lightnings operated alongside the Javelin as now the sole air defence types in RAF service. The Lightning now equipped some of the better-known pedigree fighter outfits: seventy-four 'Tigers', fifty-six 'Firebirds', and ninety-two 'Cobras'. The Hunter did have its burgeoning further operational career as a tactical support and reconnaissance fighter unlike the Javelin, which, despite its being used to provide 'show of force' low-level runs in the Far East, had no future outside the air defence camp.

At the start of 1963, having been in service for just seven years, and with its operational presence overseas expected to be extended, the Air Fighter Development Squadron based at RAF Binbrook, all the same, while ordered to retain its Lightnings and Hunters, were now to dispose of its four Javelin FAW.8s in March. The last task these jets flew for AFDS was to act as all-weather interceptors on low-level trials. The January before being withdrawn, the AFDS Javelins flew four sorties against a Royal Navy Buccaneer, which had been detached for the purpose. Three of the four were successful.

It was not until the latter end of 1964 that the first of the remaining Javelin squadrons began re-equipping with the Mach 2-capable silver monster.

Javelin FAW.8, XH979, of the AFDS (Air Fighter Development Squadron), the chosen mount of the Test and Evaluation unit. (*Ian White*)

7
Overseas Theatre

The first priority for Javelins to be deployed overseas meant Germany, so the presence of Javelins further afield could wait a while. The tension between East and West during the decades following the end of the Second World War through to the end of the 1980s ensured that the right kind of aircraft were allocated to the Royal Air Force in Germany. Essentially a tactical air force, RAF Germany did suffer all the same from the not surprising inclination to equip UK units first. This remained so up to the age of the Tornado—UK-based squadrons converted first, then Germany next. As far as the Javelin was concerned, the first were sent to Germany soon after the first couple of squadrons were re-equipped in Fighter Command, but they were hand-me-downs. So, the Germany-based squadrons still suffered a degree of prejudice no matter how high the priority that they should be considered first.

So, the initial consignment of Javelins to Germany were the second-hand FAW.1s of 46 Squadron, who were getting their new FAW.2s. Their FAW.1s were sent to 87 Squadron at Brüggen, still soldiering on with the Meteor NF.11, now looking a tad antique.

No. 87 Squadron arrived at Brüggen from Wahn on 2 July 1957. On 14 August, now under the command of Wing Commander G. C. Lamb, they held a parade to mark the inauguration of the squadron with the Javelin. Exactly a week before, the JMCU arrived from Leeming with all their kit in a Beverley and two Valettas. At the time, 87 Squadron had two Javelin FAW.1s on strength in which the JMCU people flew fourteen demonstration sorties while the aircrew attended the aviation medicine centre at RAF Wildenrath for the purpose of being fitted with the new oxygen mask type A.13A and to be afforded the opportunity of experiencing cabin pressure failure at altitude. The proceedings also included other areas of testing, including an ejector seat demonstration during which Flying Officer P. W. Ross suffered a compression fracture of the spine and ended up in Wegberg Hospital.

Wing Commander Lamb noted that the conversion programme that the JMCU were following was well-planned and would have gone extremely well but for the fact that they only had two Javelins still with a nominal amount of spares. As such, it was found impossible to carry on with the flying conversion as planned. Just eighteen months after the first UK-based unit (46 Squadron) had been paraded before the press, the first one in Germany, where some squadrons sat no further than 80 miles from the Iron Curtain, was going through something of a *Dad's Army* moment on account of having insufficient trained crews and only two jets discarded by a Fighter Command unit anyway. That said, as with aircrew, the training of the ground crew proceeded satisfactorily, with one engine and one airframe mechanic being trained on turnarounds each day.

With the Javelin still a long step from being fully deployed, 87 Squadron continued with the Meteor NFs and took part in a 'Bomex' exercise on 22 August. Although two targets were destroyed, several more Canberras were seen but could not be caught, a state of affairs which would be most unlikely with the Javelin for all its publicised faults. By September, 87 Squadron had five trained crews but still only two Javelins, pilots were training in a mock-up cockpit, not a simulator due to the lack of availability of the latter. All pilots had already flown solo, placing some store by the mock-up to provide some degree of realistic training just the same. A defining moment came the following month when, during Exercise Argus, four Meteors and a single Javelin were involved in a GCI intercept. Again, the Meteors struggled. They were vectored by GCI onto a formation of Canberras at 40,000 feet at 4 miles and simply were not gaining when the Javelin surprised them by whistling over the top and completing the intercept. Further good news, the squadron strength by November stood at ten Javelins with the Meteors reduced to six. Trips were being arranged to the public baths at Mönchengladbach, which were being made available for dinghy training; however, this brought criticism as the dinghies used were not the same as the ones carried in the Javelin's PSP (personal survival pack). In February 1958, 87 Squadron's Javelins were mounting battle flight watch during which period the bulk of the squadron were away on courses or annual leave, prompting the CO to remark that 'as a result, too many aircrew became all too familiar with cat napping in arm chairs, there were no scrambles.'

In preparation for the AOC's visit, formation flying practice became the order of the day as May approached. By the end of April, the squadron had twelve Javelins on strength. On 9 May, an aircraft was flown to Jever Air Base as a static participant in an air show. About the same time, an aerobatics competition was held at Brüggen to select a pilot to represent 2nd Tactical Air Force at air displays on the continent. No Javelins took part. When the AOC-in-C later visited 87 Squadron for coffee, he did ask for a Javelin solo display sequence to be worked up. Several pilots on 87 Squadron worked up a sequence but, for the time being, were forbidden from practicing at low level. Nose down trim was also being reported on the Mark 1s at high air speeds; to investigate, a couple of pilots from Gloster were summoned. On 21 May, they flew some of 87 Squadron's aircraft but could not find any defects.

Meanwhile, on 22 May, the squadron proved themselves in Exercise Guest, successfully intercepting USAF F-100s, B-66s, and West German and French Air Force F-84s; bearing in mind these were FAW.1s, the Javelin was proving itself able to give a highly respectful account of itself in these early times. As always with flying military high-performance aircraft in the era when so many snags and unforeseen technical problems were yet to be stumbled upon and dealt with, tragedy frequently cast its

Meteor NF.XIs formation with one of the squadron's new(ish) FAW.1s. These were one-year-old hand-me-downs from 46 Squadron in 1957. (*Brian Henwood*)

Nice study of a Javelin FAW.1 of 87 Squadron *c.* 1957. (*Brian Henwood*)

shadow on those charged with making new and unfamiliar aircraft work according to plan. On 5 June, a Javelin returned with an engine flame out; both pilot and navigator had ejected. Flying Officer Jackson ejected first and was taken to Wegberg Hospital; the pilot, Flight Lieutenant Breakwell, ejected but his chute failed and he was killed on impact. Tragedy goes hand in hand with military flying especially during this era. This was nevertheless an interesting age with a variety of radically original fighter designs: bigger and heavier yet sleeker and out-of-this-world futuristic looks possessing significantly higher levels of performance.

These beasts, straight out of the Marvel comics of the era, were appearing in public with a degree of variety that would convince the latter-day enthusiast that he had died and gone to heaven. Therefore, whenever the opportunity arose to see some new or exotic types from overseas, previously seen only in glossy magazines, that opportunity attracted many with a professional interest as well as the usual hardcore enthusiasts. So, on 27–29 June 1958, ten of 87 Squadron's aircrew headed off to the Belgian airbase at Bierset, near Liege, for their International Air Display, where two new American types were being shop-windowed to the various European NATO countries, namely the F-8 Crusader and the F-104 Starfighter. In due course, the former did not get much of a look in succeeding in being sold only to the French Navy. The latter sold across the air forces (including the West German Navy) of the continent with few exceptions and to fulfil every conceivable role short of search and rescue and in the process developing, such notoriety for crashing that black humour spread like hogweed about its reliability; one joke doing the rounds was how easy it was to start up a scrap metal business in Northern Germany, 'simply hire a field and wait for a formation of Starfighters to come your way'. Nicknames such as 'Widow Maker' and 'Flying Coffin' became familiar references to the 'hooter', the F-104's other perhaps more engaging and charitable nickname, on account of the curious eerie oscillating howl emitted from the J79 engine in certain flight conditions. Yet for all this, the F-104 remained the mainstay of all those European air arms into the 1980s before the next generation F-16s and Tornados began to replace them. Training of Javelin crews in 2nd TAF involved a degree of surface attack training, which their UK brethren were less concerned with. To meet this, 87 Squadron flew sixteen ground attack sorties during July. Such was the eagerness of some, one Javelin, piloted by Flight Lieutenant Brian Henwood, was struck in the port ventral tank by a ricocheting piece of debris. Pilots' notes for the Javelin FAW.1 were being rewritten and 87 Squadron, now the sole operator of this model, were approached for their input covering the following:

1. Layout and design of Pilots' notes
2. Aircraft approach limitations
3. Range endurance statistics
4. Forward visibility in rain
5. Crosswind landing techniques
6. Flight with hydraulic pump failures
7. Prohibited manoeuvres

This was passed to visitors from the Handling Squadron based at Boscombe Down.

In July 1958, 96 Squadron moved their mark XI Meteors from Alhorn to Geilenkirchen and from the end of August, two of their crews, Flt Lts J. and P. Wilson were on their way to RAF Leeming for a Javelin conversion course, 'at last' as the ORB had printed in brackets. The start of conversion did mean, of course, that the total number of flying hours allotted to the squadron were down severely, although those who remained managed to increase their total for the month. The squadron received its first two officially assigned Javelins, both ex-41 Squadron Mark 4s on Friday, 19 September 1958.

These were XA750 and XA762. The following Monday, 22 September, Wing Commander D. W. B. Farrar DFC AFC became the first 96 Squadron pilot to fly one of them, with Flight Lieutenant I. D. Heavers as his navigator in XA750. Indeed, these two Javelins had pitched up one month ahead of the transfer schedule and as a result, it was decided to speed things up with more ground crew being packed off to 87 Squadron at Brüggen, while other crews were detached to 96. The aircrew were despatched a month early to the UK to begin conversion courses. Brian Henwood was on 87 Squadron when he began his own conversion onto the Javelin in November 1957:

No. 87 Squadron class photo following conversion, Brian Henwood at centre of second row back *c.* 1957. (*Brian Henwood*)

I completed my Javelin 1 conversion at Brüggen in November 1957. After one radar conversion exercise I found myself North of base at 40,000 feet, a height to which we were not accustomed in our Meteors, looking forward to a pleasant trip home in good weather. En-route I noticed well below us a Canadian CF-100 Canuck, estimated at about 20,000 feet and which we were overtaking. I decided that now we were no longer the underdogs I would show this Canadian what an aeroplane could do. I started a steep descent with full power planning to level off and flypast close to starboard then climb back up to 40,000 feet perhaps a 'twizzle' or two. As the estimated time arrived to commence the level-off I eased the stick fully aft. I contemplated using the trim but abandoned that for fear of overstressing the aircraft. Meanwhile, with airbrakes extended and throttles fully back, we passed the Canuck virtually out of control in a steep dive, just in time to see two heads glance in our direction with both the crew thinking, I'm certain, 'What the hell was that?' We eventually regained control at about 15,000 feet when the indicated air speed produced a lower mach number. Unfortunately, the Javelin had a variable incidence tailplane with an elevator at the back. As our Mach number increased in the dive the shock wave moved forward across the tailplane rendering the elevator useless. Subsequent Javelin Marks were fitted with the full-flying tail, but unfortunately no such irresponsible opportunities ever arose.

Such was the rather slipshod development, the squadron, at times, had no one actually available. Wg Cdr Farrar did not expect the situation to be resolved and the squadron fully staffed and with a full complement of Javelins before January or February 1959. They were expecting to have seven Javelins all together by the end of October 1958, so the Meteor NF.XI was still the principle fighter. New crews arrived on the squadron from the UK during November, but had to take the retrogressive step of converting onto the Meteor NF.XI and AI.1 radar in order to familiarise themselves with the local area, due to the lack of sufficient Javelins which were in high demand by the crews freshly converted. Meanwhile, the build-up of the Javelins with operational crews proceeded slowly, the main hold up being radar serviceability—there was no second line servicing for the AI.17 sets available. The end of November brought just two fully trained crews from home. Nothing more was anticipated then until the end of February or the beginning of March.

The squadron commander hoped to see all the Meteor NF.XIs gone by mid-November, subject to the number of Javelins received, the very thought of which was giving squadron morale a 'considerable boost'. Yet training continued to drag due to a lack of AI.17 spares. Flying training through November was also severely restricted by the weather with fog and low cloud being unusually persistent. In another step to get some greater momentum, more aircrew were detached to Leeming while some already experienced Javelin crews were posted in from the UK, including Flt Lts T. Balfour and E. Forbes, both from 41 Squadron at Wattisham. This improved the aircrew situation with more operationally experienced personnel being posted in, but on the ground, the technically experienced personnel levels were worsening and the AI.17 continued to present problems. All this was impacting on flying across 2nd TAF.

By 13 December 1958, 96 Squadron had received its sixth Javelin. This prompted the CO to decide to concentrate now on Javelin operations and give up the Meteors. From the first day of Javelin-only flying, trouble started with serviceability. Flt Lts Balfour and E.A. Forbes had a number one and two hydraulic failure, for which Flt Lt Balfour, the pilot, handled the situation well considering his lack of experience on the type. A week later, Flt Lt J. M. C. Morgans, and Sgt Littlefield as navigator, had the same problem. By the Christmas stand down, five of the six Flat Irons were out of action requiring between them six hydraulic pumps, two nose wheel struts, and a ripple eliminator for the hydraulic system. There was nothing the ground crew could do until spares arrived for everything. So the Meteors, luckily not yet despatched, were taken out of mothballs and used as targets for the one remaining serviceable Javelin. This aircraft managed to remain serviceable for the three days of the month following the Christmas break and provided ten most useful sorties, the only weapons training carried out being some air to ground training sorties flown on 9 December. At least by the end of December, 96 Squadron were clocking up more hours on the Javelin than on the Meteor NF.11 (slightly fewer if you threw in the day hours accumulated on the Meteor T.7). Wg Cdr Farrar finished his final entry in the DOR for 1958 thus: 'I think it is true to say that Squadron morale is good and that we look forward to and will achieve, better aircraft serviceability in the New Year.'

No Sooner said than three weeks into January, 96 Squadron had probably the worst period with the Javelin yet, very bad weather threw everything at Geilenkirchen; rain, snow, ice, fog, low clouds, or very strong cross winds, the period 9 to 18 January presented the only window in which flying was possible at all. Secondly, of the eight Javelins on strength, no more than two at best were ever available, again due to the ongoing farrago of maintenance faults and a shortage of spares. What little flying they achieved was dedicated to practice intercepts. At that, they had to use the T7 Meteors as targets to ensure that as many as possible got a shot at radar intercept training, not ideal. On the other hand, all the ground crew got their servicing certificates on the Javelin. Some officers took the extra time afforded to take promotion exams while everyone attended lectures on the usual subjects with a few films thrown in. Then on 21 January 1959, in keeping with the unsettled state of affairs with the RAF's frontline of the day, 96 Squadron disbanded and on the same day were rebadged as No. 3 Squadron. No official recognition was given to the disbandment of 96 Squadron and 3 Squadron kept their silver. The squadron strength stood at twenty-two aircrew including a flight sergeant navigator, a sergeant radar observer and sixty-three ground crew and now holding the record for the shortest served Flat Iron unit.

Toward the end of the decade, and while 87 Squadron were still equipped with the Mark 1 cast offs from 46 Squadron, a report was issued on the fatigue life of the Javelin on 29 October 1959. The report determined that the fatigue life of the Mark 1 Javelin was 1,800 hours based on high level training. To wit, all of the ten Mark 1s on 87 Squadron's inventory were fatigue expired and instructions were passed to the squadron to ground their ten jets. One senior officer cynically suggested disbanding a squadron anyway in anticipation of further cuts, likely as more pressure from the Ministry of Defence was quite predictable. To ameliorate the situation, it was proposed to keep 87 Squadron flying by simply begging, stealing, and borrowing from everyone else; that meant the units of Fighter Command, who were to supply eleven Mark 4 and 5s drawn from other units, or alternately looking at the possibility of losing another squadron from Fighter Command. VCAS did not regard this as a serious step, however, the problem was rather more complex by the end of 1959, with the new Federal German Air Force (*Bundes* Luftwaffe).

Specifically, the task of defending West German airspace remained in the hands of the Allied air forces. The Germans were not yet ready to take on the task so the likely extension of Javelins and Hunters in Germany through beyond the end of 1960 was being looked at, but no one was planning for RAF air defence units to still be in Germany by the start of 1961. There were calls to extend Javelin airframe life beyond 1,800 hours, but there was not much desire to do this as of December 1959. With that said, AOC Fighter Command cut out low-level training and live firing pertaining to Javelins operated by his Command in order to preserve airframe fatigue life. AOC-in-C RAF Germany, Air Marshal Sir Humphrey Edwardes-Jones KCB CBE DFC AFC AE, was advised by Air Marshal Sir Charles Elworthy OBE DSO MVO DFC AFC to consider keeping two Javelin squadrons running until mid-1961. It would turn out to be a bit longer; indeed, QRA remained in the hands of Allied air forces until the 1980s despite the Luftwaffe being equipped before hand with adequate air defence forces, the reason being best described as political. A signal sent on 28 October 1959 detailed the selection of aircraft from Fighter Command units to re-equip 87 Squadron:

One Javelin FAW.1 from IRS
Two Javelin FAW.4s from 72 Squadron
Four Javelin FAW.4s from 41 Squadron
One Javelin FAW.5 from 151 Squadron

The aircraft already on 87 Squadron were to be grounded for about four weeks pending a decision on fatigue life. If possible, aircraft that had some fatigue life left were to return to flying; the rest would be returned via 41 Group for fatigue extensions.

In January 1960, airframe fatigue life spans on all Javelins were determined:

Sortie Profile:	
Mark:	Hours:
High-altitude interceptor 1, 2, and 4	2,400
High-altitude interceptor 5 and 6	2,130
High-altitude interceptor 7, 8, and 9	1,323
Low level and demonstration 1, 2, and 4	277
Low level and demonstration 5 and 6	245
Low level and demonstration 7, 8, and 9	141
Air-to-air firing 1, 2, and 4	176
Air-to-air firing 5 and 6	158
Air-to-air firing 7, 8, and 9	96

The above figures pertain to the Ministry of Aviation recommended increase in fatigue life according to sortie profile and mark of Javelin, following the problems experienced by 87 Squadron. The then VCAS, Sir Edmund Huddleston, was dismayed at how few the hours were on the later model Javelins, especially the Marks 7, 8, and 9 airframes. The answer was the latter models had the same wing area and strength as the earlier models but were heavier and so gust loads would be heavier. The original figure of 1,800 hours for the earlier Javelins, at high altitude, were increased to 2,400 hours and the prospect was that even they may need to be upgraded to 3,000 hours. The VCAS was reassured that the Marks 7 to 9s were nowhere near their limits and, in any case, would not be engaging in the fatigue hour gobbling practice of firing guns, as they were missile carriers. This at least by way of a short answer is what the DCAS, Sir Charles Elworthy, told his Permanent Secretary, Mr D. A. J. West, to tell him.

The rundown and other problems besetting the RAF Fighter Force during this period were being noticed elsewhere. The British Ambassador to Bonn got involved over the affair with 87 Squadron, and sent a letter to the Foreign Office stressing the importance of retaining an adequate Fighter Force. Courtesy of UK Defence Policy, fighter squadrons were being disbanded with unseemly haste. Among the points he raised was concern about German reluctance to take on a share of the 'zonal border patrol' currently, and for many years to come, a responsibility jointly shared by the RAF and USAF. The Germans themselves were only just putting an air force together after years in the wilderness. To add to the problem, there was not a lot of airfield space left in West Germany as everything was occupied by American, British, and Canadian Air Force squadrons. The German Defence Minister earlier in the year had suggested that with the current running down of RAF squadrons, that some airfield space might be available to accommodate a couple of German F-86 squadrons.

Meanwhile, 87 Squadron, for all the effort expended on keeping the unit operational, did not have a long history (relatively speaking) with the Javelin. They were to keep the same CO throughout until disbandment at Brüggen in January 1961. During the intervening period, they were joined by 3 and 11 Squadrons at Geilenkirchen and finally 5 Squadron at Laarbruch. All the squadrons based in Germany were now issued with mostly FAW.4s and 5s. Before the Javelins arrived in Germany, the night fighter Meteors operated a slightly different profile to the UK based aircraft; their focus here had a more tactical flavour with the greater likelihood of intercepting lower level intruders. In addition, although not that it was in any sense a particularly prominent role, was the utility to be made available for low level attack or offensive air support, for which reliance upon the four 20-mm Hispanos was all that could be brought to bear. However, with the arrival of the Javelin, the focus for those squadrons was more to do with confronting head on the large numbers of Warsaw Pact air forces, which it was expected may try to overwhelm their NATO adversaries.

Brüggen was one of several similar bases built in the post-war era to similar specifications. These airfields, among others in the NATO Central Region, housed either tactical air superiority, support, reconnaissance, and ultimately strike (nuclear-armed) squadrons to sit vigil. These post-war airfields existed to meet a specific purpose and, as such, had substantial runway length, dispersals, and the most up-to-date and comprehensive facilities. They sat out of view from the public roads and were accessed by long roads taking the visitor off the beaten track. The units based on these airfields would live under the highest level of peacetime readiness to confront an initial assault across the inner German border by Warsaw Pact forces. The level of readiness was quite unlike that experienced on military installations in the UK. The high tempo of exercises and maintenance of high security levels would be the routine through to the end of the 1980s and the Cold War.

The third, or rather fourth, squadron in Germany to re-equip with the Javelin was 11 Squadron, which was already at Geilenkichen. Sqn Ldr A. F. Peers, 'B' Flight Commander of 11 Squadron, was able to log in June 1959 that they could expect to begin conversion to the Javelin in the coming October.

At the time in question, Mk 8 and Mk 9 Javelins were being sent to UK units with Mk 7s having first become available the previous year. Nevertheless, Peers told his squadron that ground school courses had been arranged at Leeming from 4–14 August and 31 August–11 September. As many as five crews would attend each of the courses in Leeming, leaving the squadron still operational but with a much-reduced capacity. No. 11 Squadron received their first T3 on 31 August to begin the re-equipment programme. They were also kindly loaned another one from 3 Squadron, their next-door neighbours at Geilers. During September, 11 Squadron functioned twofold as an operational Meteor flight and a Javelin conversion flight. On 17 September, Wg Cdr Sanderson, the CO, experienced a complete port engine failure after only six minutes flying time, resulting in Category 2 damage. On the upside, all aircrew bar one had flown solo in the T3 by the end of September and nine aircrew were sent out to 228 OCU to begin the short Javelin conversion course. Meanwhile, everyone was being rotated through the Aviation Medicine Centre at RAF Wildenrath for lectures and demonstrations of the oxygen equipment used in the Javelin and ejector-seat demonstrations.

By early October, it was expected that five pilots and nine navigators would be fully trained on the Flat Iron. As it turned out, October was an unseasonably good month for weather, with cold temperatures, rain, and wind arriving only toward the end of the third week, resulting in no more than a single night sortie exercise being cancelled. By the end of the month, they had received a single FAW.4 and all were queueing up to take it aloft. In the meantime, everyone else had to keep their hand in with the old Meteors. Typically, squadrons would remain operational on their old aircraft in order to maintain currency and readiness rather than lose an operational squadron from the line for any length of time, which appears to be the preferred 'political' option today.

In 1959, capability gaps were not the way to go. A couple of mishaps arose early in the new year, first with Sgt Chamberlain of 11 Squadron, flying FAW.4 XH765, experiencing a booster pump failure at night on return to base. He relit the engine on descent to the airfield, but as soon as he released the relight button, the engine flamed out again. He succeeded in carrying out an asymmetrical landing without further incident. A few days later, Wg Cdr J. G. Croshaw, who had just taken over command of 11 Squadron, experienced a fall in oil pressure while carrying out night PIs at 42,000 feet. The correct action was taken and the aircraft was landed, again in an asymmetrical configuration, without any further incident. Next, Flt Lt Jones had a near miss with a Canberra from 59 Squadron, which was also based at Geilenkirchen.

The Canberra was under approach control. Flt Lt Jones was instructed by same to take avoiding action, which was done resulting in no more than a near miss report being filed. A further incident resulted in disciplinary action being taken against a ground crew airman when Sqn Ldr Evans, one of the flight commanders, experienced pressure instrument failure on take-off. This was caused by cross-connected static and pitot lines, which could be traced to the airman working on these components prior to the aircraft, XH765 again, being declared ready for flying. By March, they had twelve FAW.4s and conversion was complete. Only a 'battle flight' commitment from 15 to 29 March prevented them from achieving their target of 295 flying hours that month.

Battle flight for 2 ATAF was now being rotated between three of the RAF clutch bases: 87 Squadron at Brüggen; 5 Squadron at Laarbruch; and 3 and 11 Squadrons at Geilenkirchen. All now with Javelins. The Hunter squadrons in Germany were all now concentrated on tactical support and reconnaissance; the age of the front line day fighter was virtually at an end. Through to September, Flt Sgt Chamberlain experienced a number of other incidents while flying, including two boost pump failures (each on separate occasions) and a damaged wing out board of the gun port

No. 11 Squadron three-ship of FAW.4s operating from Geilenkirchen c. 1960. Overseas squadrons were usually the last to receive new equipment, no matter how much they could justify being favourably prioritised. (*Crown Copyright*)

in March; this was believed to be a bird strike while flying XA720. On 5 September 1960, he was flying XA727 when he heard a thump and thought a panel had come off during take-off. The take-off was aborted and on return to dispersal, it was noted that the AI access panel was missing. Both the pilot and the airman responsible for servicing were held responsible. Even though he ended up on the carpet initially, Flt Sgt Chamberlain was still recommended for a commission, subject to meeting the requisite medical fitness standard.

One young chap embarking on his career in the RAF at the time, and just as the Cold War was truly getting into its full 'Mexican standoff' between West and East was Keith Deal. Keith had just completed training as an 'L Fitt AR' (Electronics Fitter Air Radar) to use the terminology of the RAF of the day, at No. 1 Radio School, based at RAF Locking near Weston-super-Mare. A regular, Keith had finished training just as the peacetime National Service-era was coming to an end. Keith was posted to Germany about the time that postings to places like West Germany were becoming quite sought after:

> As a brand new Junior Technician Air Radar Fitter I arrived at RAF Geilenkirchen, 2 TAF, Germany on 26 Feb 1959.
>
> Three squadrons were operational there; 3 Squadron flying Javelin Mk 4 N/Aw aircraft, 11 Squadron flying Meteor NF.11 night fighters and 59 Squadron flying Canberra Mk 8 Interdictors.
>
> The Canberras were either loaded with a nuclear bomb or an under belly gun pack of four 30-mm cannons, we reckoned they had split personalities not knowing if they were bombers or fighters. As I had been trained on AI 17 Interception Radar and GEE Mk 3 Navigation Radar, both used on the Javelin Mk 4, I was sent to 3 Sqn.
>
> 3 Sqn consisted of a large Hangar, which could house five aircraft, with an area of hard standing outside, beyond that a big caravan which was the Ground crew Line Hut and then the Flight Line of twelve Javelins. In fact there never were twelve on the Line the most would probably be seven - the rest in maintenance or fault rectification. At the back inside the hanger were rooms allocated to aircrew and the various aircraft trades.
>
> The Javelin was a bit of a brute and quite high off the ground which meant changing some of the heavy radar equipment in the nose required strong muscles.
>
> To change the radar Dish, the nose radome had to be removed.
>
> A trestle on wheels had to be pushed under and strapped to the radome which could then be unbolted and moved away from the aircraft.
>
> Later marks of Javelin had a radome which unlatched and swung to one side.
>
> In the Nav/Rad rear cockpit was the AI 17 Display and Control Units and the GEE 3 Control Unit, which were relatively easy to change. Behind the windscreen in the front cockpit was the Gunsight display and superimposed on it the 'collimator' display (a small green dot which showed the target in relation to the Javelin for night use).
>
> I was one day sitting in the rear cockpit running up an AI 17 radar, after replacing a u/s dish, the radome was off and the dish scanning from side to side on auto.
>
> If you switched to manual the dish stopped and you could move it left or right and up or down with a small joystick on the Control Unit.

Out of the corner of my eye I noticed the Discipline Flight Sergeant walking to cross in front of the aircraft.

I switched to manual and swung the dish to point at him and as he moved I followed him.

He stopped and looked at the dish so I stopped and then he walked on so I carried on tracking him. This happened another couple of times until he noticed me, with a big grin, in the cockpit. He did not see the funny side, even though I assured him the Transmitter was not switched on, and I had to do the next two Battle Flight duties.

Keith went on detachment to the West German Air Force Base at Nörvenich for an airshow being held there on 20 June 1959. They took two aircraft with them: XA750 and XA635; one was assigned to the static park and the other to the flying display and to be put through its paces by the squadron aerobatics pilot and navigator duo. Whatever is said about the Javelin and aerobatics, Flt Lts P. Wilson (pilot) and J. Wilson (navigator) were officially recognised in April as the best 'Javelin aerobatics display crew' in RAF Germany.

It is the nose of their display mount in the picture. The other aircraft (XA 750) was sadly lost at the end of the day, as Keith recalls:

A day out to a NATO Air Display at German Air Force Nörvenich was not so good.

Two Javelins, one to give an air display and the other for the crowd to look at close up, and a ground crew were sent to Nörvenich.

At the end of a good day's flying the aircraft took off to return to their home bases but our static display aircraft crashed on take-off.

I watched it accelerate down the runway and lift off.

As soon as it got airborne it banked sharply right, which I had never seen before, then disappeared behind some trees.

Both crew were killed.

The aircraft came down two miles north-west of Nörvenich, just after taking off to return to Geilenkirchen. The take-off into a turn to starboard was quite normal until about 500 feet. Then, the aircraft, XA750, started to roll to port (left) until it was inverted, the nose dropped, and the aircraft stalled then spun into the ground. The accident report stated that the pilot, thirty-five-year-old Flt Lt Wilfred Smith Jacques, was attempting an 'unauthorized and unrehearsed slow roll and was unable to recover from the inverted position'. His navigator, Flying Officer David Alexander Ritchie, was twenty-three.

Keith witnessed a handful of other accidents involving the Javelin while serving in Germany. Some did have a happy ending of sorts:

Another accident at night at Geilenkirchen was a pilot who landed with the loss of most of his hydraulic systems, which meant no flaps or brakes.

The aircraft went straight down the runway and was still going very fast when it reached the end.

Above: No. 11 Squadron B Flight display team, left to right: Pete Simpson (navigator), John Galley (navigator), Peter Goodwin (pilot), Alan 'Taf' Evans (navigator), Pete Deakin (pilot), Les Bradley (pilot), Mike Harris (navigator), and Keith McRobb (pilot). (*Peter Goodwin*)

Below: No. 11 Squadron air and ground crew with two Mk 9 Javelins to frame the shot *c.* 1963; again, NCO aircrew are still notable in the line-up. (*Peter Goodwin*)

We went out in a Land Rover to find it and came across tyre marks in the grass, then some broken landing lights, then a hole in the camp boundary fence, then tracks across a field and a road into another field and found the Javelin parked in a wood with trees growing through it.

There was no sign of the crew but they were soon found with no injuries in a nearby farmhouse drinking Dutch gin.

The aircraft was a write off.

A very impressive accident was a pilot landing with the right under carriage leg refusing to come down.

The word got round and many people went out to watch.

The Javelin came in low and slow and every one crossed their fingers.

The pilot gently touched down on the left wing wheel and the aircraft went smoothly down the runway on it with the nose high in the air to reduce speed.

When the aircraft was so slow it could not sustain the nose up the pilot gently lowered it and was then on the left wing and nose wheels but still going quite fast.

At a point where the right wing could no longer be held up the pilot gently lowered it to the ground, the Javelin stopped and everyone uncrossed their fingers and breathed again.

The Javelin had the undercarriage fault sorted, a new wing tip and was soon flying again. Everyone reckoned the pilot did an outstanding job landing 'fifteen tons of screaming scrap metal' (as we called the Javelin) on one wheel.

There were also events that were too tragic and inexplicable:

On the day I left, I had signed myself off from the Hospital, Library, Corporals Club, Guardroom and other places, handed in my bedding and went down to 11 Squadron to hand in my tool kit and say goodbye.

I then drove up to the Station Headquarters to get documents for arriving at my new camp, which was A&AEE Boscombe Down.

As I walked out of the Headquarters two aircraft flew overhead quite low, they were Mk 8 Javelins of 41 Squadron on detachment to Geilenkirchen for a while, banking round to land.

Suddenly one just exploded into pieces and all I could do was stand there with my mouth open and watch all these pieces fall out of the sky.

I got in my car and drove out of Geilenkirchen for the last time heading for the car ferry at Ostend.

The Javelins from 41 Squadron had arrived on 12 August 1961 to reinforce the other units and take their place on the 'battle flight'.

The RAF in West Germany spent most of the Javelin era a step or two behind in modernisation, not that the Javelin itself was necessarily obsolescent but the other smaller NATO air forces were better equipped. Much of what the 2nd TAF could call upon was, by 1961–1962, a comfortable step ahead of the Javelin in terms of agility and speed; the only aircraft to truly compare, indeed edge the rest aside, when it first arrived in 1965 was the English Electric Lightning. The Hunter in the tactical reconnaissance role brought a respectable performance. By the beginning of the 1960s, while the RAF began deploying its first Lightnings back home, the air forces contributing to the 2nd and 4th TAFs were fielding their own truly supersonic types: F-100s, F-101s, F-102s, F-104s, and from France, the Super Mystère and the first of their Mirage series.

RAFG (Royal Air Force Germany) seemed to fall behind particularly during the 1960s where the tactical strike and attack roles were concerned, meaning during the early half of the decade, the three principal tactical aircraft in RAFG were the Hunter, the Javelin, and the Canberra. By the end of the decade and once the RAF had extricated itself from the debacle over TSR-2 and F-111, it was able to proceed quickly to modernise with far more realistic and eminently more suitable types, meaning much more formidable Buccaneers, Harriers, and Phantoms, yet not before these types fully equipped the squadrons of Strike and Air Support Commands then the first of RAFG's vulnerable Canberra fleet was replaced.

When the RAF could not wait to take the strain off the Jaguar squadrons in the strike role with the new, far more competent Tornado, the first went to the replace the Vulcan fleet, which perhaps was better placed to wait their turn. The Javelin squadrons deployed in Germany initially followed a logic of a single air defence unit to each of the four clutch bases along the Dutch border. Other air defence squadrons with the Hunter made up the remainder, remembering that in 1957, there were nine RAF air bases in Germany (just three years later, there were five). When the Soviet authorities threatened to close the Berlin air corridors in the run up to Christmas 1961, in order to place the best assets the RAF had for the particular role of escorting military and civilian transport aircraft in and out of West Berlin, Mk 9 Javelins, already equipping most Javelin squadrons in Fighter Command, were deployed to Germany rather than rely on the non-missile equipped Mk 4 and Mk 5 aircraft of what were by then, only two interceptor units assigned to RAFG. Oddly, the real hot-ship 'Flat Iron' was the Mk 7. Able to carry Firestreak and powered with 11,000-lb thrust Sapphire engines, it could reach an altitude of 45,000 feet in comfortably under seven minutes and was arguably the most agile (ok a mean achievement) of the breed.

Then again, the heavier reheat engined Mk 8s and Mk 9s, while rather more sluggish below 20,000 feet due to the enforced restrictions on the use of reheat, could turn and climb more impressively than the Mk 7s when above 20,000 feet if they used their afterburner. That said, many senior officers were not happy with young Javelin crews turning and burning up in the stratosphere given the wear and tear on the airframes.

No. 5 Squadron stationed at Laarbruch still had the FAW.4s they had originally equipped with in January 1960. They started to go at the end of 1962 as they received, by the time already obsolescent, FAW.9s direct from 33 Squadron at Middleton St George. This also brought a move to RAF Geilenkirchen. Naturally, this also brought about a transfer of many ex-33 Squadron aircrew who flew the Mk 9s straight into Geilenkirchen effectively the new squadron. No. 5 Squadron themselves had provided a home for former members of 87 Squadron at the start of 1961 when that unit disbanded. The previous two-and-a-half years had been crowned with the winning in 1961 of the Duncan Trophy, the premier award for air-to-air gunnery in RAF Germany. The year 1961 also brought significant changes to the deployment of RAF squadrons in Germany, particularly fighter units, although the strike and reconnaissance units were not getting off scot free.

The AOC-in-C RAFG had attempted to retain what he could and while other restructuring was already approved, the request to retain two day fighter units equipped with Hunter F6 at half strength each or a single whole squadron was yet to be decided upon. However, of the then three Javelin AW squadrons deployed at each of the clutch bases along the Dutch border, two (namely 3 and 87 Squadrons) were to disband; of the four day fighter squadrons, 4 and 94 Squadrons based at Jever and 20 and 26 Squadrons based at Gütersloh were to be disbanded as soon as possible after January 1961. However, the RAF's policy of retaining the most senior squadrons to maintain historic longevity as far as possible meant that the losers were other units with higher numbers, if not fighter squadrons. No. 59 Squadron based at Geilenkirchen in the strike role with the Canberra B (I) 8 was to be rebadged as 3 Squadron. No. 79 Squadron, a fighter reconnaissance unit at Gütersloh, was to be rebadged as 4 Squadron. No. 2 Squadron based at Jever would leave for Gütersloh, which would see Jever removed from the RAF Germany list of assets. Despite the expected comparable shortcomings of the earlier model Javelins in November 1961, in one day during Exercise Roulette, four Javelin FAW.5s from 5 Squadron claimed kills against no fewer than eighteen other NATO types, including: CF-100 Canucks, F-101 Voodoos, F-84 Thunderstreaks, F-104 Starfighters, and an F-102 Delta Dagger.

It was during 1961 that the CO of 5 Squadron expected his outfit to go the same way as many of the earlier squadrons (including 46, 87, 141, and 151 Squadrons), but they were saved by a yet another deterioration in East–West relations and as a result, the plan to replace the bulk of the Fighter Force with surface-launched missiles, which had not followed an entirely balanced transition, now unsurprisingly found little faith among both politicians, the military, and air chiefs alike. So not only did 5 Squadron receive a stay of execution, but they were actually expanded from fourteen to eighteen aircraft, making it the largest on strength at Laarbruch.

There was also the added tiny insult to 5 and 11 Squadrons during the Berlin Corridor crisis of 1961, when Mk 9 Javelins from UK-based squadrons deployed to ensure there were Firestreak-armed aircraft, to ensure missiles were carried at all times by the QRA. Further drops in temperature in East–West relations through 1962 saw 25 Squadron called upon to deploy from Leuchars to Gütersloh in West Germany in preparation yet again to ride shotgun for Allied transport aircraft flying in and out of Berlin.

Peter Goodwin was a pilot on 25 Squadron at the time during this particular detachment to RAF Gütersloh in 1962:

> 25 Squadron were sent to RAF Gütersloh, May 26 1962, to ensure the Centre and North Corridors into Berlin were kept open during Russian 'Sabre Rattling'.
>
> I shared an empty married quarter with another Javelin crew Flt Lt Chris Cowper—we arranged for our wives to join us.
>
> One night the 'Alert' sounded and we both rushed off to the airfield, on arriving at the Guard Room we were informed is was not the 'Alert' but a siren from the prison—slightly embarrassed we returned to our quarters for a beer or two....

Gütersloh was used by Goring during the war, the Officers' Mess had a small room at the top of a tower—in which was a beam in the ceiling—the story was that when any pilot 'exaggerated' a hidden lever was pulled and one half of a beam in the ceiling crashed down about 3 feet….

Some years ago the Officers' Mess at RAF Gütersloh was burnt down.

By 1962, the positioning of squadrons in Germany was moving more toward a particular format whereby the stations were less mixed but each assigned units with a comparable or at least complimentary role; all air defence responsibility by now fell to the two Javelin squadrons, 5 and 11, at Geilenkirchen with more Javelins being deployed from the UK as required. The tactical strike units now partnered with the tactical reconnaissance squadrons, essentially, Brüggen, Laarbruch, and Wildenrath. This left the fighter reconnaissance units to be concentrated at Gütersloh, often because maintaining a large number of units addressing various roles placed the wrong emphasis with undue weakness in certain areas. Therefore, by the end of the year, RAF Geilenkirchen had become the air defence hub for want of a better description, but ironically still housed No. 3 Squadron, which had since re-equipped with Canberras and was now identified as a tactical strike (nuclear) squadron while its neighbour, 11 Squadron, continued as a tactical all-weather fighter unit with the Javelin. They took turn at holding 'battle flight usually twice each a month, with 5 Squadron at Laarbruch. Battle flight was, for fighter squadrons in Germany, the equivalent of QRA in the UK. QRA in Germany referred to the strike squadrons who throughout their existence maintained live nuclear-armed aircraft, ready to respond in very much the same vain as the V-bombers when dispersed back in the UK, quite simply a scramble for them was a particularly heart in mouth affair, especially once confirmed.

Scrambles of the battle flight never presumed to cross the Iron Curtain; anything they were going to intercept would certainly be in Allied airspace, over the Federal Republic of Germany itself. Therefore, any intercepts that turned up anything interesting would hopefully be benign. On 21 March 1962, an 11 Squadron Javelin intercepted a USAF aircraft. On another instance, it was a Caravelle jet liner. As long as the quarry was never more interesting than this then that was okay. No. 11 Squadron were replacing their Mk 4 Javelins with the Mk 5. Later in the year, they would begin receiving Mk 9s when they would be joined first by 5 Squadron. In 1965 they would be joined by the Lightnings of 92 Squadron, arriving from Leconfield in Yorkshire, as the RAF rejigged its ever dwindling if better equipped order of battle. These were rapidly shifting times and both 5 and 11 Squadrons had but a short time remaining with the FAW.9.

In the run-up, to getting the Mk 9s, significant changes had to be made. In November, 11 Squadron sent several of their FAW.5-rated aircrew to North Luffenham in Leicestershire to undergo a course in the use of pressurised breathing equipment, not necessarily significant, but on top of this, eight aircrew were posted out; this accounted for a sharp fall in flying hours. No. 11 Squadron were also taking their turn providing the 2nd Tactical Air Force 'battle flight' commitment except on 21 November, when the weather at Geilenkirchen was so bad that the duty had to

Above: No. 25 Squadron at Waterbeach about 1961, before the move to Leuchars. Top row: Baz Horwood, John Rust (later joined the Red Arrows), unknown, Hank Hemming (RCAF), Ken Bassett, John Lucking, Mel Evans, and Mike Gautrey. Centre row from left: Bill Akister, Keith McRobb, Mike Harris (later killed in a Phantom), Larry Parakin (RCAF), Ivan Symonds, 'Cobber' Edwards, Laurie Manns, unknown, Bob Arnott, Paul Hodgson, 'Pop' Parsons, and Brian Whitely. Seated from left: Roy Houghton, Norman Glass, unknown, Pete Mossman (also known as 'Bossman'), 'Black Jim' Walton (CO), John Chick, and 'Paddy' Macilwrath; the last two remain unidentified. The CO, Jim Walton's initials are on his aircraft, XH880, at the rear. (*RAF Museum, Hendon*)

Below: No. 5 Squadron Javelin crews walk from their mount after a sortie over the Federal Republic of Germany *c.* 1965. (*Crown Copyright*)

No. 25 Squadron formation: three FAW.9s led by an FAW.7 about 1961. (*Peter Goodwin*)

be transferred to the USAF base at Soesterberg in the Netherlands. Elements of 5 Squadron began arriving with Mk 9 aircraft while 11 Squadron crews started ferrying their own Mk 5 jets back to the UK. Commenting in the Geilers Station ORB, one officer described the respective squadron areas as resembling a maintenance unit rather than an operational station. On the upside, work was now almost complete on a new QRA revetment and work commenced on a project adjacent to the hangars of 11 Squadron, and now 5 Squadron, on a small hangar at each to house the battle flight aircraft. Curiously, it was envisaged that all 2nd ATAF battle flights would be mounted from Geilenkirchen in future. With the RAF, together with the USAF, being solely responsible for West German peace time air defence, it was agreed would continue to be so and still was well into the 1980s when West Germany still had to accept a whiff of being overseen by the wartime allies.

Roy Evans, serving with 25 Squadron alongside his pilot mate Bob Kelly, effectively transferred from Leuchars to their new unit at Geilenkirchen by arriving with one of the new squadron's new jets:

> In December 1962 Bob Kelly and I, along with another 10 crews, left No. 25 Sqn at Leuchars and took all the squadron's Mk. 9 Javelins to re-equip No. 11 Squadron at Geilenkirchen. After a few weeks at our new base the weather clamped-in and very little flying took place. As so often is the case when the flying line failed to climb up the wall, the bosses got restless, so we ended up flying in worse conditions than we originally

stopped for. On January 23 1963, we were briefed for HLPIs (High Level Practice Intercepts) and got airborne at 1330, but our No. 2 developed 'stick-shake' (due to air in the hydraulic lines which had accumulated due to non-flying during the bad weather) Our wx. was Amber 2, pretty grotty, our No.1 wx diversion was Gütersloh some 104 nautical miles away; consequently the fuel state to enable this diversion was 2,000 pounds each side, a goodly amount under normal circumstances. We climbed to 40,000 feet and as no other aircraft came to join us we elected to do a practice-diversion to Laarbruch, EDUL. After completing our let down to Laarbruch, we overshot and again climbed to 40,000 feet. looking for some 'trade', any other aircraft which we could engage! Soon we espied four F-84Fs, slightly below us, so we 'bounced' them, eventually getting behind a pair of them whilst the other pair tried to do the same to us!

After a merry 'circle of joy' lasting about five minutes, the 'enemy' decide to break off and go home, leaving us with a rather empty sky. A quick Gee-fix put us 60 nms NNE of base, with fuel of 2,200 lb each side, so in order to reach base with our 'Bingo' fuel of 2 × 2,000 lb we elected to do a fuel-conserving 'glide' on 1 engine at 220 kts IAS. This was quite a bit slower than our normal recovery speed, and we seemed to be tracking 10 degrees right of track, so we corrected this and continued the glide to FL 250 on our dive-circle (a cardiac-shaped rough circle). Coming to this circle, we descended on it to FL 150 then turned in to intersect the extended centreline for R/W 27, continuing our descent

Air Marshal Sir John Grandy inspects the rear cockpit of one of 5 Squadron's newly acquired FAW.9s, looking on from the right are; OC 5 Squadron, Wg Cdr C. R. Gordon MVO, left of him; Gp Cpt P. Del le Cheminant DFC. (*The National Archives*)

to 3,000ft on the QNH. To my great surprise, all Gee-signals disappeared at 8,000 feet, most unusual as normally we kept sight of them until we landed!

I told Bob about this and we levelled off at 4,000 feet, just about our safety height. We tried to contact Geilenkirchen Approach frequency ... SILENCE! We again tried, still silence! By now that little word all aviators dread came to mind ... LOST! After about 20 minutes on a South/South-West heading, I reckoned we were in the South West quadrant from base, and a check on the base ILS (Instrument Landing System) localizer indeed said we were south of an East-West line through Geilenkirchen.

We called on 243.0 freq. then prefixed our call with 'MAYDAY, MAYDAY, MAYDAY'—still no answer! I told Bob to turn onto a North-East heading, and this is where my guardian angel came into play. My wife and I were living on the married quarters in Wildenrath with a cousin of hers and his family, he was a Corporal Medic there, and whilst we were having a social drink in the Sergeants Mess one evening, I chanced to talk to a Chief Technician who told me that a new, superior ariel system had been installed at ATC to improve the CADAF (direction-finding kit) performance. Our own CADAF at Geilers had been U/S for weeks, but I swiftly pulled out my RAFAC (Navigators' Bible) found the APC (Approach freq) for EDUW (Wildenrath. Bob dialled this up, we called Mayday again, and this time a very faint voice answered saying 'A/C calling, steer 040 degrees and repeat callsign!' We complied of course and all the time we were peering through the fog/mist to try to see the ground, no such luck.

Just then a Belgian F-84F flew alongside, I assumed this to be a Battle-Flight ship, the pilot was pointing vigorously downwards; he wanted us to follow him and descend to his base. 'What shall we do?' said Bob. By this time I had turned up the 'Gain' (volume) on my AI set and gained a negative response across our track which I hoped was the river Maas, putting us approximately 25 nautical miles from Wildenrath we again called APC they asked us to 'Squawk Ident', then they said they could see an echo 30 nautical miles away, on our heading—it had to be us, no other a/c was to be seen. We slowly descended to 2,000ft to intercept the ILS glideslope for R/W 09. Down we went and after three minutes, Bob said he had the approach lights dead ahead. We landed at 14:55, a sortie length of 1 hr 25 mins, when we normally only flew for 1 hour. A BUA (British United Airways) Viscount on a charter flight had waited for us for a quarter of an hour whilst we landed downwind, our sole engine running on AVTUR fumes! All our Comms, kit, Gee, Radios etc were removed and put on test by RSF(Radio Servicing Flight). When I called in there a bit later, nobody was to be seen and my Gee-box had overheated, but the report went back to the squadron that all was 'S' (serviceable), but this was not the case! To cut a long story short, after a shepherd aircraft was sent to fly with us back to Geilers, my aircraft had a succession of navigators twiddling the analogue counters on my Gee-box until eventually one of them detected a 'jump' on the C-signal counter. This was John Galley who is also a member of 11sqn Association; he saved my good name and although I went on what was a 'Chop-Check' with the CO the next day I knew I was in the clear and flew with a happy heart! I passed my checkout okay, flew with the Boss again that night and got the OK to continue. I went on to gain an 'Above Average' assessment and happily never got lost again!

Above: Following the restructuring of the late 1950s and very early 1960s, 3 Squadron had taken over the Strike Canberras of 59 Squadron at Geilenkirchen while 11 Squadron converted to Javelin FAW.9s. They were joined by 5 Squadron from Laarbruch. Two Javelin FAW.9s of 11 Squadron formate on a 3 Squadron Canberra B (I) 8. (*Barry G. Mayner*)

Below: A comprehensive gathering of 5 Squadron personnel, air and ground crews, for a squadron photo at Geilenkirchen shortly after arrival and re-equipment with the FAW.9 on 20 April 1963. (*The National Archives*)

Roy Evans and Bob Kelly were involved in a particularly sensitive incident a couple of years later while both still on 11 Squadron, crewed again with Flt Sgt, later, Master Pilot Bob Kelly:

> In March 1964 a well-known TV character named Hughie Green, who had been a ferry pilot during the war, had flown a light a/c into Berlin, Tempelhof I think it was, and in doing so had come under fire from Soviet forces! Hughie said he was flying back to UK, the Soviets said that he wasn't!
>
> As East Germany, close to the West German border, was simply crawling with SAM sites, armoured divisions, infantry and several hundred fighters, I think the Soviets were right, Hughie was to stay put where he was! However, the NATO chiefs decided otherwise, so operation 'Quicksand Patrol' was dreamed up, consisting of four F-105s of USAF, four Mirages of the French air force and four Javelin 9s of No. 11 Squadron, RAF. On March 10 1964 we deployed to Celle airbase, in the ADIZ and were billeted with the Irish Guards regiment who were gearing up to celebrate Saint Patrick's Day. As we navs carried Top Secret Authentication Kits, I tried to find a Secure Safe to stash mine in overnight, but had no joy. Accordingly I called the Regimental Duty Officer, who was not impressed that a little English Sergeant, in flying kit, had got him out of bed, but he grudgingly agreed to stash my kit in his safe. That evening all the RAF crews went into Celle town for a few jars on a terrace cafe, watched by a few German customers. The native population were so scared that the Ruskies might invade them, but seeing foreign aircrew whooping it up so cheered them up that when we asked for our bill the waiter informed us that a little old man, sitting near us, had insisted on paying all of it. We thanked him, promised to look after the population of Celle and retired to bed. Come 13 March 1964, we got airborne, joined up with the four yanks, the four Force de Frappe chaps and proceeded to perform a large circle of joy just west of the Central Corridor into Berlin! With our four shiny white Air to Air Firestreak missiles, we quite fancied our chances, oh the folly of youth! I can't remember what armament the other eight aircraft carried, but in retrospect I don't think we really stood a chance of coming out on top. Anyway, after about 30 minutes waiting for Hughie to cry out 'Help', whereupon we would all cry 'Tallyho!' and rush off to help, we were ordered to RTB, which we did without further ado, where we heard Hughie had seen sense & returned to Heathrow on a line flight of BEA (British European Airways), now defunct.

No. 29 Squadron deployed out to Nicosia in Cyprus in March 1963 to relieve 43 Squadron, which now concentrated on the ground attack role and moved to Khormaksar in the South Arabian Peninsula where the local Guerrilla Forces were determined to physically drive out the occupier who had a set policy of maintaining the Aden Protectorate. The British Government had announced the previous year to continue the policy of maintaining a garrison here, this policy would be reversed when the Wilson Government took office in 1964 through the 'nothing east of Suez' policy. The result of course was the retention of the occupier's forces and a long drawn out counter-guerrilla/terrorist campaign by British Forces against the two principal guerrilla groups: Flosy (Front for the Liberation of South Yemen) and the

NLF (National Liberation Front). This in turn therefore provoked this new rejig of HM Force deployments until a clean hand over followed by the British Forces leaving Aden and sailing or flying off into the sunset in 1967. No. 29 Squadron, now based in Cyprus, were unaffected by the events elsewhere but shortly after arriving in the Mediterranean, they were called upon for public duty when they were requested to provide a flypast over Malta as part of the formal ceremony to mark the day of independence of Malta within the British Commonwealth on 21 September 1964.

They moved out of Nicosia and into Akrotiri during October, largely due to the former's unsuitability for housing such operational units being the island's principal airport.

The year 1964 continued to be a busy one for flying the flag duties for 29 Squadron; Barry Mayner was still flying with the Squadron at the time and describes the trip to Iran, which followed in order to participate in the Iranian Armed Forces Day display:

29 Sqn were asked to take a display team to Iran for the annual Armed Forces Day for the Shah of Iran. We had worked up a display with four aircraft and deployed on 14 October 1964. Supported by a 70 Squadron Hastings (Nicosia Based) for ground crew and a Canberra from the Akrotiri Wing for route checks and weather reports, we were a bit short legged as we did not fit any wing tanks. The dates, all October 1964, and legs flown were:

1. 14 Akrotiri-Diyarbakir, 1.15
2. 14 Diyarbakir-Tehran 1.20
3. 15 Tehran-Shiraz 1.00
4. 16 Display practice in Exercise area 0.45
5. 17 IIAF ARMED FORCES DAY DISPLAY FOR SHAH 0.55
6. 17 Shiraz-Tehran 1.00
7. 19 Tehran-Hamadan Shirokhi 0.30
8. 19 Shirokhi-Diyarbakir 1.15
9. 19 Diyarbakir-Akrotiri 1.20

The display area was a four-mile-wide bowl in the hills a few miles outside Shiraz. We rehearsed a fifteen-minute display which included a Box 4—Finger 4—orbit in Finger 4 with gear and flap down—line astern for a final run along the display line at 480 Knots at 300 feet we arrived in 'Box' and lowered the gear and flap when we were top up to the VIP stand.

We did aircrew turn around at Diyarbakir. My pilot Keith Fitchew and I quickly realised that we were short of fuel; one of our ventrals (Bossom Tanks non-jettisonable under the fuselage) refused to accept any fuel.

We went into a huddle and I worked out if the forecast was reasonable then operating as a singleton, we could make Nicosia.

The Hastings support aircraft was about two hours away. The Boss, after going through all the options with us, agreed to us proceeding as a singleton with the option to divert into Incirlik Adana if we had any doubt about reaching Nicosia safely.

Publicity release with photograph of Peter Goodwin dismounting. (*Peter Goodwin*)

HRH Prince Philip, the Duke of Edinburgh, visiting 11 Squadron at Geilenkirchen, 4 December 1964. He is seen here with Wg Cdr Marriot, OC 11 Squadron, only partially seen to the right is Geilenkirchen Station Commander, Gp Capt Rixon. (*The National Archives*)

The Canberra got airborne and was to contact the Hastings after we all got airborne to say 'no need to land Diyarbakir'. We got airborne 10 minutes behind the other Javelins so that we could operate independently.

All worked as planned and by cutting a few corners, Keith and I were able to stay at height (we had cruise climbed to 45,000 feet).

We contacted Akrotiri and were cleared for a no diversion recovery to Base. Yes we pushed the limits but all the tweaks and careful handling of speed, fuel and engines worked. An aside is air traffic and ops at Sharoki said we were the first jets to land on the new airfield.

We got a bit of a fright watching our Canberra leap frogging the approach end CHAG (Chain Hydraulic Arrester Gear) which was rigged but required us to land past the cable, which was designed to catch the undercarriage if you needed it.

The accompanying photos here were taken by Barry himself.

In 1965, the squadron, now moved to Akrotiri, practiced both high, medium, and low-level intercept sorties. Exercises here included practicing low-level attacks on surface vessels at sea as with the Javelins deployed to Germany, RAF Javelin squadrons overseas found themselves practising all manner of tactical roles. Good relations continued to be evident and that year, 29 Sqn worked up an impressive formation display for King Idris of Libya at RAF El Adem, to take place on 15 September. This had to be reduced to a flypast due to limitations on engine wear and tear at the time obliging lower thrust settings which meant the display would rather lose its sparkle.

On 11 November, another part of the old empire started to rupture and break away. This time, it was a declaration of independence. However, this was not a native population looking to sever links with British imperialism; this was the white government of Ian Smith making his now infamous unilateral declaration of independence, not that independence from London was not on the cards, but only if the Rhodesian government was prepared to admit more native people to positions within the government and elsewhere as Smith was effectively presiding over an apartheid state. The declaration was followed by a statement from Mr Smith:

> There can be no happiness in a country while the absurd situation continues to exist where people, such as ourselves, who have ruled themselves with an impeccable record for over 40 years, are denied what is freely granted to other countries.

On 19 November, all routine flying ceased and the squadron was ordered to fit long-range tanks to all aircraft and prepare to move at short notice; all personnel were ordered to pack for the Tropics and to remain at twelve hours standby. In the meantime, as many Javelin Mk 9s as could be mustered were fuelled, and then flew off to Luqa to land, refuel, and return to Akrotiri. These were proving trips to determine turnaround speed. By 24 November, there were ten Javelins in their long-range fit. On 26 November, they were told they were going on exercise to Masirah.

The following day, the squadron received a visit from AOC-in-C MEAF, Air Marshal Sir Thomas Prickett KCB DSO DFC, on the crisis in Rhodesia, and informed

Fine forward view study of an FAW9 R on golf dispersal at Akrotiri c. 1965. (*Barry G. Mayner*)

Dayglo Meteor T7, possibly the squadron hack, with a Javelin under what appears to be either a setting or rising sun in Akrotiri c. 1965. (*Barry G. Mayner*)

that the Squadron might fly to Zambia. The route was planned immediately following the C-in-C's brief. It would take the Javelins to Diyarbakir (Turkey) to Dezful Vahdati (Iran) then to Masirah. Eight aircraft reached Masirah one had to divert to Muharraq and another delayed at Dezful Vahdati. From Masirah, they were to fly on to Muharraq (Bahrain) then to Khormaksar (Aden), Nairobi (Kenya) then to the eventual destination, Ndola in Zambia. All ten jets in the deployment eventually reached Khormaksar in Aden on 29 November and all were held there awaiting orders. They were supported by three Hastings from 70 Squadron based at Nicosia. From Khormaksar, they were to fly out to Nairobi; two days later, 29 Squadron were still in Aden waiting for orders to proceed.

By 9.30 a.m., they were off, getting airborne in pairs, all had arrived by midday and were in position to fly off again. Meanwhile, the political situation over Rhodesia continued to unfold. Finally, on 3 December, orders were received to proceed to Ndola in Zambia where, on arrival, they were met by Mr Bottomley, the Commonwealth relations secretary, a sizeable gathering of press reporters, and all the attendant people and paraphernalia. Nothing much transpired until 9 December, when four Javelins were flown down to Lusaka to set up a defensive readiness state (QRA). Given the propensity toward public display flying at the time, when President Kaunda visited Lusaka on 17 December, two Javelins were launched to demonstrate a practice intercept, which the President watched on a radar screen provided courtesy of No. 1 ACC (Air Control Centre), which deployed from RAF Wattisham. After the intercept, the two Flat Irons returned to fly an impromptu display over the airport. The crews were Flight Lieutenants, P. F. C. A. Thorn, M. D. Steel-Morgan, P. Frewer, and Flight Sergeant M. S. F. Staples. Otherwise, flying was severely restricted for the rest of the month owing to the shortage of fuel available in Zambia. On arrival at Ndola, there was no technical accommodation. Within four days, tents were erected for servicing control and first line servicing with two telephone lines installed.

Initially, all squadron personnel were billeted at the Lusaka college of Further Education, which was described as good if crowded. This was only temporary, however, as they moved to the showground in January 1966. Initially, the number of crews in Zambia was maintained at the maximum possible in case they were called upon to move to provide twenty-four-hour readiness. This was not a 'sit back and wait tour'. Due to a lack of available admin officers, the squadron aircrew took on one or more secondary duties until a secretarial officer could be despatched. A criticism in the post deployment report was that ordinarily, a small admin unit would be expected to deploy if anything ahead of the squadron aircraft, thus allowing the aircrew to concentrate on preparing for going on an operational state. The first rotation of aircrew came on 21 February, allowing for ten Javelins and twelve aircrews remaining in Zambia.

By May 1966, the squadron were still in Zambia and being surrounded by rumours, one quite astonishing one by a local lady who claimed airmen were being regularly attacked and beaten up by local gangs while on detachment to Lusaka. This was roundly refuted by Air Commodore E. James, the British Commander in Zambia.

No. 29 Squadron Javelins were dispatched to Iran in October 1964. They are photographed by Barry Mayner during a pit stop at Diyarbakir airbase in Turkey. The Squadron markings, the triple 'x', are removed for political reasons. Note the Turkish F-84s and accompanying Hasting in the background. (*Barry G. Mayner*)

No. 29 Squadron Flat Irons parked up at Shiraz airbase in Iran before their display in the National Air Day on 14 October 1964. (*Barry G. Mayner*)

Javelin FAW.9, XH891 'R', of 29 Squadron at Akrotiri, ready for a long trip somewhere or having just arrived from one. (*Ian White*)

However, the squadron's lack of challenge meant that there were calls, not least from the Defence Secretary himself, for 29 Squadron to return to Akrotiri, but this was politically sensitive even though the RAF had to deny to locals that their presence was in any way to do with defending Ian Smith and Rhodesia. President Kaunda himself had felt it possible for the Javelins to be withdrawn but had been persuaded by the British Government that withdrawal at such an early stage could be seen as a sign of weakness by the Rhodesian Government. The Javelins had been deployed in the first instance to meet the request for British assistance from President Kaunda and partly in order to pre-empt any request for military assistance by the Zambian Government to other foreign nations, which may prove quite disagreeable. In fact, the Westminster Government wanted the Javelins out as soon as possible, but were deeply concerned about how this would appear politically. The last thing they wanted was to be seen as weak or to precipitate the very response from Smith that 29 Squadron at least symbolically guarded against. If it came to it, the Rhodesian Air Force would be out matched by the Javelins, hence their presence was enough, should there have been any designs on Zambia in the first place.

In April, Judith Hart MP was appointed Commonwealth Affairs Minister. One of her first tasks was to seek President Kaunda's full agreement to the withdrawal of the Javelins and associated equipment, the concern being that he might attach unacceptable conditions. The truth was that Prime Minister Harold Wilson had chosen now to negotiate with the UDI leader in Rhodesia, Ian Smith. There was also the suggestion that Wilson risked a mutiny as many British commanders felt more

Not what God intended the Flat Iron for, nor the Air Ministry or RAF, but here is one from 29 Squadron carrying out low-level strafing runs off over the Mediterranean c. 1965. (*Barry G. Mayner*)

than just awkward about attacking the Rhodesian Forces; many of their commanders were personally known to the senior British officers and were possibly inclined to be more sympathetic to Smith's position than to that of their own Government, which had initially reacted swiftly to President Kaunda's requested for military assistance from the UK for fear of possible Rhodesian aggression.

Hart flew out to Lusaka in July 1966 to negotiate with President Kaunda for the withdrawal at the earliest opportunity. This was not a happy deployment as 29 Squadron reported two cases of undercarriage failure, which were possibly attributable to the standard of the Zambian airfields they were operating from; the shortness of the runways, difficult taxiways, high temperature, and high altitude were problematic. This made it all the more desirable to get out of Zambia. In order to make this possible, Judith Hart's main objective was to convince Kaunda of the need to intensify negotiations with Smith.

While negotiations proceeded, an embarrassing incident unfolded, the results of which were innocuous enough but raised a complaint from the Zambians over the effectiveness of the RAF's air defence screen. On 15 August, a Royal Rhodesian Air Force helicopter inadvertently landed in Zambia as a result of a navigation error in the dark. The chopper was on a mercy flight for a sick patient and landed 15 miles inside Zambian territory, somewhere in the region of Victoria Falls. The pilot evidently got out to speak to someone to ascertain his whereabouts and when realising his error, got back in the helicopter, took off, and landed this time in Rhodesia at Victoria Falls. The RRAF CAS, Air Vice-Marshal Hawkins, asked that his sincerest apologies be communicated to the proper authorities. The initial reaction by the Zambian Permanent Secretary of Defence was to call for a report on the RAF's failure to intercept the RRAF helicopter. The detachment commander, when communicating the outcome to ACAS Ops back in London, stated:

> He has had the facts of life explained to him, Impossibility of radar pick up at low level at two hundred miles range and unsuitability of Lusaka for night operations by Javelins. No reaction from press as yet, have discussed with Commander ZAF and we are both of the opinion that it is difficult to believe that crew could have failed to see the Zambesi, even in the dark.

In return, there would be increased British assistance in other areas, such as renewed civil airlifts designed to mitigate the impact of British sanctions against Rhodesia.

An agreement with President Kaunda to withdraw 29 Squadron came on 20 August 1966; the agreement with the Zambians came following the offer of a separate aid programme. The amount of RAF effort from other commands to withdraw the deployed force was planned to include: ten Britannias and thirty crews (Transport Command), eight Argosies (Transport Command), three Hastings (NEAF), six Argosies (AFME), and four Beverlies (AFME). No. 29 Squadron flew out to stage back to Cyprus on 31 August and 1 September.

Problems with the Sapphire engine were not unknown and when the aircraft had been in hotter climates for but a short time, problems began to materialise. In

No. 29 Squadron Javelin, XH890, low level over the Mediterranean shadowing a naval vessel. (*Barry G. Mayner*)

No. 29 Squadron Javelins at RAF Luqa, Malta, with Vulcan B2s in the background. The furthest example is painted in its anti-flash white dating the photo to 1964. (*Barry G. Mayner*)

1964, compressor blade failures were becoming a quite regular occurrence. This was especially prevalent within the squadrons based in Cyprus and Tengah. There had been twelve failures reported from Tengah in Malaya. The aircraft in Cyprus had suffered failures in the blade root whereas the jets in the Far East experienced problems with the blade form. The remedy was a simple one and applied to both problems: the blades of the first stage compressors were twisted a further five degrees; this reduced stress on both the blade form and root. That said, it was expected to take at least another three months before the first modified engines would reach the squadrons. With an expected output of twenty modified engines per month, the first prioritised to receive the new engines unsurprisingly were 29 and 60 Squadrons, respectively based at Akrotiri and Tengah. Yet at this rate, they would not be fully modified until around March or April 1965, with the rest of the Javelin force (now very much run down) being re-fitted during the period July to September. This followed hot on the heels of the centre line closure problem.

In June 1961, 60 Squadron's colours were returned to the UK for repair and cleaning. The following month, they received their first Javelin FAW.9, remaining operational with the Meteor NF.XIV. The CO, Wing Commander P. Smith, together with Flight Lieutenant J. W. Betts took up XH841 for an acceptance air test with Squadron Leader I. S. MacPherson and Flight Lieutenant B. S. Clifford in XH717 and Flight Lieutenants E. N. Gosling and B. G. Unsted in XH757.

Conversion exercises locally began from 28 July and AOC 224 Group led the welcoming party, bringing in a further five Javelins. Wg Cdr Smith noted that 'this must be about the first time that a Far East Squadron has received aircraft which are as good as those issued to UK Squadrons, and which are not somebody else's cast offs. Morale rose almost visibly.' One of their first problems was finding somewhere on the Javelin to paint the Squadron markings; the sides of the aircraft were too small so the fin had to do to carry everything. Between the tricolour flash and the tailplane, they painted the broad horizontal black bar and the superimposed horizontal silver stripes with the Markhor's head below.

One thing the Javelin afforded was a genuine leap in ceiling performance. Smith remarked about how interesting it was to see Singapore now from 45,000 feet. The unit's Meteors continued to fly alongside the Javelins until the final Meteor sortie on 31 August 1961. There was tragedy afoot: two of six Javelins were lost *en route* to Singapore. One blew up on the ground at Malta while being started. The other crashed in the jungles of Pakistan near the mouth of the Ganges river. The pilot, Flt Lt Owens, was killed; however, his navigator, Master Navigator Melton, was found alive after three days.

Since 20 January 1963, alongside the emergency in Aden came tension between the yet to be formally recognised state of Malaysia (Federation of Malaya, Singapore, Northern Borneo, and Sarawak) and Indonesia, with the latter objecting to the creation of the former, which the Indonesian President, Sukarno, regarded as an attempt to resume British Imperialist rule. Much of the involvement of the RAF revolved around the Javelins and their contribution to protecting the borders against what air threat Indonesia's Air Force, the AURI, had at their disposal. The Javelins

No. 29 Squadron FAW.9s during return to Akrotiri via Malta following the Zambia emergency in 1966. (*Barry G. Mayner*)

therefore spent the next three years maintaining aircraft on 'state' continuously. Due to the geographic lay out, the territory for the Flat Irons to defend was wide and fractured and contested along its entire length. To the west, the peninsula was threatened by the island of Sumatra, then across the sea, the territories of Sarawak and British Borneo were contested by: north, west, east, central, and south Kalimantan. No. 60 Squadron despatched 'B' Flight to Labuan airfield in North Borneo in 1964 to cover this area. QRA and border patrols were routine and soaked up the bulk of flying activity. As with fighters at Leuchars in Scotland, the Javelins at Tengah found themselves scrambling a number of times and shadowing AURI (Indonesian) Tu-16s along the 'fence', as it was known.

On 20 November 1963, while 64 Squadron were on their way to an exercise over India with their air force, four of their jets were instead diverted to RAAF Butterworth where they were later joined by four more Javelins deployed from the UK on 30 January 1964. This then formed 'C' Flight of 60 Squadron as part of the squadron's expansion. At the time, this made 60 Squadron the largest fighter squadron in the RAF with a UE of twenty-four Javelins. Through the month of January, 60 Squadron maintained what was termed the 'Tramp' commitment, which required a readiness state of seven minutes during the day and fifteen minutes at night at Tengah while a fifteen-minute night time QRA was maintained at Butterworth. Although the Badger was the bomber that the FEAF were most concerned about during the confrontation era, the Indonesian Air Force were far more likely to attack with B-25 Mitchells and P-51 Mustangs. This posed a problem for what were, after all, modern, guided, missile-armed fighters. It was thought that the Firestreak missile might not work against Second World War-era aircraft as well as against modern jets given that piston engines give off far less heat than jet engines. However, trials with the Firestreak against piston-engined aircraft showed promise and further trials against American Hercules aircraft powered by turbo-props proved that the Firestreak was effective against piston and turbo-prop engines, providing attacks were adjusted to target speeds of 200 knots.

In February 1964, fighter engagement rules for the Javelins at the Tengah bases were amended, giving Javelin crew captains the authority to engage and destroy Indonesian aircraft overflying the ADIZ (Air Defence Identification Zone) if they were engaged in supply-dropping, propaganda, or other purposes without prior authority being obtained after a sighting. Mobile radar was put in position at Labuan and the Hunters of 20 Squadron, which meant a fifteen-minute alert during daylight hours while also providing three border patrols a day. The Javelins detached to Kuching in Sarawak worked without the benefit of radar control and flew intensive border patrols, reaching eight sorties per day.

At the time, any requirement for offensive support and tactical bombing, should it have come to it, would have fallen to the Hunters of 20 Squadron and the Canberras of 45 Squadron, also based at Tengah. The Javelins in the meantime were being relied upon as a good visible deterrent and 60 Squadron's crews were kept sufficiently busy to warrant detachments from the UK from 1964. On 24 April, 23 Squadron Javelins flew out from Leuchars. With in-flight refuelling, they transited via El Adem, Aden, Gan, and Butterworth in order to reinforce 60 Squadron. Air Defence exercises continued just the same with 60 Squadron taking part in a high-level adex against Bomber Command Victors and also playing host to four F-100s of the 612th TFS from the USAF Tactical Air Command. Next came Exercise 'High up' on 16 April during which five Tengah Javelins claimed seventeen kills in eight sorties against Royal Navy Sea Vixens and Buccaneers and locally based Canberras. Flying hours for the Far East Flat Irons were quite high, in April 1964: 500 hours and forty minutes with just fifty-seven in the simulator.

In May 1964, for the first time since North Borneo operations started, an aircraft was fired upon being hit by small arms fire from Indonesian Ground Forces. On 31 May, while on a routine patrol, Fg Officers D. W. Barden and G. M. Warden were on a routine patrol along the border when they felt a thump. They continued the sortie and on return to base, a bullet hole about .303 inches in size was found under the port engine nacelle. The bullet was believed to have passed into the intake about level with the AI in the nose and exited through the nacelle about 8 inches from the cockpit. Another hole was noticed 3 inches away but could not be determined as a second bullet or another hole made by the first bullet. At the time of the strike, the aircraft was flying at 310 knots and 300 feet above ground level.

By September, reinforcements were needed again. No. 64 Squadron, based at Binbrook, were ordered to cancel an armament practice camp to RAF Valley in order to send eight of their Javelins to Tengah. To support this, four Britannia Transport Aircraft were organised to fly out all ground crew and those aircrew not required to fly the Javelins to Tengah.

By February 1965, 60 Squadron maintained operations in Borneo at Kuching and Labuan and had established a standard format, of four crews and three aircraft, at each airfield. No. 64 Squadron, which had provided periodic reinforcements earlier, were about to become permanently assigned. The selection of 64 Squadron for this role perhaps was not the wisest choice. The squadron did not have many Javelins left, having been ordered to send six of 'B' Flight's eight jets to the NEAF to join 60 Squadron.

On 1 April 1965, 64 Squadron arrived to share the responsibility of providing 'fence' patrols and QRA at Tengah and the various outer lying posts on Borneo and at the Royal Australian Air Force Base at Butterworth, now on a more permanent footing. Following the run down at Binbrook of 'B' Flight, replacements were quickly scratched together from personnel drawn from the UK, Germany, and the Far East and now amounted to 155 airmen and twenty-six officers, initially drawing aircraft from the recently expanded 60 Squadron. Such a reconstitution of the unit meant many of the new aircrew had been drawn from units that were not equipped with Javelins and therefore had not flown it. Others had not flown for months. Very few had experience of low-level work. It was the same with the ground crews; many had never worked on Javelins before.

The task before the new 64 Squadron was to be divided into two: the defence of Singapore and the Malaysian mainland against both high and low-level air attack, which they shared with 60 Squadron and the Borneo commitment. The latter were the British Territories of Borneo, essentially the northern half of the island and known today as Eastern Malaysia. These were also to be guarded against air attack and any patrol and escort duties that would be required in that area. Of the two bases which the Javelins deployed to Kuching (Sarawak) and Labuan (Sabah), the latter airfield was on a small island just off the coast of Sabah in the north-east of Borneo, but all fell within the declared Malaysian sovereignty.

Despite the problems with the hastily accrued squadron, they took on their commitments in full by June 1965. Naturally, this and QRA commitments left little scope for training though training sorties had to be fitted in. Through the previous month, many training sorties were lost due to technical problems, mainly with hydraulic, radio, and radar faults. Total hours managed were 210 hours and thirty-five minutes. Despite the problems, all crews got a turn at practising low-level intercepts and cross-country. By July, 64 Squadron were settled in; however, training schedules were restrictive. The training programme had been drastically altered to comply with FEAF interim Javelin SFI/65 instructions, which limited all training sorties to a base height of 10,000 feet. As a result, no worthwhile low-level training was flown, which was considered essential. Further problems were encountered regarding the squadron detachments to Kuching and Labuan. Hastings transport aircraft would ordinarily have ferried everyone back and forth for rotation of personnel to allow for leave, but these were grounded for a period.

May 1966 brought another round of peace talks concerning the Malay/Indonesian confrontation. Singapore television went so far as to declare an end to the confrontation. However, 60 and 64 Squadrons remained on 'state'. Otherwise,

The approach to Labuan airfield in north-east Borneo, Malaysia. This airfield was used by detachments from both 60 and 64 Squadrons Javelins through much of the 'confrontation' to defend British interests on the island. (*Barry G. Mayner*)

Javelin of 'B' Flight, 60 Squadron, on dispersal at Labuan in 1965. (*Barry G. Mayner*)

training continued as normal with Vulcans posing as high-level targets, 'their height and speed proving an invigorating challenge' as the entry in the ORB said. Yet the CO of the Vulcan Detachment was 'suitably chastened' to be shown film of his big deltas being intercepted by the small ones at 48,500 feet, however rare the instance.

On 9 July 1966, due to two recent cases of control jamming on the elevator, all Javelins were restricted to flying above 3,000 feet except for operational purposes. Both incidents revealed a defect with the Hobson unit in the tail. These were believed to be isolated incidents just the same but in order to be sure, further investigation was called for. In order to determine whether any of 60 Squadron's aircraft were affected ahead of modification A343, all were grounded on 12 and 13 July for inspection of the Hobson units. All bar two aircraft—XH779 and the Sqn T3—were found to be clear. The modification was applied to both and each were cleared to fly again by 28 July. The T3 had been grounded for three weeks before due to a litany of serviceability problems, including an engine flame out on the 8th. On 3 February 1967, Sqn Ldr N. D. Cameron led four Javelins at 1,000 feet, from 60 Squadron, over Tengah at night and in reheat in order to present a farewell gesture to the departing AOC 224 Group. Air Vice-Marshal C. N. Foxley-Norris was attending a farewell party thrown by the Squadron. This was regarded as another first for 60 Squadron. They flew a second formation, a diamond nine on 14 February, this time to welcome the new C-in-C Far

Labuan airfield during a quiet moment—ground crew with Javelin of 60 Squadron and 205 Squadron Shackleton MR2. (*Barry G. Mayner*)

East General Sir Michael Carver KCB CBE DSO MC. Although hampered by low cloud, Wg Cdr N. H. Miller positioned the formation at the correct time overhead. This was a month of flypasts. Next, on the 23rd, four aircraft led by Sqn Ldr Cameron again were returning from Butterworth, where regular detachments of aircraft and personnel from the Javelin Squadrons were maintained during the *Konfrontasi*, and were bounced by five more Javelins from Tengah, which then converted into another diamond nine formation.

No. 64 Squadron aircrew appear to have just dismounted or even posing for a candid publicity shot at their home base Binbrook c. 1964. At the time, they were making regular reinforcement detachments to Tengah to back-up 60 Squadron during the 'confrontation'. I say a staged shot as they appear to have walked passed a line of aircraft with closed canopies and no ground crew activity around them. (*RAF Museum Hendon*)

No. 64 Squadron FAW.9s about the time they were based at Tengah, near Singapore, Malaysia. (*Barry G. Mayner*)

The air defence of Singapore was backed-up during the confrontation by the Bloodhound missiles of 65 Squadron, seen here on their specially-constructed launch pans at RAF Seletar in July 1964. (*The National Archives*)

8
Staying On

No sooner had the Javelin OCU disbanded in 1961 than the Air Staff were facing growing concerns about the planned phasing out of operational Javelins from Germany by the end of 1961, with other units disbanding shortly thereafter. Now, the units in Germany were to be retained until the end of 1962. Other delays were expected largely due to the not as yet arrived English Electric Lightning F3. This then created an open-ended problem to maintain the already depleted fighter numbers, even though many Hunter and earlier Javelin units had already or were on the point of disbanding. The immediate situation did not demand an instant resumption of Javelin crew training—there were sufficient available—however, there was little faith in the Flat Iron not having its operational service extended again. In January 1962, the last operational Javelin squadron was expected to disband at the end of June 1963 at the latest. By March 1962, the Defence Committee's planned global fighter force pattern had changed. Now, the two Javelin squadrons in Germany, so recently expanded by an addition of eight aircraft, were to be retained until the end of 1963. If that was the case, there would be no need to resume the Javelin OCU; however, there would be a need to train and provide refresher training for station, squadron, and flight commanders, as well as nav/rad leaders, and also keep those younger pilots who may be selected for the Lightning current. The biggest concern at that time was slippage in the delivery of the Mk 2 and Mk 3 Lightnings. On top of this, it was proposed that an additional twelve Javelin crews should be trained up to plug any gaps. The Air Ministry were able to provide about eighteen pilots; ten of these were to be ex-first tour QFIs, suitable to go on to the Lightning in due course. The remaining eight, while considered suitable for Javelin operations, were deemed to be unsuitable for converting to the Lightning, but it was thought they could take the place of a comparable number of younger Javelin pilots, who could go to the Lightning much earlier than would otherwise be possible. All together with the returning flight commanders, this would amount to thirty additional pilots and a small number of navigators, which would not pose too much of a problem. To do this, they planned retention of eight Javelin FAW.5s and two T3s together with two Canberra T11s from the Target Facilities Squadron, which would suffice to provide training.

By 1964, operations in the Mediterranean, Middle East, and Far East convinced the Government to review the rundown of the Javelin force. This was Britain in its

Javelin T3 of 228 OCU struts its stuff over RAF Finningley during Battle of Britain Day on 18 September 1965. (*John Wharam*)

Above left: While further north, the unit's display team strut over the homestead at Leuchars. (*R. A. Stitchell*)

Above right: The OCU team make another pass over the Leuchars crowd on 18 September 1965. (*R. A. Stitchell*)

final throes of empire. The new Government headed by Harold Wilson, while not opposed to meeting the demands of maintaining the nation's Defences, did perhaps enter office with a reordered sense of priority, which placed the needs of social security, state health, and education before national security. The official line has always been 'Defence of the Realm first'; however, the rationale of most governments sympathises with the need to have something worth protecting before they go about protecting it. Shortly after entering office, the Wilson Government was determined to identify exactly what was needed and what could be dispensed with. Adding to the debate was the determination to wrap up and dispense with all the remaining British controlled states and provinces east of the Suez Canal, thereby releasing those military assets and personnel, which otherwise could be redeployed in the north-west European and North Atlantic theatres, for instance, where the continued threat of Soviet military-backed hegemony was about the only identifiable threat requiring a substantive military posture.

More likely, much of what was to be brought back could justifiably be labelled surplus to requirements. Even so, the withdrawal from certain areas was not always possible in any kind of seemly fashion and was taking longer and transitioning less than smoothly resulting in the need to retain a degree of military posture which the government had expected to have eased sufficiently to allow the withdrawal of substantial military forces. The retention of some overseas Javelin squadrons in addition to the smaller number of Lightnings envisaged was accepted as the path of least resistance in order to provide the right balance of air cover for operations against guerrilla forces.

The last operational Javelin squadrons assigned to defend United Kingdom airspace directly were 23 and 64 Squadrons. The former began re-equipping with Lightnings and remained at Leuchars, while 64 Squadron transferred, along with many of 23 Squadron's former Javelins, to Tengah in Malaya. Even with the number of Lightnings entering service not being expected to stretch quite to the original plan of twelve squadrons, delays to the delivery of the Mk 3 Lightning, raised political concerns. A knock-on effect from this was an unexpected, indeed, unpredicted shortfall in suitable pilots to convert onto Lightnings. This was caused by pilots on the Javelin now being retained operationally in sufficient numbers beyond the time expected. Many of these, it was hoped, would be eligible to convert onto the later Lightnings. However, because of the entry into service delays, it was now feared that many Javelin pilots would have become unsuitable due to either age or due to insufficient time left to serve to be of any use. This was understood as early as 1962 after the OCU had disbanded. Now that Sandys' missiles were not going to prove to be quite the panacea and that the RAF were not going to receive as many as twelve squadrons of Lightnings and that deployment of Lightnings overseas was still some way off, the Javelin was to be retained overseas.

Originally, the pattern planned for just nine Javelin squadrons remaining in Fighter Command as of 1961 was down to seven in 1962, five-and-a-half in 1963, two in 1964, and none by 1965, by which time eight Lightning squadrons would alone fulfil the Fighter Command task of defending essentially the V-bomber bases, a marginally

Above: Two No. 29 Squadron jets over Malta on 22 September 1964. (*Barry G. Mayner*)

Below: No. 29 Squadron officer and NCOs of 29 Squadron on C Dispersal at Akrotiri enjoy a liquid lunch or happy hour *c.* 1965 at Akrotiri. (*Barry G. Mayner*)

optimistic figure. As far as overseas theatres were concerned, the Javelin was to be gone by 1962 from Germany but a single squadron would be deployed in the Far East until 1964; most curiously of all, there would be no air defence fighter for the RAF commitment in Germany, this may have been based on the expectation of the Luftwaffe resuming this commitment, which did not happen almost certainly for reasons of political sensitivity.

The long-term rundown of Fighter Command even following the implementation of the Sandys review policy was still quite severe; a fighter force of 228—Hunters, Javelins, and Lightnings as of March 1961—was to become settled at ninety-six Lightnings by March 1965 for very much the rest of the decade. The all-important missile force was already planned to reduce significantly after reaching a peak of twelve squadrons by June 1961, with an allocation of 352 missiles, to three squadrons of ninety-six missiles by March 1966. Even this rapid long-term planned contraction proved to be an optimistic forecast for those who imagined that Duncan Sandys meant what he said about missiles being the future.

It was also acknowledged, by the Air Staff, that the Javelin's own appointed direct replacement, the English Electric Lightning, had certain pronounced weaknesses. There were intentions to improve upon the shortcomings still because, like the Javelin, it had to be replaced and in a foreseeable period of time. The Lightning would still serve alongside the Javelin, exploiting its greater assets, heavier armament, and greater range, while the Lightning's scintillating speed in the climb and greater ceiling performance, not to mention overall supersonic capability, remained a draw. By 1966, the Lightning's own expected successor was, despite various offers of new designs, for the sake of economy, with the balance of good performance, more likely to be the McDonnell Douglas F-4M Phantom—as close as anything to a combination of the best of both. In order to make keeping the Lightning on a more viable prospect, various options were considered, including angle of attack indicators to be fitted to all remaining Lightnings at an estimated cost of £180,000–£190,000. Further, at a cost of £190,000, fitting a cold air unit to sixty-one Mk 6 Lightnings in order to improve low-level performance was considered. The expectation was that two squadrons with Mk 6 Lightnings would remain in the Far East until at least 1972–1973, one of which would almost certainly have been 60 Squadron.

This was not to be with the Government's proposed end to any interests east of Suez, which meant the disbandment of 64 Squadron followed by 60 Squadron on 30 April 1968, then the one deployed Lightning unit—74 Squadron—going in August 1971. There were, by 1966, Bloodhound Mk 2 missiles deployed in the UK and Far East, but in a complete reverse of the predictions of Mr Duncan Sandys, the RAF did not regard the Bloodhounds as anything other than complimentary to the fighters. The Javelins in the Far East had, since deploying out there, spent a great deal of time on low-level border patrols. The Mk 6 Lightning was seen as ideally suited to move into the Far East, but with its short-legs, the Lightning was described as a very poor performer, with regards to low-level interceptions or any kind of low-level operation due to its lack of a 'look down' radar and guns, the Mk 6 had guns but in place of the forward third of its ventral fuel pack. The mark 2/2A carried guns in the nose, but the Lightning was seen as unsuited. The gun armament, the only armament which it could bring to bear at low altitude was regarded as secondary. As such once the Phantom entered service, the Lightning's future was also open to question. However, the demands on the Phantom Force would be heavy before encroaching on the Lightning world, with ground attack, reconnaissance and air defence responsibilities with the latter as a tertiary consideration. Therefore, approval was given for certain modifications including; cockpit cooling system, guns in the forward fuel pack for the Mark 6 Lightnings and new angle of attack indicators to all operational Lightnings in order to maintain a credible air defence force into the 1970s.

Re-opening an operational conversion unit for an aircraft type supposedly on the run down is quite unprecedented. The usual form in recent times has been to abbreviate an OCU by reducing it to a single enlarged flight of aircraft or embedding it in an operational squadron, if ever a decision is taken that no form of *ab initio* or refresher training is called for its usually heralded retirement for the aircraft in question. This was indeed an unusual case. To minimise cost, a number of options were considered; one was the possibility of turning an existing squadron into the training unit as the majority of Javelin squadrons at the time were still UK-based. Another option was to reduce the size of the remaining squadrons, thus negating the need for any Javelin training, except on a very small scale. However, the Germany-based squadrons, at least, had only recently been increased to a unit establishment of sixteen, an OCU composed of the following would be required: ten Canberras and fifteen Javelins. This was carefully calculated and it was also considered that by simply reducing the two Germany squadrons back to their original UE of twelve aircraft, then an OCU of just six Canberras and ten Javelins would suffice.

Also looked at was the idea of disbanding the Germany units altogether, necessitating a training flight of just seven Javelins for what was left. It was expected that this would also eliminate the need to train more navigators. A similar situation has been arrived at in more recent times following the SDSR, which has seen the end of navigator training for the Tornado GR4, the last aircraft in RAF service that used navigators. Another solution was to reduce the established aircrew to aircraft ratio from 1.25:1 to 1:1. This it was reasoned would mean only training requirements for flight and squadron commanders. However, Fighter Command were strongly opposed to this as it would weaken the effectiveness of the squadrons, which would be reduced, and it would be difficult to reinforce an overseas deployment without seriously denuding the remaining squadrons. There being just the one mark now operational, the comparable, perhaps some would argue superior, Mk 8 with its American radar, had been removed completely in line with the RAF's move toward a largely missile air defence system with 41 and 85 Squadrons having retired their Mk 8s, then gone through a re-tread: 41 Squadron as a Bloodhound SAM squadron and 85 Squadron in the target facilities role with a mix of Meteors and Canberras. The reformed OCU was just about ready to receive its first students when two of the five remaining overseas squadrons disbanded. Nos 5 and 11 Squadron at Geilenkirchen were both gone by the start of 1966; 29 Squadron at Akrotiri would go in 1967 with 64 Squadron at Tengah leaving 60 Squadron disbanding in April 1968. It all seems hardly worth the

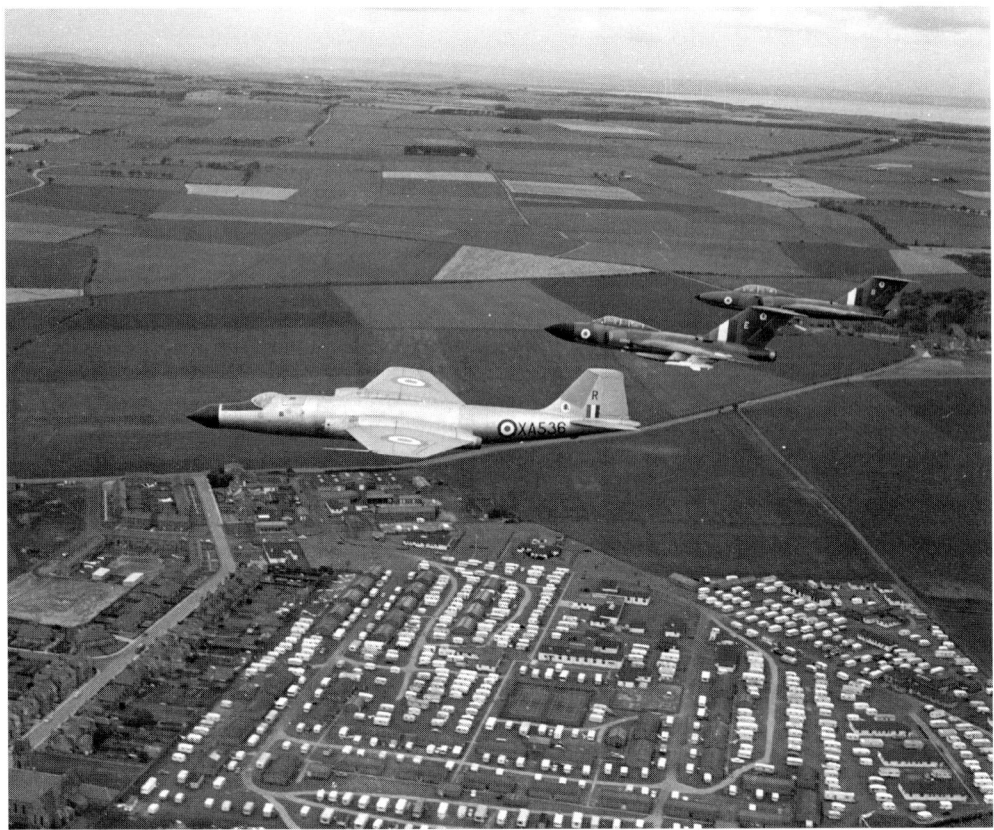

No. 228 OCU aircraft operated at Leuchars from 1965–1966. From nearest camera: Canberra T11, Javelin FAW.9, and Javelin T3. The small white disc on each fin contains the two eagle crests of 11 Squadron, which following disbandment had been assigned as the shadow number plate. (*Crown Copyright*)

resumption of a fully functioning OCU but they kept busy enough including lending their operational effectiveness to the Leuchars Fighter Wing during exercises as 11 Squadron, the shadow identity assumed from early 1966.

Arguments favouring the resumption of the Javelin OCU dated as far back as late 1961–early 1962. Back in August 1961, the Prime Minister, Harold McMillan, after he had authorised the dispatch of eight additional Javelins to the last two squadrons in Germany. Not long after, there were calls to reintroduce the OCU due to what now looked increasingly like the need to retain the Javelin longer than the post Sandys forecast. The developing political situation, in particular the tension over the Berlin Corridor, was not promising to disappear shortly, yet it was situations like this that were both being used to justify the reintroduction of the OCU and the very reason getting in the way of this happening. With the pro-OCU lobby wanting the Germany squadrons reduced to a UE of twelve apiece again in order to use the returned aircraft to form the new training unit; meanwhile, the very tension over the Berlin Corridor precluded this idea from being entertained. A further option envisaged a run on of the

Javelin to a single squadron in Fighter Command by June 1965. All this depended on a far more stable and agreeable political environment overseas and further reliance on a greater number of Lightnings.

The preference of Fighter Command was to use an existing squadron, all of which were eligible, except 85 Squadron, which had Mk 8s and therefore Mk 22 AI (APQ-43) radars; everyone else had Mk 17s. This meant 85 Squadron, due for disbandment at the end of the year, could not be retained as the resumed OCU. More so, having dismissed the idea of a small training unit simply to provide refresher training for flight and squadron commander replacements, the RAF would need to restart training of first tour Javelin pilots. The focus was already falling on West Raynham, current home of 85 Squadron. In anticipation, Canberras being returned from 75 Squadron RNZAF were diverted there. It would take six months to get a first tourist through *ab initio* training for the Javelin so a decision was needed urgently, but in anticipation, Fighter Command proceeded at least as far as preparations short of works services and moving personnel was concerned. The OCU received approval and began to form not at West Raynham, which instead took in two Hunter squadrons that had been reassigned to Transport Command to provide an embedded tactical offensive support wing, but instead was to reform at Leuchars and began working up there in May 1965. The run-down plan for the Javelin expected to see seven squadrons in the UK by March 1962, one squadron in the Far East with none in Germany. As things stood, there were not any in the Mediterranean, not even under the revised plan that now envisaged retaining two squadrons in Germany.

The early plan forecast expected that a single Javelin squadron would be operational by March 1965 and that it would be in the Far East. The rethink looked to have three units in Fighter Command in addition. By March 1965, two squadrons (5 and 11) would still be in Germany; a single squadron (29) in Cyprus; and two squadrons (60 and 64) in the Far East at Tengah in Malaya, or Malaysia as it had been officially declared on 16 September 1963, which included Singapore (location of RAF Tengah).

Herein lay the chief concern: President Sukarno, a Communist sympathiser, anti-imperialist, and ruler of Indonesia considered the new Malaysian state to be a British conspiracy and therefore a threat. This in turn resulted in an era of skirmishes (described as an undeclared war) and a defined air threat, which kept the Javelins of 60 and, from 1965, 64 Squadrons busy. The Lightning would have re-equipped five Hunters and a single Javelin unit in the UK by the end of that year. The time it took to get the resumed OCU at Leuchars to the point of production again took about as long as the unit lasted once back up and running. It probably filled any gaps that threatened to appear among the remaining operational units abroad, but on reflection, it seems to have been an expensive way of keeping the Javelins going when it may have been to a much more economic advantage had the inevitable full deployment of Lightnings taken place sooner.

Nevertheless, new crews were churned out from midway through 1965 to the end of 1966 when the OCU, following its short rebirth, was disbanded again. During this time, three of the remaining squadrons disbanded. Nos 5 and 11 Squadrons at Geilenkirchen both folded by February 1966, the former to re-equip with the new

Mk 6 Lightning while the latter became the shadow number plate of the OCU until such time as it disbanded, leaving 11 Squadron to form on Lightnings in 1967.

The new OCU, back as 228 again, officially reformed on 1 May 1965 at RAF Leuchars with Flt Lt Geoffrey Roberts as acting CO. No. 228 OCU also incorporated the JIRF (Javelin Instrument Rating Flight), Javelin Simulator and Emergencies Section, and the RAF Leuchars Station Flight. This gave the unit an inventory of seven aircraft at the time, including four Javelin T3s, two Hunter T7As, and a single Meteor T.7, the latter being used as the unit 'hack'. The two Hunters, representing the station flight, were in fact the property of the two resident operational squadrons: 23 and 74 Squadrons, who also provided the ground crew and therefore were not part of 228 OCU. When Leuchars had its official annual formal inspection on 19 May by Air Commodore R. J. P. Pritchard CB CBE DFC AFC, 228 OCU were able to participate in the flypast with one Javelin and one Hunter. Two days later, on 21 May, Sqn Ldr George Beaton AFC took over command of the unit. On 26 May, three crews, including one master navigator, flew out to Geilenkirchen and returned to RAF Binbrook with three Mk 9 Javelins, where they underwent a modification programme prior to reallocation to the OCU. With emphasis on lectures and *précis* work began on getting ready for the first basic course due to begin on 5 July but the unit was now prepared for what Sqn Ldr Beaton described as 'the onslaught' while work to prepare some buildings in time continued.

On 3 June, HRH Princess Margaret visited Leuchars to present a new standard to 74 Squadron, who (together with their chums on 23 Squadron) put together something of scintillating air display. The new OCU were able to contribute in some form by providing two Javelin T3s for the flypast and a recently arrived Canberra and another T3 for the static display. After ferrying three to Binbrook in May, the first Mk 9 Javelin, XH912, did not arrive until 11 June, but this was just temporarily as the aircraft was required at 27 Maintenance Unit at RAF Shawbury, from whence it came. Two Javelin FAW9s—XH767 and XH716—arrived on 17 June. XH716 had a corroded crack in the starboard main spar, requiring tests by a visiting metallurgist to determine whether or not the aircraft was a write off. However, a visiting team could not reach a definite conclusion either way.

While the new unit was building up strength accruing both personnel and assets, the new CO, Sqn Ldr Beaton and two other officers, Flt Lts Horning and Roberts, headed off to Binbrook on 30 June to discuss with 85 Squadron personnel and intercept controllers from the MRS (Master Radar Station) at Buchan in Aberdeenshire, the purpose being to agree the profile of sorties flown by the new unit. No. 85 Squadron were flying Canberras and Meteors in the air defence target facilities role, much the same as the Hawks of 100 Squadron today, therefore their involvement with the OCU's Javelins would be a regular feature. This day also marked a milestone of sorts with 228 OCU providing a fully armed Javelin FAW.9 for QRA duty from 1.30 p.m. onwards; a hand-held camera was also made available. The QRA duty in this case, however, was restricted to day time alert only and was stood down again at 10 a.m. the following day, 1 July, with the first basic course starting on 5 July. This began with two weeks ground school with actual flying training beginning on 19 July; despite aircraft and flying time being at a premium in August, aircraft, time, and fuel were still found to allow practice by a four-strong display team for the forthcoming Battle of Britain 'At Home' day, even though the aircraft establishment at best extended to seven Mk 9 Javelins. One aspect affecting the Canberras of the OCU was the modifications required to fit the AI 17 equipment in the rear cockpit extended into the ejection line of the left-hand seat, meaning that long-legged navigators were out from here on in, including Flt Lt Morgan, one of the instructors.

The situation regarding accommodation provided something of a challenge, requiring that 228 OCU share the aircraft servicing platform (ASP) with the Lightnings of 23 Squadron and any visiting aircraft. Whether they would all fit remained to be seen and so someone may have to move, should it all become crowded. Monday 5 July came and the first course began with a fortnight's ground school, with the first flying training sorties planned for Monday 19 July. These started well and progressed satisfactorily; however, the few Mk 9 Javelins on strength provided constant headaches. XH912 was returned to 27 MU at RAF Shawbury for modifications while another (XH909) arrived only to be returned again as it was showing loose rivets in the fin.

This prompted a difference of expert opinion. The aircraft was seen by staff from 60 MU, based at Leconfield, who declared the aircraft to be Category 2 (limited damage), which 228 OCU's OC Eng disagreed with. Another (XH716) having been inspected by a metallurgist, was flown back to Shawbury as a Category 3, classed as a 'fly away'. This was on the 11th. A couple of days later, another FAW.9 arrived (XH883) straight from Shawbury, but because the aircraft had been given an unsatisfactory respray, it had to be returned as well two days after arriving. The one that arrived on 1 July and stayed was XH907; it required an engine change before the end of the month.

By the end of August, the unit had, after much ebb and flow, managed to accrue an establishment of five Mk 9 Javelins, three Canberra T11s, a Javelin T3 (XH397), and lost Meteor T.7 (WE816), which headed off to join 85 Squadron at Binbrook.

After the usual demands of September, the new unit was ready to start training its first intake. No. 1 course had begun and completed the first two weeks of ground school on 8 October. Flying training conversion stumbled on into November 1965. The unserviceability of the Canberras, due to long periods waiting for replacement parts, meant that course leave was being cancelled once the aircraft were available. No. 2 Course were sent to the Aviation Medicine Centre at RAF North Luffenham with twelve air exercise sorties still outstanding. They returned to Leuchars on 29 November instead of going on leave. The problems of operating military aircraft safely, especially when night training was required, was very much dependent on suitable diversion airfields. RAF and Naval air units based in Scotland have always faced challenges, certainly in post-war years, which do not arise for units based elsewhere in the UK and Germany, even in 1966, an era in which active military airfields were all the more widespread than in 2016. The availability of diversions back in November 1965 was described as 'seriously hampered' as far as Leuchars was concerned. Night flying for OCU student crews on 8 November was facing typical winter conditions.

Turnhouse, still a military airfield, was unavailable as a crash diversion, but was often closed anyway due to strong cross-winds and/or an icy runway not available. Aircraft were to return to Leuchars with enough fuel on board, at the point of overshoot, to divert to either Lossiemouth, Prestwick, Machrihanish, or indeed, further afield, RAF Valley was also used as a diversion for Leuchars. The measure of weather conditions in the RAF was summed up in overview by colour states; red being the most severe then graduating through amber, yellow, green, white, and blue, the last suggesting barbeque conditions and on occasion accompanied with the abbreviated phrase 'CAVOK', meaning cloud and visibility okay (that is if the sky was gin-clear). A further colour state, 'black', referred to the airfield being out of use for other reasons, such as runway obstruction.

For 228 OCU's Javelin students in 1965–1966, during night exercises, if Turnhouse was out, as it quite often was, then so long as Lossiemouth deteriorated to no worse than 'green', it was possible, with everything else running smoothly, to fly two exercises with the fuel available; any other problems with the weather (and it was only one, while flying on Saturday) was likely in order to catch up. For some unexplained reason, student crews appeared to hit a bad patch mid-way through night flying. This plus everyone going down with colds on the courses meant further delays in getting anyone through to successful completion of training. Ultimately, the first course passed out just before Christmas, with the students throwing a party for the staff of the OCU at St Michael's Hotel on 2 December. No. 2 course held a similar party at Pitmilly Hotel on the 8th of the month. Although the first course passed through successfully, there were (as mentioned before) a number of exercises missed; however, this did not affect matters much and were more than made up for by the number of repeated exercises flown by students.

With the first course of the resumed OCU ready for distributing to the remaining operational Javelin squadrons, the bulk of postings were originally intended for the Far East; however, as often transpires, the political climate dictated otherwise and the crews of No. 1 course 228 OCU instead had their postings changed to 29 Squadron based at Akrotiri in Cyprus just prior to Christmas. The understanding on the OCU at the time was that 29 Squadron's existing crews were on extended deployment to Zambia in response to the situation there with the Rhodesian UDI.

In February 1966, the OCU were told they would officially become the recipient of the No. 11 Squadron plate. In due course, once permission was granted, the two Eagles were painted onto the fins on white discs. This was seen as something of a morale booster for all on board. Nos 3 and 4 courses began and by June, they graduated. The observation was made that No. 3 course were 'under trained' compared with their predecessors. This was not a reflection of the calibre of the young men in question but simply the result of all things, including a lack of sufficient darkness for night training during May. That said, it was duly noted that they were unique in receiving ECM training if only in the simulator and that this made up for the lack of night flying training.

In August, as No. 5 course was beginning, the OCU received news that they were due to disband. The next course, No. 6, had been in the planning but with the breaking news about the OCU's long term future, No. 6 was cancelled before any of the students had been put together. So, the immediate future for the Javelin was becoming clear. Yet whatever the future held, 228 OCU still ran refresher courses, including a returning former station commander at Leuchars, Group Captain Harbison, who needed to get a refresher course under his belt before moving on as OC Ops at Fighter Command.

Established line-up of instructors on resumed 228 OCU at Leuchars. The aircraft in the background is a metallic-finished Javelin FAW.9. The initials are those of the CO, Squadron Ldr George Beaton, sat centre wearing leather gloves—on top row from the left; Bob Rogers, unknown, Buck Buckingham, Brian Henwood, unknown, Bill (or Tony) Hawes, unknown, Mick Crosland, and Jock Shields. Seated row from left; Roger Long, unknown, John Farrell, unknown, George Beaton (CO), Pete DuPlessi, and Flt Lt Turner (first name unknown); the last two remain unidentified. The photo is *c.* 1965. (*RAF Museum Hendon*)

By September 1966, the OCU staff now facing redundancy were informed that they were yet again surplus to requirements and that their impending disbandment loomed in the foreseeable future. They were relied upon quite heavily that month to provide the now increasingly rare Flat Iron to put in appearances on Battle of Britain 'At Home' day. Naturally, the home base got the bulk of attention, with just two of 228 OCU's Javelins being made available for static displays at Coltishall and Finningley, while Leuchars had two on static alongside one of the T11 Canberras, while a Javelin four-ship formation display team and a solo flew in less than perfect weather conditions. Altogether, this meant providing nine out eleven Mk 9 Javelins, as Sqn Ldr Beaton commented 'that's no mean feat by anyone's standards, especially as so many of the chaps were required for other duties around the station.' October brought the last course, No. 5, and what was described as a special effort was made to get them off to a good start. Flying training began on the 10th of the month and, in spite of hold ups due to weather, progressed smoothly until the last day. On 31 October, the aircraft situation was in a poor state with only two exercises achieved. This left the course seven exercises behind schedule by the start of November. The students were uneven by one pilot; this was Flt Lt Bowman, who was crewed with a staff navigator, an arrangement that would stay until an RN observer student would arrive (expected at the end of November). Bowman was already a week behind the rest of the course at the start of November as he had a week's leave at the end of October to get married. Another pilot, Plt Off Beckley, was sent to 229 OCU at RAF Chivenor to convert to the Hawker Hunter as it was now determined they had one pilot too many for the Javelin; clearly, everyone was, by this stage, expected to succeed. A considerable number of refresher training courses were also carried out in October despite the expected run down. On completion, Wg Cdr Neil was sent to 29 Squadron as their new CO.

October also saw the start of winding things down. Postings for the staff were not yet known but everyone had a good idea of their fate; initially, it was not good. They mostly hoped to move on to the F-4 Phantom, it seemed not to be, with just three navigators with any indication they were moving in that direction. It took some effort by Sqn Ldr Beaton to bring whatever influence he could to bear, but he managed to get the postings changed, resulting in everyone being reasonably happy as at least almost all were going onto flying posts.

The unit's three Canberras were delivered to Binbrook where they were to become assets of the new 85 Squadron in the air defence target facilities role. They also unintentionally lost two Javelins; one was landed on two wheels, sustaining only Category 3 (minor) damage, which was subsequently changed to Category 5 (severe). On 21 October, one of the instructors, having managed to avoid a stranger (conflicting aircraft) over Dundee, found that he had rather overstressed the airframe. This left the unit establishment at the end of the month at nine Mk 9s, four Mk 3s, and two wrecks.

A message transmitted to RAF Leuchars on 23 December 1966 carried the following passage:

> After some twelve years we have come to the end of the Javelin's life in Fighter Command. For most of this period No. 228 OCU has been responsible for the training of many hundreds of Javelin aircrews. The task has now been completed and your unit now disbands. But this does not mean that 228 OCU is lost to us forever for with the introduction of Phantoms at Coningsby in the not too distant future it will again come into being to take over the training task. On this, the last day of your unit, I send you and all personnel of 228 OCU my best wishes for the future and my appreciation for a job well done.

It was not quite over there as Squadron Leader Beaton noted in the unit records as late as January 1967:

> After a month of make do and mend, the place is rather like a morgue. Where previously the happy laughter of instructors mingled with the groans of tormented students, now a sombre silence pervades all. Even the air smells different. The foetid odour of burning rectifiers from the simulator has been replaced by a burning paper and new polish smell. The Hangar is clean and tidy; the ground equipment either returned to stores

No. 228 OCU Display team rehearsing for their final appearance in September 1966 at the then annual Battle of Britain air display at RAF Leuchars. This would also be the final appearance in public by RAF Javelins in the UK. (*Brian Henwood*)

or in neat rows, newly painted. Only the simulator awaits its fate. MOD cannot make up its corporate mind on what to do with this fascinating, expensive and completely worthless piece of equipment. No doubt I shall recognise pieces of it in Lyle Street shops in a few weeks. Only Pete du Plessis and myself await jobs; we have both been posted supernumerary to RAF Leuchars to keep the paperwork straight. We must try and find ourselves a small room with a power and water supply, where we can drink coffee and play Uckers until something turns up.

I shall leave the F540 duplicates in store at Leuchars SHQ until such time as No. 11 Squadron reform here. They might provide some continuity for the squadron history; they will certainly contain evidence of the esteem in which we all held the squadron, and the pleasure we felt at having been given the honour of continuing its life.

The postings out brought some curious and interesting destinations, nobody going to either Hunter of Lightning OCU, but one officer to Kuala Lumpur, Malaysia another to Lindholme then home of the Bomber Command Bombing School, one to Stradishall, No. 1 Air Navigation School, one to Scampton, and two heading to Binbrook, possibly following the Canberras there.

No. 29 Squadron returned to the UK to convert to Lightnings then moving to Wattisham. No. 64 Squadron disbanded, leaving 60 Squadron as the last operational Javelin squadron in the RAF. With the Government's desire to end the British military presence east of Suez, to all intents surplus to requirements, they did not have too long to wait before the inevitable.

9

The Last Days

From April 1965, the Javelin ceased to form part of the operational commitment of Fighter Command and by early 1966, the last Javelins had left Germany this left the Middle and Far East commands as the last remaining operators of the Flat Iron: 29 Squadron at Akrotiri in Cyprus with 60 and 64 Squadrons both at Tengah in Malaya. All three were relied upon from time to time to prepare for action if not actually called upon to fire shots in anger. At Tengah, they found themselves scrambling a number of times and shadowing AURI (Indonesian) Tu-16s along the 'fence', as it was known.

On 11 August 1966, Indonesia officially recognised the new state following peace talks. The confrontation had involved British, Australian, and New Zealand Forces. Now, continuous 'state' was at an end. The arrival of 1967 brought the end within site for the Flat Iron. The OCU that had reformed in 1965 to meet the unexpected demand for additional Javelin crews had now disbanded once and for all, presaging the last days for the last operational units. Over in Cyprus, 29 Squadron were replaced in August with the arrival the Lightnings of 56 Squadron from Wattisham. This left the last of the Javelins in the Far East and as relevant to the future of British Defence Policy as their location. No. 64 Squadron disbanded hot on the heels of 29 Squadron, but a return to full operational status was not around the corner for the Scarabs; they did live on as the shadow reserve identity to the then soon to be reformed 228 OCU, this time to train up the RAFs future force of F-4 Phantom crews.

The final unit, 60 Squadron, marked the finale of the Javelin, the RAF's first truly all-weather fighter, thousands of miles from home after scarcely twelve years of operational flying, which saw a total of nineteen squadrons formed (if you include the first shadow of the OCU, 137) and nine marks flown, one of which, the T3, was a pilot trainer; navigators remember focused their skills on anything else to hand from Valettas to Canberras before venturing into the rear cockpit of the real thing. No. 60 Squadron had been the last unit in the RAF to fly Meteors operationally and again out in Malaya, one of the old Meat boxes was kept on as a gate guard outside the squadron office in Tengah. With the signing of the peace agreement between Malaysia and Indonesia, 64 Squadron were looking forward to returning to normal peacetime training for the first time since they had first deployed to Tengah from Binbrook as an emergency deployment in March 1964 in direct response to the *Konfrontasi*. Rumour

No. 64 Squadron Box-4 formation low and fast over the Malaysian jungle c. 1967. (*Barry G. Mayner*)

had been rife on 11 August 1966 that 64 Squadron without the role, which took them to Malaysia in the first place, were for the chop and many braced themselves for possible redundancies, a mindset quite prevalent in the HM Forces of the era. There was some relief when they were told that for the immediate future, they would simply reduce to an establishment of twelve Javelins and sixteen crews. This was to take effect from 19 September 1966, with the few crews to be made redundant being repatriated by 1 November.

On 12 May 1967, Mr John Dahn from the Central Office of Information visited 64 Squadron at Tengah. Just before disbandment, tragedy struck. Two of 64 Squadron's ground crew were given the opportunity, as was extended from time to time, to enjoy an experience flight in the back of a Javelin, on 30 May 1967.

One aircraft, XH708, was flown by Flying Officer William Brendan Kay; at age twenty-one, he was possibly the youngest and in all likelihood, possibly the least experienced pilot on the squadron. His passenger was Corporal Kenneth Ashbee, aged twenty-three. Getting airborne the same day was XH896, flown by Flying Officer

P. McKellar; his passenger was Senior Aircraftman M. Lokanadan. The two jets were in a stream of six aircraft, taking off in pairs at twelve-second intervals. Kay and Ashbee were the No. 4 in the formation, in line ahead and below the No. 3, McKellar and Lokanadan, and just behind the lead pair. This positioning was held for a few seconds, then XH708 started to climb up and slot back momentarily. Nos 3 and 4 struck and both dived into the ground.

McKellar and Lokanadan both managed to eject safely from XH896 but Kay and Ashbee left it too late. This could suggest the No. 4 was perhaps more adversely affected in terms of control of attitude in the precious few seconds left. Altogether, eighty-five Javelins in RAF service were lost—a sizeable number due to engine fires while running on the ground. Many could be explained, such as centre-line closure or mid-air collisions during manoeuvring. Sometimes, it was unbelievable rotten luck. One crew from 64 Squadron, having returned from a sortie, decided to continue with some circuit training. The procedure included approaches to the runway breaking off at 300 feet when the throttles were opened up and the aircraft accelerated to 250 knots and entered a climbing turn onto the downwind leg where the throttles were closed and the downwind leg checks made. The pilot, Flt Lt J. J. Jackson, then attempted to open the throttles, which would not move no matter how many attempts. The crew ejected successfully. The navigator, Flt Lt P. J. Hart, was making his second successful ejection from a Javelin. Javelins lost on the ground due to engine explosions were spectacularly high; usually, the starter cartridge was a typical cause, so much so that Wg Cdr M. H. Miller, the CO of 60 Squadron, remarked following such an incident involving a starter explosion resulting in an engine fire in which the ground crew were commended for acting swiftly enough to put out the fire. Miller's resigned observation was simply to say 'This type of starter failure seems to be yet another feature of the Javelin that we have to live with'.

In June 1967, 60 Squadron were allocated twelve of 64 Squadron's FAW.9Rs to replace twelve of their own. A few days before taking 64 Squadron's jets on charge, 60 Squadron were tasked with sending four 9Rs to Hong Kong on Exercise 'Gas Iron One'. These changes affected the flying programme for the month but practice intercepts and cine training continued together with ground attack sorties and air-to-ground gunnery training over the China Rock and Ulu Tiram ranges.

Another big flypast opportunity came this month: the celebration of HM Queen Elizabeth's birthday. This involved ten Javelins of 64 Squadron and nine of 60 Squadron, all nineteen led by OC 60 Squadron with Wg Cdr B. E. De Iength, OC 64 Squadron, as his navigator. Flt Lt C. V. Holman left the formation after the flypast to carry out an impressive low-level aerobatics display, which was not bad given the Javelin's restrictions on aerobatics. This flypast was acknowledged as the last time that as many Javelins would be seen in the air together.

No. 60 Squadron continued to operate alongside the Lightnings of 74 Squadron, which had since replaced 64 Squadron, until their own disbandment, which while involving fewer aircraft was somewhat more imaginative. Taking place in April 1968, the details of the final flypast are as detailed in the squadron ORB below.

The end is nigh: nine FAW.9s and a T3 from No. 64 take the lead with nine FAW.9s in diamond formation marking the disbandment of 64 Squadron in April 1967. (*Barry G. Mayner*)

The nineteen-strong Flat Iron formation seen from below as they run-in as part of the 64 Squadron disbandment ceremony; the diamond is made up of jets from 60 Sqn. (*Barry G. Mayner*)

Who said the Flat Iron was non-aerobatic? No. 60 Squadron upward bomb burst manoeuvre over RAF Tengah, marking the end of the Javelin's operational career with the RAF in April 1968. (*The National Archives*)

The final 'night disbandment' flight on 30 April 1968. (*The National Archives*)

No. 60 Squadron final flights flown on 2 May 1968 from Tengah as entered in the Squadron Operational Record Book. (*The National Archives*)

10
Javelin Postscript

For many years following the final touchdown of wheels on tarmac of the last airworthy Javelin, the beast disappeared into history with little comment, not exactly forgotten completely but certainly not the subject of any attempt to salvage at least a single remaining airworthy airframe. The Javelin did not have a future as an icon of air power or stand in for theatrical productions in film and television depicting fighter aircraft—not even as much as a cameo appearance. Instead, the Hunter and Lightning reaped that reputation.

The last word on the Javelin perhaps should go to one of its test pilots, Jerry Lee, when speaking of the French Mirage in comparison, an aircraft he also had experience of: 'it was a different class of aircraft, stacks of thrust, a thorough fighter pilot's machine'.

Finally, of the Javelin; 'It was a gentle old lady, with its Second World War cockpit and lights all over the place. It didn't like going too fast or turning—but five years later it could have been a Mirage!'

Appendix I
Flat Iron Comparisons

FAW.1
Engine: Armstrong Siddley SA6 turbojets: two 8,000-lb static thrust
Radar: AI.17
Armament: four 30-mm Aden cannons
Performance: ceiling: 52,500 feet; maximum speed at sea level: 711 mph

FAW.2
Engine: Armstrong Siddley SA6 turbojets: two 8,000-lb static thrust
Radar: APQ-43/AI.22
Armament: four 30-mm Aden cannons
Performance: ceiling: 52,500 feet; maximum speed at sea level: 711 mph

T3
Engine: Armstrong Siddley SA6 turbojets: two 8,000-lb static thrust
No radar
Armament: four 30-mm Aden cannons
Performance: ceiling: 46,000 feet; maximum speed at sea level: 640 mph

FAW.4
Engine: Armstrong Siddley SA6 turbojets: two 8,000-lb thrust
Radar: AI.17
Armament: four 30-mm Aden cannons
Performance: ceiling: 50,700 feet; maximum speed at sea level: 702 mph
New feature introduced: all-moving tail fin.

FAW.5
Engine: Armstrong Siddley SA6 turbojets: two 8,000-lb thrust
Radar: AI.17

Armament: four 30-mm Aden cannons
Performance: ceiling: 50,100 feet; maximum speed at sea level: 704 mph
New feature introduced: additional internal fuel capacity in wings.

FAW.6

Engine: Armstrong Siddley SA6 turbojets: two 8,000-lb thrust
Radar: APQ-43/AI.22
Armament: four 30-mm Aden cannons
Performance: ceiling: 50,100 feet; maximum speed at sea level: 704 mph
New feature: as FAW.5 but with APQ-43 AI radar.

FAW.7

Engine: Armstrong Siddley SA7 turbojets: two 11,000 lb
Radar: AI.17
Armament: four 30-mm Aden cannons and up to four Firestreak infrared homing missiles
Performance: ceiling: 52,800 feet; maximum speed at sea level: 711 mph
New feature: as FAW.5 but with uprated SA7 engines and capability to carry and launch Firestreak missiles.

FAW.8

Engine: Armstrong Siddley SA7r turbojets: two 11,000 lb with reheat; two 12,390 lb above 20,000 feet
Radar: APQ-43/AI.22
Armament: four 30-mm Aden cannons and up to four Firestreak infrared homing missiles
Performance: ceiling: 52,000 feet; maximum speed at sea level: 702 mph
New feature: as FAW.6 but with ability to carry drop tanks and Firestreak missiles with reheated SA7r engines (although restricted to use above 20,000 feet due to inefficient fuel pump and distribution when reheat engaged at low level, performance for both FAW.8s and 9s was significantly improved at higher altitude, where it mattered, but wear and tear on airframes and engines alike, was seen as costly when used excessively.)

FAW.9

Engine: Armstrong Siddley SA7r turbojets: two 11,000 lb with reheat; two 12,390 lb above 20,000 feet
Radar: AI.17
Armament: four 30-mm Aden cannons and up to four Firestreak infra-red homing missiles
Performance: ceiling: 52,000 feet; maximum speed at sea level: 702 mph
New features: As for FAW.7 but with reheated SA7r engines, same impact on performance at altitude as for the FAW.8; however, the FAW.9 was the only version to be fitted with fuel probe for IFR and was the heaviest of all Javelins.

Appendix II

Javelin Squadrons and Post-History

No. 3 Squadron

FAW.4: January 1959–December 1960
Squadron crest: Cockatrice, the first creature to fly according to ancient folklore.
Colours: Green bar sometimes with yellow or white edging.

No. 3 Squadron has an arguable claim to being the first operational RAF Squadron. By the Battle of Britain, 3 Squadron was operational with Hurricanes and, on D-Day, were being led on fighter sweeps, with Hawker Tempests from the UK, by Roland Beaumont, who among other things went on to test fly the Canberra, Lightning, and TSR-2. As the transition from the Meteor and Vampire era passed, 3 Squadron re-equipped with Hunters before a change in direction in January 1959 when they were reassigned as an N/AW fighter unit. They operated Javelins for almost two years until a continued restructuring of the RAF front line re-tasked them in the tactical strike role, following the decision to rebadge 59 Squadron as 3 Squadron. No. 3 Squadron changed roles again to tactical fighter support with the Harrier from 1971 while remaining in West Germany. In 1998, they returned to Cottesmore in the UK and later, in 2005, became the first operational Eurofighter Typhoon squadron, the type which 3 Squadron currently operate, from their current base at Coningsby in Lincolnshire, in the dual air defence, air superiority, and tactical attack fighter role.

No. 5 Squadron

FAW.5: January 1960–November 1962; FAW.9: November 1962–October 1965
Squadron crest: Canadian maple leaf.
Colours: A broad red bar with either; white, green or no edging.

In December 1965, 5 Squadron became the first to form on the Mk 6 model of the English Electric Lightning at RAF Binbrook, continuing in the air defence role policing the approaches to UK airspace. In October 1987, 5 Squadron became the second unit to equip with the Panavia Tornado F3 at RAF Leeming in North Yorkshire. In 2003, 5 Squadron was disbanded, arguably to help pay for the folly of the invasion of Iraq. However, 5 Squadron re-formed in 2007 at RAF Waddington, with the Raytheon Bombardier Sentinel R1 to meet the requirement for airborne battlefield surveillance reconnaissance targeting over Iraq and Afghanistan. Since Allied Forces have been withdrawn from these two theatres, the Sentinels of 5 Squadron were, following SDSR 2010, supposed to have been disbanded but the demand for the aircraft's unique contribution to the Battlefield picture has brought about a stay of execution.

No. 11 Squadron

FAW.4: October 1959–March 1962; FAW.5: January–December 1962; FAW.9: December 1962–January 1966
Squadron crest: Two eagles in side view attacking as a pair.
Colour: Horizontal black bar containing a yellow diamond, split in the middle by an interceding white disc containing a letter identity code. On the Mk 9 Javelins, the bar stretches across the top of the fin containing a half diamond tapered to the rear and containing the two eagles at the broad end.

Initially following the unit's disbandment in West Germany, it was assigned as the shadow number plate of the resumed Javelin OCU, No. 228. Following the standing down of 228 OCU in December 1966, 11 Squadron reformed on the English Electric Lightning F6 during the summer of 1967 at RAF Leuchars. In 1972, the squadron took its Lightnings to Binbrook where they joined 5 Squadron again. No. 11 Squadron were the last operational RAF unit to equip with Lightnings, jointly with 29 Squadron, eventually disbanding on 1 May 1988. They were the last on type as well, then reforming on the Panavia Tornado F3 at Coningsby before moving to Leeming in July. No. 11 Squadron disbanded again in 2004 then reformed in 2006 on the Eurofighter Typhoon at RAF Coningsby, becoming the second such unit equipped with the Tiffy. Like 3 Squadron, 11 Squadron's current role is air defence, air superiority, and tactical support attack.

No. 23 Squadron

FAW.4: March 1957–July 1959; FAW.7: April 1959–July 1960 and April 1962–September 1962; FAW.9: April 1960–October 1964.
Squadron crest: Red eagle descending toward prey with wings spreading.
Colours: Alternating red and blue square blocks forming a solid bar.

No. 23 Squadron had a long pedigree as a night fighter unit reaching back to the Battle of Britain when they were equipped with Bristol Blenheim 1Fs. Being an early convert to the Javelin, they hold the distinction of being the first Javelin squadron to re-equip with the Lightning. From March 1963 to October 1964, they flew Javelins from Leuchars then converted to the English Electric 'Frightening' until disbandment in October 1975. No. 23 Squadron lived again after reforming on the McDonnell Douglas F-4M Phantom II at RAF Wattisham. Following the Falklands Campaign in 1982, 23 Squadron were chosen in early 1983 to take up permanent station at Port Stanley then Mount Pleasant in the Falklands, but with a much-reduced UE.

Matters returned to normal by October 1988 when they became the fourth operational Tornado F3 unit in the RAF and the second to form a part of the new F3 air defence wing at Leeming. Post-Cold War defence cuts and the conventional arms reduction in Europe treaty meant the end of 23 Squadron as a fighter unit. The squadron was reformed around 2000 as an additional squadron number for the E-3D Sentry airspace warning and control aircraft based at Waddington. In the run up to the SDSR 2010, 23 Squadron disappeared once and for all. Its current status is disbanded.

No. 25 Squadron

FAW.7: December 1958–January 1961 and April 1962–September 1962; FAW.9: December 1959–December 1962
Squadron crest: Bird of prey perched on falconer's glove with wings ready to take flight.
Colours: Horizontal silver/metallic bar with black edging, often seen with the full squadron crest at centre. The CO's aircraft sported an especially broad bar on the fin.

One of the later converts to the Javelin and to a later model, the FAW.7 made for a greater jump in capability than for the early converts to type. Again like 23 Squadron, 25 Squadron were a pioneer night fighter unit of the Second World War. Disbandment came as what appears to have been a final round of cuts started in 1957 and promptly became a missile unit. Shortly thereafter, when the rolling up of the missile force began, 25 Squadron survived and moved to Brüggen in Germany in 1970 where the squadron was deployed in 'A', 'B', and 'C' Flights based at Wildenrath, Brüggen, and Laarbruch. They returned to the UK, still with Bloodhounds, in 1983, this time operating from Wyton with other flights at Barkston Heath and Wattisham. In 1989 came the chance to be a fighter squadron again when they reformed on the Panavia Tornado F3 at RAF Leeming. They remained there until 2008 when the UK Defence Budget was being squeezed by conflict in Iraq and Afghanistan, the squadron was disbanded again.

No. 29 Squadron

FAW.6: November 1957–August 1961; FAW.9: April 1961–May 1967
Squadron crest: Two birds of prey, an eagle dispatching a hawk.
Colours: Three red crosses, in Roman numeral form, on a white horizontal bar with red edging.

Another traditional night fighter unit, 29 Squadron began with the Javelin Mk 6 (APQ-43 radar) at RAF Acklington just as the Sandys axe was completing its first swing; on the way back, the axe caught Acklington and 29 Squadron moved to Leuchars in July 1958. They remained there until March 1963, when, by now operating the FAW.9, they moved again to Nicosia in Cyprus. One of the later Javelin units to disband, they did so in 1967, at Akrotiri, before becoming one of the joint last two squadrons to convert to the Lightning (the other being 11 Squadron). They moved back to the UK and RAF Wattisham. They converted to the F-4 Phantom following a move to Coningsby in 1974. In 1987, they notched up another first as they became the first fully operational Tornado F3 squadron. They fell to the spending axe of the Blair Government's first defence review, SDR (Strategic Defence Review), in 1998. They then resurfaced as the shadow to the Eurofighter Typhoon OCU, their current status.

Legend has it that during the 1920s, an officer asked a young airman to paint the squadron number on their aircraft in Roman numerals. The young lad asked what that entailed and was told correctly, 'x, x, one, x'. Misreading this to mean two 'x's then one more, off he went and completed a fine job on all fuselages with three bright red 'x's. Yet it remains nothing more than rumour, the other being the 'x's are derived from the brewer's tradition of marking kegs of extra strong beer.

No. 33 Squadron

FAW.7: July 1958–January 1962; FAW.9: October 1960–November 1962
Squadron crest: A stag's head face on.
Colours: Horizontal light blue bar on fin, with dark blue edging and interceding red stripe.

A long standing cold war fight fighter squadron, after converting the FAW.7 at Leeming, this unit moved to RAF Middleton St George at the end of September 1958 where they remained until disbandment at the end of 1962. That was it for 33 Squadron until 1 March 1965, at a time when the Bloodhound missile squadrons in the UK were fast running down. They reformed on Bloodhounds in Malaya, based at RAF Tengah. They disbanded again on 30 January 1970 as part of the Government's 'nothing east of Suez' policy. On 14 June 1971, they reformed as a tactical transport unit equipped with the Aérospatiale SA330 Puma, their current role and type. Today, 33 Squadron are based at Odiham in Hampshire operating the Puma HC2.

No. 41 Squadron

FAW.4: February 1958–February 1960; FAW.5: August 1958–February 1960; and FAW.8: November 1959–December 1963
Squadron crest: Cross of Lorraine in red
Colours: Horizontal red bar with white borders of equal thickness.

Prior to converting to the Javelin, 41 Squadron were based at Biggin Hill with the Hunter, you could say it was the Sandys effect which saw them re-equip with the Javelin and move to Coltishall. The squadron was disbanded the same day as 141 Squadron at Coltishall, 31 January 1958; the next day, 141 Squadron became 41 Squadron and so the tradition of preserving the older units pressed on. No. 41 Squadron then moved to Wattisham in July where it remained throughout its Javelin era until disbanding again at the end of December 1963. Thereafter, it had a sabbatical until September 1965 when resurrection in the air defence role came, this time at West Raynham, but with the Bloodhound surface-to-air missile. No. 41 Squadron were by now the sole Bloodhound (indeed, sole SAM) unit deployed by the RAF as a component part of the UK Air Defence ORBAT—so much for the plan to put a screen of SAM units along the east coast from Manston to Buchan.

From 19 September 1970, 41 Squadron became 85 Squadron. Having been airbrushed out of the present once again, 41 Squadron reformed on 1 April 1972, but departing the air defence role essentially forever, now equipped with the latest fighter in service of the day, the McDonnell Douglas F-4M Phantom II at Coningsby assigned to 1 Group Strike Command in the Tactical Reconnaissance role. They very much retained this posture through a change to the BAC SEPECAT Jaguar and a move to Coltishall in 1977. They were settled then until 2006 when they disbanded due to defence cuts imposed by the Government under the title 'Delivering Security in an ever-changing world'. They were not beaten yet, and the Cross of Lorraine has since reappeared on the fins of altogether five fast jet types and variants: Harrier GR9, Tornado GR4, Tornado F3, Jaguar GR3, and Typhoon FGR4, back at Coningsby since 2010, as the shadow number plate for the FJ&WOEU (Fast Jet & Weapons Operational Evaluation Unit). Today, the unit continues with this role but now only in respect of the Typhoon.

No. 46 Squadron

FAW.1: February 1956–October 1957; FAW.2: August 1957–June 1961; and FAW.6: May–October 1958.
Squadron crest: Three scarlet arrow tips, or indeed, Javelins soaring together.
Colours: Usually a white arrow tip with red edging.

The first of the first with the Gloster Javelin, formed on the Mk 1 at Odiham, Hampshire in February 1956. The squadron moved to Waterbeach in July 1959, before disbanding in June 1961. It was resurrected one more time as a tactical troop transport unit equipped (first again) with the Hawker Siddeley Andover at Abingdon at the end of 1966. They moved to Thorney Island in 1970 where they were disbanded, this time the conclusion of another public finance-driven review was that there were too many transport units, so 46 Squadron disbanded once and for all in September 1975. It was mentioned somewhere that 46 Squadron was chosen to become the shadow for the Lightning training flight at Binbrook in the 1980s should push come to shove, but evidence of this remains elusive.

No. 60 Squadron

FAW.9: July 1961–April 1968
Squadron crest: Head of a springbok face on.
Colours: Large horizontal black bar with silver/grey borders and interceding horizontal silver/grey stripe at centre.

Based in Singapore since virtually the end of the Second World War, 60 Squadron had transitioned at Tengah from Spitfires through to Meteor NF.14s before upgrading to the ultimate Javelin, the FAW.9 in July 1961. Although the last with the Javelin, 60 Squadron had the most stable period with the type—one base location, one variant, and the most advanced and the longest period of unbroken service lasting until the final disbandment parade on 30 April 1968, which included a spectacular flypast (see photo on page xxx). After Singapore, 60 Squadron reformed on 3 February 1969, like many ex-fighter units of the era, as something quite different. Assigned to the VIP communications role, 60 Squadron now sported Pembroke C1s at RAF Wildenrath in Germany. This was their lot for the rest of the Cold War. No. 60 Squadron operated other suitable types for this role, including the Heron C4 and Andover C1 and CC2, the latter as sole type from 1987 after the last of the Pembrokes went.

Disbandment came in 1992 following the end of the Cold War and the contraction of the RAF in Germany. There was no justification for a specially assigned VIP transport unit for the shrinking command. They did reform, however, as a helicopter tactical support squadron with the Wessex HC2 at Benson. This last incarnation lasted until 1997. They since became the identity of the RAF element of the all service defence helicopter flying school at RAF Shawbury.

No. 64 Squadron

FAW.7: August 1958–October 1960; FAW.9: July 1960–June 1967.
Squadron crest: Scarab beetle.
Colours: White diamonds with alternating red and blue borders occupying top and lower halves.

No. 64 Squadron came to the night fighter role late on, receiving Meteor NF.12s in place of their F8 day fighters in 1956. They were at Duxford when they received the Javelin FAW.7 in August 1958. The contraction of Fighter Command brought the closure of Duxford in 1961, which brought the relocation of 64 Squadron to Waterbeach on 17 July and remained there until August 1962. They moved again, to make way for the new tactical Hunter wing, to Binbrook operating from here until 1 April 1965 when they departed for Tengah in Malaya. Again, like many of the latter units to convert, they lasted longest with it, perhaps due to their being armed with the more capable definitive marks.

They disbanded in June 1967, this time as the RAF presence in the Far East began contracting. They returned to operations of sorts in August 1968 at RAF Coningsby, this time as the reserve squadron for also newly reformed 228 OCU, responsible for the training up of the RAF's planned F-4 Phantom force. One more move came in April 1987 when the F-4 OCU moved to Leuchars; at the time, they were expected to remain in business there until the end of the 1990s. However, the end of the Cold War and the introduction of the Conventional Arms in Europe Limitation Treaty meant the F-4 became surplus to requirements under the 'Options for Change' defence review so the OCU (including 64 Squadron) disbanded for the last time on 31 January 1991.

No. 72 Squadron

FAW.4: August 1959–June 1961 and FAW.5: June 1959–June 1961
Squadron crest: Blue swallow in a dive
Colours: either a blue bar or arrow tip with red edging.

No. 72 Squadron were, along with 64 Squadron, equipped with Spitfires during the Battle of Britain. Likewise, they remained a day fighter unit up to February 1956 when they swapped their Meteor F8s for Meteor NF.12s and 14s. After being converted to Javelins while still based at Church Fenton, they moved to Leconfield on 28 June. When their illustrious career as a steely eyed fighter squadron came to an end in June 1961, they rose again as a helicopter battlefield support squadron in November 1961 at RAF Odiham, where they were equipped with Bristol Belvedere C1s, a prototype for the Boeing CH-47 Chinook if ever there was.

In 1964, the Belvederes were replaced with the Westland Wessex HC2, a flight of which were detached to RAF Manston to provide SAR cover, until a dedicated SAR Flight was available. Still with the Wessex, they moved to Benson in April 1981, then to Aldergrove later that year. In January 1997, they were operating both Wessex and Puma HC1s until being disbanded in 2002. In July that year, the squadron number plate came alive once more as one of the shadow squadrons of the No. 1 Flying Training School providing basic flying training on Short Tucano T1s at Linton-on-Ouse. This remains the current status of 72 Squadron. No. 72 Squadron were a gift squadron, that is the existence of the squadron is owed to sponsorship by paying for aircraft assigned from a province of the British Empire, in this case Basutoland, and this therefore forms a part of the squadron's title.

No. 85 Squadron

FAW.2: November 1958–March 1960; FAW.6: November 1958–June 1960; and FAW.8: March 1960–March 1963
Squadron crest: A hexagon, usually with white borders against a dark back ground.
Colours: Orange and black chequered bars.

A Hurricane squadron at the start of the Second World War, 85 Squadron were among the first RAF fighter squadrons to be sent to France in September 1939 to provide air defence for the Advanced Air Strike Force—effectively the air element of the BEF (British Expeditionary Force). They continued with Hurricanes after the Dunkirk evacuation and through the Battle of Britain. In January 1941, 85 Squadron became an early night fighter squadron. They worked their way through the war with first Boulton Paul Defiants, then, A-20 Havocs until things really started developing, in terms of the air war over Europe, in August 1942, they converted to DH Mosquito NF.IIs from here through the rest of the war. No. 85 operated a farrago of Mosquito night fighter variants through to the end of the war including: Mks XV, XII, XIII, XVII, and XXX.

They were operating NF.36s in 1951 when they converted to the Meteor NF.11 then later NF.12 and 14. As often happens, they did not convert to the Javelin so much as 89 Squadron operating both Mks 2 and 6 Javelins at Stradishall were renumbered 85 Squadron. They moved to West Malling in June 1959 before another move to West Raynham in September 1960. They were one of the last units to be trimmed away by the Sandys axe in 1963.

The day after disbanding as a fighter unit, they became the number of an Air Defence Target Facilities Squadron at West Raynham on 1 April 1963. Before the end of the month, they were off again to Binbrook where they settled down until January 1972. During this time, they operated a variety of marks of Canberra: B2, PR3, T11, and T19, as well as Meteor F8s. After disbanding yet again, their squadron number was moved in 1975 to replace 41 Squadron as the sole Bloodhound squadron in the UK, bringing a move back to West Raynham again.

They eventually disbanded in July 1991. At that time, they had missile flights at North Coates, West Raynham, and Barkston Heath; Bawdsey, Wattisham, and Wyton had absorbed the missile flights of 25 Squadron in 1989. They reappeared in 2008 as a university air squadron shadow number at Church Fenton before disbanding finally in 2011.

No. 87 Squadron

FAW.1: August 1957–October 1960; FAW.5: September 1958–October 1960, and FAW.4: November 1959–January 1961
Squadron crest: Snake, head and tail embowed, rather as the buckle of a snake belt.
Colours: Horizontal white bar with interceding black bar in centre, superimposed over this is an oscillating green line on either side of nose roundel with a red dagger on the fin.

No. 87 Squadron shares the honour of being one of the very first of the few squadron, flying out to France in September 1939 as part of the BEF air element with 85 Squadron. Flying Hurricanes at the time, it took until 1943 before they re-equipped with another type, the Spitfire, of which Mks Vb, Vc, VIII, and IX were flown. By 1944, they settled on the IX; this is the aircraft they finished the war with.

After the war, they returned to West Germany in January 1952 as part of the 2nd Tactical Air Force placing them very much so at the sharp end of the cold war.

Based at RAF Wahn, they moved to Brüggen on the Dutch border in 1957, just before converting onto the Javelin and in so doing, became the first with the new type in Germany replacing its Meteor NF.11s, which had been acquired in 1952. When rationalisation came about, 87 Squadron were surplus to requirements and disbanded in January 1961.

No. 89 Squadron

FAW.2 and 6: October 1957–November 1958.
Squadron crest: A Wyvern transfixed by a bolt of lightning
Colours: Horizontal light-blue bar with interceding dark-blue stripe.

No. 89 Squadron had a rather hit and miss history. They were formed on 1 September 1917 then disbanded shortly before the end of the Great War on 4 July 1918. They did not reform until 25 January 1941 as a result of wartime expansion. They disbanded again in 1946, then, due to the short expansion period extending from the Korean conflict, they reformed in 1955 with the Venom NF.3. At the end of November 1958, they were lost to history as they officially became 85 Squadron.

No. 96 Squadron

FAW.4: 12 February 1958–21 January 1959
Squadron crest: A lion in defensive pose with several stars appearing on body representing constellation of Leo.
Colours: Blue bars with yellow edging and five yellow stars line abreast in each with the centre star dominant totalling ten stars. There does not appear to be any images of Javelins wearing 96 colours.

An early convert to the night fighter role after the Battle of Britain, when it reformed on Hurricanes. It flew then NF Hurricanes and Defiants Havocs and Mosquitos. The squadron adopted a variety of roles through, including, transport and anti-submarine warfare, latterly flying Dakotas and Halifaxes. In 1958, the unit began converting from Meteors. They had not gained full recognition as an operational unit when in January 1959, they were rebadged as 3 Squadron. No. 96 Squadron has never been resurrected.

No. 137 Squadron

FAW.5 and T3: January 1957–September 1961 (Shadow to 228 Operational Conversion Unit)
Squadron crest: Horse's head, prominent mane usually on blue disc with red edging.
Colours: Light blue and red

Early in the war, they were one of the first squadrons to be equipped with the Westland Whirlwind twin-engined fighter, but later were operating the older Hurricane before transferring onto the Hawker Typhoon 1b and were deployed in Normandy in 1944 to 45. Shortly after the end of hostilities in Europe, 137 were disbanded, they had also laid dormant between the end of the First World War and February 1941. They were disbanded once again in August 1945. They made one more return, January 1957, when they returned as the Javelin OCU at RAF Leeming, initially with a motley collection of aircraft for the purpose of initial air navigation training; Canberra T11, Vickers Valetta, and Meteor. In September 1961, they laid up their colours.

No. 141 Squadron

FAW.4: February 1957–January 1958
Squadron crest: Head of white lion face on with mouth open.
Colours: Black square pierced by white arrow tip from each end, usually head of lion or service roundel intercedes at centre.

No. 141 Squadron flew Defiants, initially in the day fighter role alongside 264 Squadron, during the Battle of Britain and suffered heavy casualties such that they were both withdrawn from day time operations and flown in the night fighter role where they enjoyed a degree of success. They maintained their night fighter role throughout the war operating Beaufighters and Mosquitos, eventually finishing with the Mosquito NF 36 in 1951, six years after the war. The then transitioned to the Meteor NF.11 then the Venom NF.3. In February 1957, they received their first Javelins, making them the second unit to re-equip with the Flat Iron, they perhaps unexpectedly had the shortest period of operations with it as well, disbanding eleven months later. They were reformed as a Bloodhound squadron at Dunholm Lodge on 1 April 1959 enjoying a less brief period of activity continuing as a SAM unit through to 31 March 1964 before laying up the colours for the last time.

No. 151 Squadron

FAW.5: August 1957–September 1961
Squadron crest: Crossed sabres with owl head forward with wings spread in attack profile.
Colours: Since reforming at Leuchars in 1952, the saltire made up of traditional blue and white.

Another Battle of Britain veteran equipped with Hurricanes at the time and like many of the other Javelin Squadrons their lineage in all-weather night fighter operations was developed during the war. No. 151 Squadron first moved to what was essentially the night fighter Hurricane 2C, later moving to Boulton Paul Defiants then, like so many others, took receipt of various marks of the 'Wooden Wonder', from April 1942 to October 1946 operating five different marks of Mosquito from NF.2 to NF.30. A victim of post-war contraction, they disbanded but found fortune in being resurrected during the moderate period expansion during the early to mid-1950s. They arrived at Leuchars in February 1952 with Vampire NF.10s which they exchanged for Meteor NF.11s in 1953. They moved from the Meteors to the Venom NF.3 in 1955 then took a quantum leap forward as one of the early converts to the Gloster Javelin during the summer of 1957, for which they were detached to RAF Turnhouse, today Edinburgh Airport, this being due to runway resurfacing at Leuchars and the cross-runway being unsuitable. At the end of the year they were back at Leuchars where they seemed to initially have survived the cuts imposed earlier in 1957. However, come 1961, they were slated for the chop and on 19 September 1961, mounted their final flypast before ending frontline operational flying, as a fighter unit, once and for all. No. 151 Squadron did live again the following January as a Signals Command unit equipped with Avro Lincolns flying as sigint (Signals Intelligence) platforms together with Hastings, Varsities, and Canberra B2s while based at Watton. This was a short-lived return as 151 disbanded again in May 1963.

That was not the end, however; improvements to the UK air defence posture by the Government under Margaret Thatcher brought 151 Squadron back to life again as an air defence unit, reformed on BAE Hawk T1/T1A aircraft at RAF Chivenor as a component squadron within No. 2 TWU (Tactical Weapons Unit) in September 1981. The squadron remained settled as such until September 1992 when the political climate changed significantly again and the demand for fighter pilots contracted.

Appendix III

Fighter Command Order of Battle as of 1 September 1957

Following the publication of Duncan Sandys White Paper on defence in April 1957, the following is order of battle of Fighter Command just five months later:

Squadron	Base	Type	UE	Sector
43	Leuchars	Hunter F4	16	Caledonian
222	Leuchars	Hunter F4	16	Caledonian
151	Turnhouse	Javelin FAW.5	16	Caledonian
66	Acklington	Hunter F6	16	Northern
29	Acklington	Meteor NF.11	16	Northern
92	Middleton St George	Hunter F6	16	Northern
33	Middleton St George	Meteor NF.12/14	16	Northern
19	Church Fenton	Hunter F6	16	Northern
72	Church Fenton	Meteor NF.12/14	16	Northern
131	Leconfield	Hunter F4	13	Northern
137	Leeming	Meteor NF.11	16	Northern
153	West Malling	Meteor NF.12/14	16	Western
122	West Raynham	Hunter F6	16	Western
176	West Raynham	Javelin/Venom/Meteor NF.12	16	Western
74	Horsham St Faith	Hunter F4	16	Eastern
23	Coltishall	Javelin FAW.4	16	Eastern
141	Coltishall	Javelin FAW.4	16	Eastern
56	Waterbeach	Hunter F5	16	Eastern
63	Waterbeach	Hunter F6	16	Eastern
165	North Luffenham	Meteor NF.12/14	16	Eastern
512 USAF	Woodbridge	F-86D	25	Eastern
41	Biggin Hill	Hunter F5	16	Eastern
89	Stradishall	Venom NF.3	16	Metropolitan

263	Stradishall	Hunter F6	16	Metropolitan
152	Stradishall	Meteor NF.12/14	16	Metropolitan
65	Duxford	Hunter F6	16	Metropolitan
25	West Malling	Meteor NF.12/14	16	Metropolitan
85	West Malling	Meteor NF.12/14	16	Metropolitan
111	North Weald	Hunter F6	16	Metropolitan
513 USAF	Manston	F-86D	25	Metropolitan
514 USAF	Manston	F-86D	25	Metropolitan
54	Odiham	Hunter F6	16	Metropolitan
247	Odiham	Hunter F6	16	Metropolitan
46	Odiham	Javelin FAW.1	16	Metropolitan
1	Tangmere	Hunter F5	16	Metropolitan
34	Tangmere	Hunger F5	16	Metropolitan
127	Chivenor	Hunter F1/4	16	Metropolitan

Note: 89 Squadron were, at the time, converting to the Javelin FAW.6.

Appendix IV

Chart Depicting Fighter Command Planned Deployment as of 30 September 1958

	Year Planner	1959	1960	1961
Deployment Base	6 monthly planner	1/2 2/2	1/2 2/2	1/2 2/2
West Malling		X X	X X	X 2/2 85-Javelin FAW8 + 41-Javelin FAW8
Wattisham		1/2 111-Hunter F6 + 41-Javelin FAW8 2/2 111-Hunter F6 + 1-Hunter F6 + 41-Javelin FAW8	1/2 111-Hunter F6 +1-Hunter F6 + 41-Javelin FAW8 2/2 111-Hunter F6 +1-Lightning F1	1/2 111-Hunter F6 + 1-Lightning F1 2/2 111-Lightning F2 + 1-Lightning F1
Odiham		1/2 46-Javelin FAW2 + 54-Hunter F6 2/2 46-Javelin FAW2 + 54-Hunter F6	1/2 46-Javelin FAW2 + 54-Hunter F6	

1962	1963	1964	1965
1/2 2/2	1/2 2/2	1/2 2/2	1/2 2/2
1/2 85-Javelin FAW8 + 41-Javelin FAW8 2/2 85-Javelin FAW8 + 41-Javelin FAW8	1/2 85-Javelin FAW8 + 41-Javelin FAW8 2/2 85-Javelin FAW8 + 41-Javelin FAW8	1/2 85-Javelin FAW8 + 41-Javelin FAW8 2/2 85-Javelin FAW8 + 41-Javelin FAW8	
1/2 111-Lightning F2 + 1-Lightning F1 2/2 111-Lightning F2 + 1-Lightning F1	1/2 111-Lightning F2 + 1-Lightning F2 2/2 111-Lightning F2 + 1-Lightning F2	1/2 111-Lightning F2 + 1-Lightning F3 2/2 111-Lightning F2 + 1-Lightning F3	1/2 111-Lightning F2 + 1-Lightning F3 2/2 111-Lightning F2 + 1-Lightning F3

Stradishall		1/2 85-Javelin FAW6 + 1-Hunter F6		
Duxford		1/2 64-Javelin FAW7 + 65-Hunter F6 2/2 64-Javelin FAW7R + 65-Hunter F6	1/2 64-Javelin FAW7R + 65-Hunter F6	
Coltishall		X 2/2 23-Javelin FAW7 + 74-Hunter F6	1/2 23-Javelin FAW7R + 74-Lightning F1 2/2 23-Javelin FAW7R + 74-Lightning F1 + 54-Hunter F6	1/2 23-Javelin FAW7R + 74-Lightning F1 + 54-Hunter F6 2/2 74-Lightning F1 + 54-Lightning F2
West Raynham		1/2 C.F.E. 2/2 C.F.E.	1/2 C.F.E. X 2/2 X	1/2 25-Javelin FAW7R + 56-Hunter F6 2/2 25-Javelin FAW7R + 56-Huntr F6
LIncoln " X "			1/2 X 2/2 C.F.E. + 64-Javelin FAW7R + 65-Hunter F6	1/2 CFE + 64-Javelin FAW7R + 65-Lightning F2 2/2 CFE + 64-Javelin FAW7R + 65-Lightning F2
Leconfield		1/2 X 2/2 19-Hunter F6 + 72-Javelin FAW4	1/2 19-Hunter F6 + 72-Javelin FAW7R 2/2 19-Lightning F1 + 72-Javelin FAW7R	1/2 19-Lightning F1 + 72-Javelin FAW7R 2/2 19-Lightning F2 + 72-Javelin FAW7R
Waterbeach		1/2 25-Javelin FAW7 + 56-Hunter F6 2/2 25-Javelin FAW7R + 56-Hunter F6	1/2 25-Javelin FAW7R + 56-Hunter F6 2/2 25-Javelin FAW7R + 56-Hunter F6	

1/2 74-Lightning F2 + 54-Lightning F2 2/2 74-Lightning F2 + 54-Lightning F2	1/2 74-Lightning F2 + 54-Lightning F3 2/2 74-Lightning F2 + 54-Lightning F3	1/2 74-Lightning F2 + 54-Lightning F3 2/2 74-Lightning F2 + 54-Lightning F3	1/2 74-Lightning F2 + 54-Lightning F3 2/2 74-Lightning F2 + 54-Lightning F3
1/2 92-Lightning F2 + 56-Lightning F2 2/2 92-Lightning F2 + 56-Lightning F2	1/2 92-Lightning F2 + 56-Lightning F2 2/2 92-Lightning F2 + 56-Lightning F3	1/2 92-Lightning F2 + 56-Lightning F3 2/2 92-Lightning F2 + 56-Lightning F3	1/2 92-Lightning F2 + 56-Lightning F3 2/2 92-Lightning F2 + 56-Lightning F3
1/2 CFE+64-Javelin FAW7R + 65-Ligtning F2 2/2 CFE + 66-Lightning F1 + 65-Lightning F2	1/2 CFE + 66-Lightning F1 + 65-Lightning F2 2/2 CFE + 66-Lightning F2 + 65-Lightning F2	1/2 CFE + 66-Lightning F2 + 65-Lightning F2 2/2 CFE + 66-Lightning F2 + 65-Lightning F2	1/2 CFE + 66-Lightning F2 + 65-Lightning F2 2/2 CFE + 66-Lightning F2 + 65-Lightning F2
1/2 19-Lightning F2 + 72-Javelin FAW7R 2/2 19-Lightning F2 + 72-Javelin FAW7R	1/2 19-Lightning F2 + 72-Lightning F2 2/2 19-Lightning F2 + 72-Lightning F2	1/2 19-Lightning F2 + 72-Lightning F2 2/2 19-Lightning F2 + 72-Lightning F2	1/2 19-Lightning F2 + 72-Lightning F2 2/2 19-Lightning F2 + 72-Lightning F2

Horsham St Faith		1/2 23-Javelin FAW7 + 74-Hunter F6		
Church Fenton		1/2 19-Hunter F6 + 72-Javelin FAW4		
Middleton St George		1/2 33-Javelin FAW7 + 92-Hunter F6 2/2 33-Javelin FAW7 + 92-Hunter F6 + 66-Hunter F6	1/2 33-Javelin FAW7R + 92-Hunter F6 + 66-Hunter F6 2/2 92-Hunter F6 + 66-Hunter F6	1/2 92-Hunter F6 + 66-Hunter F6 2/2 92-Hunter F6 + 66-Hunter F6
Acklington		1/2 66-Hunter F6 2/2 X	1/2 X 2/2 33-Javelin FAW7R + 46-Javelin FAW2	1/2 33-Javelin FAW7R + 46-Javelin FAW2 2/2 33-Javelin FAW7R + 46-Javelin FAW7R
Leuchars		1/2 43-Hunter F6 + 29-Javelin FAW6 + 151-Javelin FAW5 2/2 43-Hunter F6 + 29-Javelin FAW6 + 151-Javelin FAW5	1/2 43-Hunter F6 + 29-Javelin FAW6 + 151-Javelin FAW55 2/2 43-Hunter F6 + 29-Javelin FAW6+151-Javelin FAW5	1/2 43-Hunter F6 + 29-Javelin FAW6 + 151-Javelin FAW5 2/2 43-Lightning F1 + 29-Javelin FAW6 + 151-Javelin FAW5
Leeming		JAVELIN OCU	JAVELIN OCU	JAVELIN OCU
Chivenor		HUNTER OCU	HUNTER OCU	1/2 HUNTER OCU 2/2 HUNTER OCU ?
Disbandments				1 Jav Sqn (gun only armed)
Summary of				

1/2 64-Javelin FAW7R + 25-Javelin FAW7R 2/2 64-Javelin FAW7R + 25-Javelin FAW7R	1/2 64-Javelin FAW7R + 25-Javelin FAW7R 2/2 64-Lightning F2 + 25-Javelin FAW7R	1/2 64-Javelin FAW7R + 25-Javelin FAW7R 2/2 64-Lightning F2 + 25-Javelin FAW7R	1/2 64-Lightning F2 + 25-Lightning F2 2/2 64-Lightning F2 + 25-Lightning F2
1/2 33-Javelin FAW7R + 46-Javelin FAW7R 2/2 33-Javelin FAW7R + 46-Javelin FAW7R	1/2 33-Javelin FAW7R + 46-Javelin FAW7R 2/2 33-Javelin FAW7R + 46-Javelin FAW7R	1/2 33-Javelin FAW7R + 46-Javelin FAW7R 2/2 33-Javelin FAW7R + 46-Javelin FAW7R	
1/2 43-Lightning F1 + 29-Javelin FAW6 + 151-Javelin FAW5 2/2 43-Lightning F1 + LOCU + FCS	1/2 43-Lightning F2 + LOCU + FCS 2/2 43-Lightning F2 + LOCU + FCS	1/2 43-Lightning F2 + LOCU + FCS 2/2 43-Lightning F2 + LOCU+FCS	1/2 43-Lightning F2 + LOCU + FCS 2/2 43-Lightning F2 ing + LOCU +FCS
JAVELIN OCU	JAVELIN OCU?	? ?	? ?
? ?			
2 Jav Sqns (gun only armed)	1 Jav Sqn	1 Jav Sqn	

Fighter Forces				
TOTAL		1/2 20 Sqns 2/2 20 Sqns	1/2 20 Sqns 2/2 20 Sqns	1/2 20 Sqns 2/2 19 Sqns
Legend:				FCS = Fighter Combat School
	Javelin FAW7R = Javelin FAW9	X = Base under Development		
DEPICTION	Sqn-Type + Sqn-Type			

How to read the chart:
Each square contains details of units active in the order Squadron No.-Aircraft Type + Squadron No. – Aircraft Type. They are listed to show the status at six monthly intervals which are broken down, per year, in the order 1/2 (first six months) 2/2 (latter six months). The vertical column to the left shows the bases corresponding to the units assigned to them, to the right and cross-referenced with the time line above

Appendices

1/2 19 Sqns 2/2 17 Sqns	1/2 19 Sqns 2/2 17 Sqns	1/2 17 Sqns 2/2 17 Sqns	1/2 13 Sqns 2/2 13 Sqns
OCU = Operational Conversion Unit	CFE = Central Fighter Establishment	LOCU = Lightning Operational Conversion Unit	